ONE AND FUN

ONE AND FUN

A Behind the Scenes Look at John Calipari
and the 2010 Kentucky Wildcats

AARON TORRES

Foreword By: Kentucky Sports Radio's Matt Jones

For more information on the book:
www.KentuckyBasketballBook.com
E-mail: KentuckyBasketballBook@gmail.com
Twitter: @Aaron_Torres

ISBN: 1516906586
ISBN 13: 9781516906581
Library of Congress Control Number: 2015913403
CreateSpace Independent Publishing Platform
North Charleston, South Carolina

It's only appropriate that I dedicate this book, the same way that I did my first one.

This book is for my parents, two people who have absolutely nothing in common... except for an unconditional love and support of their children.

Everything I am is because of you two. I'll never be able to thank you enough for that.

CONTENTS

FOREWORD

"**W**E WILL RECRUIT THE BEST OF THE BEST here."

During his introductory press conference in 2009 welcoming the 7th head coach of the most storied program in college basketball history, John Calipari served up notice that the game in Lexington was about to change. Calipari of course wasn't coming to create a new program in the heart of the Bluegrass, that wasn't necessary. Being the student of basketball history that John Calipari is, he knew that the legacy of Kentucky basketball extended through Adolph Rupp, seven (at the time) national championships and the most wins in the history of the sport. But he was letting UK fans know that business as usual would no longer be tolerated inside college basketball's holiest cathedral. Whereas past versions of UK basketball were about the tradition, the coaches and the fanbase, this new version would be about something completely different, the players.

Contrary to the popular mindset of the time, John Calipari would not be coaching his team for the name on the front of the jersey, but for the names on the back. He planned on bringing the best players from the around the country to Lexington and creating an environment that allowed them to blossom individually into superstars. From their individual success, team success would follow and Calipari believed, everyone would win. In a game that for too long had seen the actual talent on the floor as a fungible product, whose only importance was akin to that of clay to be molded by the brilliant coaches who reigned over the sport, John Calipari was about to fundamentally shake up the system. The mythology of college basketball was about to be shattered and with one sentence, the rest of college basketball was put on notice. The era of mega-talented players congregating in one place, likely only for one year, had begun. The game would never be the same.

I attended that initial press conference and was struck by just how perfect John Calipari was for the job of the head basketball coach at Kentucky. Unless you live in the state and are a charter member of Big Blue Nation, it is hard to describe just how much this sport means to those of us involved. It is not an exaggeration to say that there is nothing that matters more to the state's collective morale and mindset than the results of intercollegiate games played by 18-21 year old kids. That may seem silly to you if you don't live here, and I can detach myself enough to understand why. But if you are wrapped up in the joy of being a part of the Big Blue circus, rationality is the least of your worries.

Watching Calipari handle the massive media, fan and donor presence at that press conference made me realize that Kentucky had found its perfect modern PT Barnum. He loved the insanity of the UK job and he wouldn't just be able to put up with it, he relished being at its center. Calipari considered himself the lifelong outsider, always seated at the basketball kid's table, whether due to his own athletic talent (which was limited), his choice of jobs (at schools never given the budget or respect of a major program) or his reputation (adored by those who knew him and criticized by those that didn't). Like all great outsiders, he lived to ruffle feathers and defy expectations, reaching heights that his critics assured could never be obtained. But now the gatecrasher found himself sitting at the throne of the preeminent basketball program in America, with nothing to inhibit world domination.

At UMass and Memphis, John Calipari would have to beg and plead the top players in America to give him a chance at basketball outposts that were less than ideal. At Kentucky he could pick and choose. Walking to the high school recruiting buffet, Calipari didn't have to select one meat and two vegetables, he could take as many plates as he wanted and know that the next time he returned, there would be more waiting. Here the coach had a chance to not only be at the helm of the greatest program in the sport, but he could do it his way, with his set of rules. The Kentucky program's desperation (brought about by the disastrous two year stint of Billy Gillispie) meant he could mold the program with his vision and then sell it to players hungry to reach the NBA. It was a perfect marriage and Calipari went right to work.

Straight out of the gate, Calipari recruited a group that helped compose what still is my favorite Kentucky team of all time. As Aaron Torres so perfectly encapsulates in this book, the 2009-2010 Kentucky team completely changed college basketball. Calipari showed in his first year at Kentucky that basketball jibber-jabber about the importance of "building a program" and the "necessity of experience" was, at least if you were coaching at a powerhouse like Kentucky, complete nonsense. Inheriting a team that the year before had found itself in the inglorious abyss of the NIT, Calipari set about creating a group that would not only be much improved, it would become the best team in America immediately, while showcasing that if you have the "Jimmys and Joes", it is a lot easier to do the "Xs and Os." His blueprint succeeded and thereafter teams realized they had to follow if they wanted to compete. The era of "One and Done" began, with no turning back in sight.

A team that changed the fundamental nature of college basketball would be a good enough story in itself, but as Aaron so vividly showcases, this group was also an amazing amount of fun. From John Wall's first iconic dance at the season's initial practice, to DeMarcus Cousins telephonic meeting with Barack Obama, to raising over $1 million dollars for victims of an earthquake in Haiti, this Kentucky team found a way to not only be tremendously talented on the court, they were rock stars off the court. When I am asked about the most popular player of my lifetime at Kentucky, the answer is clear, John Wall. He and Cousins were Mick Jagger and Paul McCartney and the state followed their every move. Returning veteran Patrick Patterson added maturity and leadership, Eric Bledsoe eye-popping athleticism and youthful naivety (he told reporters he came to Kentucky to "get shit right") and Ramon Harris, DeAndre Liggins and Darius Miller redemption from the past coach whose personal issues stained the program. Throw in the fact that blogs and social media allowed fans to find out more details about their beloved players than at any point in the history of the program and what followed was a traveling road show of non-stop excitement and a fanbase delirious to soak up every single second.

Sitting here in 2015, the uniqueness of Calipari's first team might seem difficult to comprehend. John Calipari's revolutionary idea, that it no matter how much experience a player had, it was always better to surround your team with talent, is now commonplace. Virtually every NBA Draft sees the lottery filled with players who come from the "One and Done" mode and there isn't a program in the country that would shy from having such players on its team. Calipari has taken Kentucky to four Final Fours in six years, won one national championship and has kept the Wildcats entrenched as the most newsworthy program in college basketball. And if imitation is the most sincere form of flattery, the 2015 National Championship won by a Duke team starting three "One and Done" freshman, showcases that even arguably the greatest coach in college basketball history ultimately had to acknowledge Calipari had it right.

The recalibration of college basketball into a player-driven culture much like the NBA would not however have been possible without this first group. Calipari brought together his "Player's first" ideal to the greatest stage in college basketball and produced a team that both figuratively AND literally changed the game. The fact that team didn't win the

Championship and was upset in the Elite Eight does not diminish, but rather highlights, its importance. Who remembers the team that won the 2010 title...anyone? (Answer, it was Duke and they were boring). But everyone knows the Wall/Cousins group and even in defeat, their pre-eminence and importance was obvious even then. The 2010 UK Wildcats changed the game I loved that team more than any other in my time as a UK fan. Aaron's collection in the pages ahead will make you love them too.

Matt Jones
Kentucky Sports Radio
September 2015

Prologue: It's The Biggest Day in the History of Kentucky's Program

NEW YORK CITY isn't a place where you'd expect a college basketball revolution to take place, especially one that was rooted in Lexington, Kentucky. But on the night of June 24th, 2010, New York and its famous basketball arena were home to one of the most significant moments the sport had seen in decades.

On that night, the NBA Draft found its way to Madison Square Garden, and if you're wondering how an NBA Draft could possibly go down as one of the most important moments in *college basketball* history, well, just give me a second. I'll get there in a minute. I promise.

But before we get to the revolution, the one that happened the night of the NBA Draft, we first have to go back to a game that was played in the same building --- Madison Square Garden --- some six months earlier. That night, college basketball's fourth-ranked team, the Kentucky Wildcats took on No. 14 UConn and took them down in a thrilling 64-61 win.

On the surface the victory was important for a few very significant reasons.

The first one was the most obvious: The win was everything every Kentucky fan had hoped for when the school hired John Calipari as its head coach on April 1, 2009. In a big game, on a big stage, against a big opponent, the Wildcats pulled out a big-time victory. It was a win that simply couldn't have been imagined a season before, when Billy Gillispie was still the school's head coach, and his team fell to illustrious college basketball powers like VMI and the University of Miami, on their way to a 14-loss season, and an appearance in the NIT.

Losses like those are also what prompted the hire of Calipari in the first place: Simply put, a school like Kentucky can't lose to a school like VMI (or even Miami). Ever. And when it does, swift and immediate action is necessary.

The second reason the victory was so important was less obvious: It proved that Calipari's grand, Kentucky plan might just work after all. You know, the plan where he brought in a bunch of highly-touted high school players, didn't worry about whether he'd have them for one year or four, and convinced them all that if they were willing to sacrifice for the team (both minutes and stats), not only would the team succeed, but eventually, they'd succeed as individuals too.

Which brings us back to the night of the 2010 NBA Draft, where everything that Calipari had spent the previous 14 months preaching came true. Where his stars --- who sacrificed in ways that many of the skeptics could've never imagined --- were rewarded in the biggest way possible.

It began just moments after commissioner David Stern took the podium to open up the draft.

"With the first pick in the 2010 NBA Draft," Stern calmly said into the microphone. "The Washington Wizards select John Wall. Guard, from the University of Kentucky."

The arena at Madison Square Garden burst out into cheers, as Wall got up and hugged those closest to him. His third hug was reserved for Calipari, the coach who he'd dreamed of playing for, ever since he saw Calipari coaching Derrick Rose at Memphis three seasons earlier. The two embraced, before Wall walked onto the stage, and shook Stern's hand, before disappearing backstage.

With his selection, Wall had made history. Incredibly, he was the first player in Kentucky's storied history ever to get drafted No. 1 overall.

But while Wall's night was complete, Calipari's was just beginning.

Four picks later Kentucky's second star freshman DeMarcus Cousins --- a loveable 6'10 teddy bear, whose temper could sometimes get the best of him --- was selected fifth overall by the Sacramento Kings. Cousins' table was situated right next to Wall's in the green room, and the second he got up, there was Calipari again, ready to hand out another hug.

Calipari was there once again nine picks later when Patrick Patterson was selected at No. 14 overall by the Houston Rockets. Patterson was the only first rounder from Kentucky drafted that night who signed with and played under Gillispie; when Calipari took the job he decided to stick around, hoping to finish his degree, expand his game, and play in the NCAA Tournament after missing it due to injury his freshman year. As the 14th overall selection in the draft, and with a degree in hand that he'd earned the previous spring, it's safe to say Patterson had achieved those goals.

Beyond just the obvious however, Patterson's selection was also significant for a different reason: It marked just the second time ever that three UK players were selected in the first round. Antoine Walker, Tony Delk (who ironically, served as assistant Director of Basketball Operations on the 2009-2010 UK coaching staff), and Walter McCarty had all been taken in the first round, following a championship in the 1995-96 season.

Those '96 'Cats would be in the record books for just a few more minutes, before Oklahoma City made Eric Bledsoe the fourth Kentucky player selected in the first round. Bledsoe was traded to the Clippers within hours, but his selection at No. 18 overall was important for two very distinct reasons. One, it set the record for the most players in school history ever taken in the first round.

More importantly though, it showed just how far Calipari's system could take a player if he was willing to put in a little hard work. That's because unlike Wall and Cousins, Bledsoe hadn't come to Kentucky projected as a one-and-done player; as a matter of fact, Kentucky's staff (with the help of Wall) spent most of the previous season convincing Bledsoe just how good he could be, and even then, Bledsoe still almost decided against declaring. Safe to say that after going 18th overall (and after signing a $70 million contract in the summer of 2014), Bledsoe made the right decision.

And finally, the 2010 Kentucky Wildcats would go down in the record books nine picks later, when Daniel Orton was selected at No. 29 overall by the Orlando Magic.

The pick made waves across the entire basketball world, not just because it marked the first time *ever* that one school produced five first round picks, but also because of *who* that fifth first round pick was. Yes, Orton was an uber-talented big man that many could see developing into a first round pick *at some* point. But nobody could've envisioned it at that particular moment, not after Orton averaged just three points and three rebounds in his only season at Kentucky. Only there he was, sneaking into the first round, and securing the guaranteed contract that came with it.

Beyond just the pick itself however, Orton's selection raised a very scary question: If Calipari could get a guy who averaged three points per game into the first round, who *couldn't* he get drafted?

The whole idea left everyone speechless, even one person watching at home, who'd lived the entire 2009-2010 season first-hand.

"It was amazing to see," said Mark Krebs, a senior guard on the 2009-2010 team.

If there was one person who could probably provide a little perspective on everything that unfolded the night of June 24th, 2010 it was Krebs. He was a player who started his UK career under Tubby Smith and had survived the disastrous two-year Gillispie era, only to finish up his final season under Calipari.

In four years of college hoops, he'd literally seen it and done it all. He'd seen players and coaches come and go. He'd gone to the NCAA Tournament to the NIT and back. He'd witnessed the program go from after-thought nationally his entire junior year, to the tip of everyone's tongue as a senior.

Again, he'd seen it all. Well, except...this. Five first rounders? It seemed inconceivable.

Yet incredibly, it was what Calipari had been preaching virtually the entire season before.

"That was crazy to me that all the little things he (Calipari) said throughout the season came true," Krebs said. "He'd say little things throughout the day, before practice. He'd say 'Patrick, keep doing what you're doing. It's going to pay off. Daniel, keep giving us good minutes. It's going to pay off.' And it did."

"It's so true what Coach Cal said throughout the year," Krebs explained. "What he said was going to happen, happened."

Again, it was the vision that Calipari had sold both to returning players and new ones alike since he arrived at Kentucky.

And he couldn't help but speak his mind when he was asked about it that night.

"I'd say it's the biggest day in the history of Kentucky's program," Calipari said beaming to ESPN's Heather Cox.

The quote immediately shook up the state, and not for the reasons you might think. Fans and former players alike did not take kindly to Calipari's words, openly questioning its validity. How could *draft night* be the biggest day in Kentucky basketball history? No game had been won. No championship had been decided. This had *nothing* to do with Kentucky, and *everything* to do with the NBA.

Or so they thought. But what no one understood at the time was that Calipari wasn't actually talking about the day itself, but what it meant in the big picture.

He wasn't talking about one night, or even one moment, but instead, the birth of a potential dynasty.

"What Cal was saying was 'The championship we win, it will be because of this night,'" former Sports Information Director, and current Deputy Director of Athletics at Kentucky, DeWayne Peevy said. "And he ended up being a prophet. All the success we've had as a program, that team laid the path."

That's right. June 24th, 2010 might not have produced a championship, but it laid the groundwork for so much more. To date, the Wildcats have won an NCAA title, and played in a staggering four Final Fours in six seasons since Calipari took over.

And it wouldn't have happened without the 2010 team starting it all.

"My point was that now, they have changed the landscape of college basketball," Calipari said. "And they have. Which is bigger than Kentucky."

Indeed it was.

Not bad for a team that didn't even make the NCAA Tournament the year before Calipari arrived.

* * *

So before we go any further, I'm guessing that you're probably wondering a few things. Like for starters, why this book was even written in the first place. After all, it's not often that a book gets written about a college basketball team, period. Let alone one that just played six seasons ago.

Well, there is a rhyme and reason as to why I wrote this book. And a little back-story as well.

That story goes as follows: As you've probably figured out by now, my name is Aaron Torres (the name on the front of the book probably gave it away, huh?), but what you might not know is that I'm a writer for FoxSports. com. I cover a few different sports, but growing up in Connecticut (yes, I'm a UConn fan, meaning that 80 percent of the Kentucky fans who bought this book will probably burn it, and demand a refund. And frankly, I can't blame them), I've always had a special place in my heart for college basketball. Just like in Kentucky, college basketball is basically all we have to call our own in Connecticut. Also just like in Kentucky, we cherish our team, and at times, we probably care a little too much about their successes and failures. In our defense, that's just what we do as fans. Fan is just short for "fanatic" after all.

So anyway, I love college basketball, and one day at the beginning of this past season (2014-2015), I sat down to try and think of some story ideas for the season ahead. A few smaller-scale ones immediately came to mind, but at the same time, I also wanted to do something big. Do something fun. Do something more than just "this team will be good, and here's why." I wanted to do a story that meant something, one that would make a lasting impression.

Initially nothing really jumped to mind. The best I could come up with, was something on the five-year anniversary of the Butler-Duke championship game in 2010. But then I really thought about it, and realized "Wait a second, who would want to spend several months working on a positive story about Duke?" I'd rather do cartwheels into oncoming traffic.

So for a while there, I was stuck.

But then I went back, and really thought about that 2010 season. And when I did that, I realized that while Duke won the championship that year, Kentucky was the *story* of the entire season. John Calipari's arrival at the school signified a "perfect storm" of sorts for college basketball; a big-time coach, taking over at a big-time program, trying to find success using a highly unconventional method, by building his team around freshmen.

Again, the entire season was a perfect storm, a sociological experiment found in Nike sneakers. Everything about Kentucky --- the swagger (of both the players and the coach), the idea of building a team around freshmen, the concept of shaking up the *entire system* of college basketball --- drove the "old school" media mad. It made people like me --- people who grew up rooting for The Fab Five, UNLV, and Miami football --- want to see them succeed that much more.

And succeed they did. UK didn't have traditional "success" that year and didn't win a National Championship. But --- and this is a big "but" --- they did win a ton of games, they did completely turn around Kentucky's program, and they did shake up the entire system in the process.

Oh, and they had fun doing it.

And above all, I couldn't help but think of that word "fun" when I ended up pitching my editor on doing a story about the team.

Not only had that team completely changed college basketball, but I also couldn't help but remember how much "fun" I had watching them in the process (and I'm not even a Kentucky fan!). They were engaging and exciting and entertaining. Fans might remember that Duke won the title that year. But they would also remember John Wall, DeMarcus Cousins and Kentucky. So ultimately what would be more fun than going back, tracking down as many of those players and coaches as I could, and doing a story on them?

Nothing as far as I was concerned, which was why in October of 2014 I began the process of writing the article. The final piece came out the following March, and safe to say that it was a hit. College basketball fans in general thanked me for writing about a team that they couldn't help but love. Kentucky fans thanked me for helping them re-live one of their favorite seasons to be a fan.

And then, just as the buzz from the article was dying down, something surprising happened: A few Kentucky fans told me I should turn the article into a book.

Hmm, a book??? I mean sure, I wrote one back in 2011 but I hadn't really considered doing another one. At least I hadn't been thinking about it.

But then I started thinking about a few things. I thought about how much fun I'd had writing the article. And how much fans enjoyed reading it. Most importantly, I realized how much good stuff *got left out* of the article. Really good stuff. Funny stuff and great stories that we just didn't have space for when the final article was published.

A book, I realized, would be the perfect avenue to get it all in.

Which was why shortly after I finished the initial article, I decided to jump two-feet in, and yes, actually write a book.

All the good stuff that wasn't included in the initial article would make it this time. I would write about the team's surreal beginnings, after missing the NCAA Tournament all together in 2009. I'd write about Calipari's arrival, and how both freshmen and upperclassmen came together as a team. I'd write about the highs of the season, the visits from LeBron and Drake, and I'd write about the lows of the season too, when it all came crashing down with a loss in the Elite Eight.

But most importantly I'd write about this team, and expand on the theme of the original article: How this team changed college basketball.

How they taught everyone that young, one-and-done players could come together, could put the team before themselves and could do well in class. Then I'd write about how they could reap the benefits of their sacrifice when it was time to move onto the next level, and that neither the player nor the program would be hurt by it.

Granted, it all sounds like common sense now, after Kentucky's won a National Championship and made four Final Fours playing this way. But it wasn't common sense at the time.

Then the 2009-2010 Kentucky Wildcats changed that.

And ultimately that's why I decided to write this book: Because their story is *too good* not to tell.

This is the story of the 2009-2010 Kentucky Wildcats, told by the people who lived it all first hand, with all quotes (unless otherwise noted) coming first-hand from that Fox Sports article.

It truly was an incredible season.

And it was a fun season.

And above all, that's what I hope you get out of this book: The fun of it all.

The players and coaches had fun living it.

I had fun writing it.

And I sure as hell hope you have fun reading it.

It's Always Darkest before the Dawn: The Billy Clyde Years

To fully understand just how special Kentucky's run was during the 2009-2010 season, and why John Wall, DeMarcus Cousins, Patrick Patterson and their teammates mean so much to Kentucky's basketball program and its fans, you must first go back to 2009.

Do that, and you'll remember that in the season before John Calipari arrived in Lexington, there was no talk of No. 1 seeds, lottery picks or Final Four dreams. Instead, there were just losses. Lots and lots of losses. Even worse, they came as the program crumbled from within, under a coach who was ill-fit for the responsibilities that came with being Kentucky's college basketball coach.

As they say, "It's always darkest before the dawn." And in the winter of 2009 it was damn near pitch black in Lexington.

The funny thing is though, it wasn't supposed to be that way. Two years before the pomp and circumstance of Calipari's arrival at Kentucky, there was similar pomp and similar circumstance for a similar coach, who many believed could be the savior of Kentucky basketball. That man was Billy Clyde Gillispie, and although he arrived in Lexington under much different circumstances than Calipari did two years later, each was ultimately tasked with the same mission: Make Kentucky, Kentucky again.

In Gillispie's case, he arrived following the 10-year run of Tubby Smith. During Smith's reign, the Wildcats were never "bad," per se, but after a National Championship run in 1998 (led by mostly Rick Pitino's players) they were never really "elite" either. Smith made the tournament all 10 seasons he was in Lexington, and won a staggering 76 percent of his games, but in Kentucky --- where fans don't hope for championships, but *expect* them --- not nearly enough of those wins came when it mattered in March. After making that first championship run, Tubby never did get back to the Final Four (let alone win a title), and after back-to-back second round exits in 2006 and 2007, decided it was enough. He resigned in March of that year to take the head coaching job at Minnesota.

Although Smith never said it publicly, the logic behind the move was clear: He was getting out, before Kentucky could force him out.

It also meant that in the spring of 2007, the Wildcats would be seeking a new head coach.

They'd eventually get that man in Gillispie. And while his regime would ultimately go down as an utter failure, in defense of both the school and coach, it did seem like a good hire at first glance.

Gillispie arrived in Lexington with the reputation of a basketball lifer, a man who ate, slept, and breathed basketball. He had no wife. He had no social life. And he had no hobbies. Instead, he had basketball all day, every day. The sport consumed him, and by the time he arrived at Kentucky he had the resume to prove it. For Billy Clyde Gillispie, there was no easy road to the top of college basketball. He started as a high school assistant, before becoming a high school head coach, then a junior college assistant, and eventually a college assistant, before ultimately getting his first head coaching gig at Texas El Paso in 2002.

And when he did finally get that head coaching gig, well to his credit, he didn't disappoint. Gillispie got off to a slow start, going 6-24 his first year, before engineering one of the greatest turnarounds in *NCAA history* in year two. There he led the Miners to a 24-8 record overall (in a season that included an exhibition game win over the Harlem Globetrotters, by the way). UTEP earned its first NCAA Tournament berth in over a decade that season, and pushed Maryland to the brink, before losing 86-83.

After that NCAA Tournament run at UTEP, Gillispie left for Texas A&M. But while Gillispie's address changed, the success just kept on coming.

And it came at the most unlikely place. That's because while Texas El Paso is a school that loves its basketball team (UTEP actually won an NCAA championship, when they were known as Texas Western and beat Kentucky in 1966), Texas A&M is a football school first, second, and third, and a place where basketball, simply provides a diversion between the last football game of the season, and the start of spring practice.

Except in three short seasons at the school, Billy Clyde completely flipped that on its head. The Aggies won 21 games his first season, and by year two, Gillispie had the school in the NCAA Tournament for the first time in nearly two decades. By his third year, Gillispie not only had A&M in the Sweet 16, but did it in a way that caught every Kentucky fan's attention: The Aggies won their first and second round games at Rupp Arena, for all of Big Blue Nation to see. The fact that they beat Louisville and Rick Pitino to advance to the Sweet 16 only added icing to the cake.

Talk about endearing yourself to a fan base, huh?

Texas A&M eventually lost in the Sweet 16 that season (ironically to John Calipari and Memphis), but the Aggies' run, through Rupp Arena, and through Louisville was enough to convince Kentucky fans that Gillispie could be *the guy* to lead the Wildcats' program back to the top when the UK job came open that spring. He appeared to be the perfect fit, someone who was all about basketball, had a penchant for turning around programs (and doing it quickly), and who also was coming off high-level tournament success.

Not to mention, he was also a man who seemed to fully embrace the challenges and responsibilities that came with the Kentucky job.

At least that's what he told the crowd of fans and media members, who packed Memorial Coliseum for his introductory press conference the day he was hired by Kentucky.

"I like expectations," Gillispie told the crowd that day. "My most favorite year was this (past one at Texas A&M), when we had pressure. And that expectation, it either drives you or it diminishes your ability — and my ability isn't diminished by expectations."

It all sounded too good to be true.

Unfortunately for Kentucky, the old adage turned out to be accurate in this case: If it sounds too good to be true, it usually is.

It took just two games for the school and its fans to realize that maybe Gillispie might not be the perfect fit after all. That's because after a relatively impressive 67-40 win over Central Arkansas in Gillispie's debut, the first sign of trouble --- ok, the first sign of an all-out catastrophe --- came in just his second game as the head coach at Kentucky.

There, the unthinkable happened: Kentucky lost.

But it wasn't just any loss.

Kentucky lost to.... a school called Garner-Webb.

(Let me stop here to let that sink for a second)

....

....

Yes, you read that correctly. Kentucky, the winningest program in college basketball history, lost the second game of the Billy Gillispie era to Garner Webb, a school that few college basketball fans had ever heard of at the time, a school that even fewer could find on a map, and a school that to this day, still has yet to make an NCAA Tournament appearance. Yet there they were, walking into Rupp Arena on the night of November 7th, 2007, and walking out with a win. The fact that the loss came on Gillispie's birthday was an ominous sign if ever there was one.

And sadly, things never really got better from there in Gillispie's first year at Kentucky. There were a few more wins, before the Wildcats proceeded to lose four straight games in December (including a pair to noted college basketball powers UAB and Houston). They did bounce back with a win, before immediately following that up with a loss to San Diego at home to fall to just 5-6 overall.

Safe to say, things were getting bad for Gillispie and Kentucky. Really bad. And it wasn't just all about the losses on the court either. In addition to the win-loss record, it was becoming apparent that while Gillispie said that he "liked expectations" at his opening press conference, he might not have been totally aware of what the word "expectations" actually meant in Kentucky. Understand that in Gillispie's previous two coaching stops, his sole focus was on basketball. In El Paso and College Station, "expectations" were synonymous with wins, and as long as you had more wins than losses, nobody really bothered you. But at Kentucky, it wasn't so simple.

For starters, there were still expectations on the court.....only they were way more extreme than anything Gillispie had ever dealt with in either of his previous head coaching stops. John Calipari famously tells his recruits, "I can't hide you at Kentucky," and it's something that's applicable not only for players, but coaches too. At Kentucky, every result matters. Not in March, but all season long. And there's no football program to provide a distraction when the coach needs to work out the kinks or work through a losing streak, like Gillispie had in College Station.

More importantly however, there were "expectations" off the court too, and even more than the losses on the court, it was quickly becoming clear that Gillispie was ill-equipped to handle those either.

It's no secret that when you're the head basketball coach at Kentucky you're not just the face of the basketball team, and not even the face of the entire UK athletics department, but in actuality, you're the face of the entire state. Sure, being the Kentucky basketball coach is part X's and O's, and yes, you better win way more games than you lose. But at the same time, there are a ton of responsibilities off the court as well, to the point that you've got to have a little politician in you as well. The Kentucky basketball coach has to kiss babies. He's got to hug grandmas. He's got to pose for pictures with puppies.

Ok, maybe it's not that extreme. But at the very least, he's got to be likeable, especially when he's not winning very many games. And unfortunately for Gillispie, he was neither likeable, nor was he winning.

And it was becoming evident rather quickly that both on the court and off it, he probably wasn't the right guy to be the head coach at Kentucky.

"I think from the get-go he was in over his head," said Josh Harrellson, who played one year for Gillispie, followed by two more for Calipari. "Kentucky is not a job for a lot of people. Not many people can do the requirement of being the head coach at Kentucky. You've got to be a fan-pleaser, you've got to be a coach on the court, you've got to be this public figure. Coach Gillispie, he just wanted to coach. He didn't want to do the rest of it."

To his credit though, after the slow start, Gillispie did rally the troops. Kentucky finished the regular season at just 18-11 overall, but did manage to go a respectable 12-4 in the SEC (a better in-conference result than Tubby Smith had the previous year), and snuck into the NCAA Tournament as an 11-seed. Unfortunately once they did get into the Big Dance, their stay was short. Without Patrick Patterson in the lineup (who was out with an injury) the Wildcats fell behind Marquette early and never were able to catch up. They lost 74-66, bringing their season to an end.

It also brought the first year of the Billy Gillispie era to an end as well.

To most, the season was considered a disappointment, but at the same time, it was still in fact just one year. The team had still made the NCAA Tournament, in a season where Gillispie was a new coach, installing a new system, with new players. If the Wildcats were still able to make the Big Dance despite all those obstacles, things had to get better in year two, right?

Yeah, not so much.

That's because, if Gillispie's first season started off with a thud (by losing to Garner-Webb in the second game) the start of the following season was an all-out disaster. The Wildcats lost their opener to VMI ---yes, you read that right, V-M-freakin'-I --- in a game which Kentucky --- a team that was built on defense under Gillispie --- gave up 111 points. It was the most points the Wildcats had allowed in a single game in nearly 20 years, and the unfortunate part was that Kentucky had no time to recover. Their second game of the 2008-2009 season was against North Carolina, which just so happened to be the No. 1 ranked team in the country, and a club which would go on to win the championship later that season. The Wildcats lost 77-58, in a game that wasn't nearly as close as the final score indicated (the one silver lining for the Wildcats? A local high school star from North Carolina was in the stands that day. His name? John Wall).

And from there, it never really got better. There were peaks in Gillispie's second season (including 11 wins in the 12 games following the loss to Carolina) and valleys (another loss to Louisville), with plenty of other general, Gillispie weirdness along the way (most notably when the Kentucky coach mocked ESPN reporter Jeannine Edwards during half-time of a nationally televised game).

But mostly there just weren't enough wins. As Kentucky's season progressed, questions about Gillispie's future at the school began to circulate.

Billy Clyde was on the hot seat, and everyone started to feel it.

"I'd be lying to you if I told you that if you keep hearing it, it's not go-ing to bother you," Ramon Harris, who was a junior during the 2008-2009 season said. "As much as you try to say (to yourself) 'Whatever happens, happens' (it bothers you)."

The final straw for Gillispie may have come on "Senior Night" of that second season. Understand that "Senior Night" is a sacred tradi-tion at Kentucky, and it was all the more important in 2009. Kentucky entered the night with a record of 19-10, and sat squarely on the NCAA Tournament bubble, meaning that Georgia was a game they *had to win*, and frankly it was a game they had no excuse *not to win*. Besides the fact that Kentucky is Kentucky, and Georgia is Georgia, and the Wildcats should basically beat the Bulldogs under virtually all circumstances, this was an especially bad Georgia team. They entered the evening at 11-18 overall, with a grand total of two wins in SEC play that season. Not to mention that oh, by the way, they had also fired head coach Dennis Felton in the middle of the season, and were riding things out with an interim head coach.

Everything was lining up for an easy Kentucky win, one that would keep the Wildcats' tournament hopes alive, and keep the heat off Gillispie for at least one more day.

That is, until the Wildcats lost 90-85.

On Senior Night.

To Georgia.

In what ended up being the Bulldogs last win of the season.

To the surprise of no one, the Wildcats walked back to the locker room to a chorus of boos.

Dana O'Neil, who was working on an all-access piece for ESPN.com at the time, was with the team when they got to the locker room. The scene wasn't pretty.

The players sit alone for eight minutes. It is silent, monastery silent, vow-of-silence silent, the only noise provided by the hum of the heating unit. Gillispie and his staff meet in a private room. ESPN, which was allowed an all-access tour with the Wildcats, is asked to leave before he comes out.

Later, a university official says that Gillispie never spoke to his team except to tell the players what time practice was the next day.

With Senior Night over, the hits kept coming for Kentucky. The Wildcats lost their season finale at Florida, lost in the SEC Tournament quarterfinals to LSU, and when the NCAA Tournament brackets came out the following week, Kentucky found themselves in a very unfamiliar position: They were out of the NCAA Tournament altogether. It was a crushing blow for a school that hadn't missed the Big Dance since 1991. Even that year, it was sanctions, not a bad win-loss record that kept them out of the tournament.

What was especially disappointing though, was that the program was supposed to be beyond all this. After all, wasn't Gillispie supposed to be Kentucky's savior? Wasn't he supposed to be a step up from Tubby Smith? Even in the darkest days of the Tubby era, when the Wildcats were far from a National Championship contender, at least they made the NCAA Tournament.

But this? Missing the Big Dance, and going to the NIT? It wasn't just bad. It was literally inconceivable.

"It's easy to think about the NIT now that Kentucky played Robert Morris (in 2013)," Matt Jones, the founder of Kentucky Sports Radio said. "But (back then), Kentucky had not been to the NIT, I don't even know when the last time was. Kentucky did not go to the NIT, and then they went to the NIT."

The Wildcats were indeed in the NIT, but even then, even when everyone seemed ready to move on from Billy Clyde, the old coach didn't go down without a fight. Kentucky beat UNLV in their NIT opener (a game which wasn't even played in Rupp Arena, but instead, Memorial Coliseum), and then followed it up with a wild win over Creighton, when Jodie Meeks converted a three-point play with just 10.6 seconds to go.

Kentucky was rallying. Sure it wasn't the NCAA Tournament, but the Wildcats were playing well, and most importantly, they were winning. It seemed like maybe, just maybe, that after two years, Gillispie had finally turned a corner. Some thought it might even be enough for him to keep his job.

"All the managers, everybody's talking about 'Well, if we beat Notre Dame, Gillispie is coming back,'" team manager Chad Sanders said. "'They won't fire him.'"

Then, they lost to Notre Dame, officially bringing the 2008-2009 season to an end.

"It was kind of like 'No, they're not going to do it, they're going to give him one more year," Sanders said. "'We've got Jodie and Patrick coming back, they're not going to do it right now.'"

But then, they did.

On March 27th, 2009, the University of Kentucky fired Billy Gillispie, less than two full years after they hired him. Gillispie finished his two seasons in Lexington with a 40-27 record, and a grand total of zero NCAA Tournament wins, in one NCAA Tournament game. Gillispie never did turn out to be the savior that everyone envisioned when he was hired.

At the same time, while history hasn't necessarily been kind to Billy Clyde's time in Lexington (understandably so), with a little hindsight, it might not be quite as bad as we all remember it. Ask many who played and worked for Gillispie and they still swear by his coaching acumen.

The problem was, he just wasn't a great coach for Kentucky specifically.

"X's and O's I don't think I've ever been around a coach like him," Sanders said. "From X's and O's I was learning a lot from him, in terms of how to break down games, how he prepares teams for games. But every coach is different, and it wasn't the right fit for him with the media. With everything else at Kentucky, it isn't just about playing ball."

At Kentucky, it's not just about playing ball. It was a concept that Gillispie probably hadn't fully understood when he took the job, but in his defense, it's something that the Kentucky administration hadn't fully considered when they hired him either. At Kentucky, it's not enough to just hire a "basketball coach." You've got to hire someone who understands the X's and O's, sure. But you've also got to make sure the same guy understands all the off-court demands --- from the fans, alumni, media and everyone else around the program --- that come with it too. You can't have one without the other.

It also meant that as the school pursued another head coach, they couldn't make the same mistake twice. They had to find someone who knew basketball, but also knew how to handle the maniacal fan base.

Many wondered if such a person existed.

"I think there was a malaise about it, but also kind of a slight panic," Jones said. "During the end of the Tubby Smith era, the last five or six years or so, the team was always good, but not great. Then with Billy (Gillispie) there was a little rejuvenation of energy, and then when he failed I think there were some Kentucky fans that felt like 'Will Kentucky ever be Kentucky again?'"

It was the question that was on everyone's mind as the school pursued its next head coach.

This time though, there could be no screw ups.

The school had to get this hire right.

And immediately, the search centered around one man.

It's just not the man you might think.

Then, Fate Sort of Interjected

BILLY GILLISPIE WASN'T technically fired until the morning of Friday, March 27th, 2009, but long before it became official, rumors began to circulate on who might replace him. And while no one is quite sure the exact moment that John Calipari's name was first linked to the job, one of his former assistants remembers exactly where he was, when he first heard Calipari's name brought up as a possible replacement for Gillispie.

That man is Josh Pastner, and before he became the head coach at Memphis, Pastner worked as an assistant coach and recruiting coordinator under Calipari for one season at the school. Memphis was good in the one season Pastner served as an assistant in 2009, the problem was, that just a year after playing for a national title, they weren't "championship good." The Tigers 2009 season ended in disappointment with a Sweet 16 loss to Missouri in the West Regional semifinals in Phoenix.

After the game Pastner and the Memphis basketball traveling party did what every team does when they lose in the NCAA Tournament. The coaches and players fulfilled some quick media obligations, showered and headed to the airport for a long, cross-country flight that absolutely no one was looking forward to. As Pastner settled in, he was hoping to just sit back and relax for a minute; a long off-season was ahead, one that would be especially busy for him personally. That summer, the 31-year-old assistant coach was getting married.

But as the flight took off and Pastner flipped on the radio, a huge story broke. It was a story that would rock both his own personal life, and the entire sport of college basketball in the coming days.

"I remember they had radio on the airplane ride home from Phoenix," Pastner said, from his office in Memphis. "They're all talking about Coach Calipari's name being swirled around as the next Kentucky coach."

There it was: Kentucky was planning on firing Billy Gillispie the next morning and they needed a man to replace him. And to no one's surprise, John Calipari's name was one of the top names on Kentucky's list. After all, how could Calipari *not* be a candidate? The guy had taken Memphis from a middle-of-the-pack Conference USA club, and turned it into one of the top programs anywhere in the country.

However, just because Calipari's name was *on* the list, doesn't mean it was at the *top*. Instead, Kentucky's administration actually preferred someone else.

"Everybody was talking about Billy Donovan," team manager Chad Sanders said, when asked about the early stages of the Kentucky coaching search.

Oh, Billy Donovan. You forgot about him, didn't you? But despite how history played itself out, and despite the fact that John Calipari has had one of the most successful runs in college basketball history at Kentucky, it was Donovan who was actually the school's first choice. And in defense of both Kentucky's administration and its fans, there was good reason why. At the time Donovan was just 44-years-old, but already had a championship pedigree after turning Florida from a college basketball afterthought to super power. He had made his first Final Four in 2000 at just 35-years-old, and by 2007, had not only won one National Championship in Gainesville, but back-to-back titles in 2006 and 2007.

Donovan's resume was plenty impressive. But for Kentucky fans it wasn't just about what he did at Florida. It was also about what he'd done *before* he got there as well.

That's because prior to his arrival in Gainesville (and prior to his first head coaching stop at Marshall) Donovan had served as an assistant on Rick Pitino's coaching staff at Kentucky. During his five years at the school he helped Pitino push Kentucky through crippling NCAA sanctions, and rebuild it into one of the most formidable teams in college basketball.

Therefore, unlike Gillispie, Donovan would (at least in theory) understand all the "big picture" stuff that came with the Kentucky coaching job. While Gillispie's problems at the school stemmed from his inability to handle all the external pressures of the gig, Donovan was not only aware of those pressures, but had seen it first-hand in his five years there as an assistant.

From both a coaching standpoint and a management one, Donovan appeared to be the perfect fit for Kentucky. That's also why his name was on the short list of potential candidates that Kentucky hoped to interview, the weekend after Gillispie was fired.

"If anyone would be honest with you --- and they might not be --- there were three candidates for the job," Kentucky Sports Radio's Matt Jones said. "They were going to interview Billy Donovan, Tom Izzo and John Calipari."

"Then fate sort of interjected," Jones said.

That's because before Kentucky could ever sit down with Donovan, he withdrew his name from the coaching search, deciding instead to stay at Florida. And with the pool whittled down to two logical candidates, fate stepped up again; just when Kentucky's brass thought they would get the chance to sit down with Izzo, his Michigan State Spartans squad pulled off an upset in the Midwest regional against Louisville.

The win meant that --- whether he wanted to be or not --- Izzo was essentially out of the running for the Kentucky job. `

"A lot of people don't talk about that, but Izzo was almost the coach here," Jones said. "But when Tom Izzo pulled off the upset in the Elite Eight, it meant that to interview him, they would have to wait a week, until after the Final Four."

The thing was, there was no need for Kentucky to wait. In the process of _hoping_ to interview Izzo, they actually _did_ interview Calipari, whose NCAA Tournament had ended with that Sweet 16 loss to Missouri.

And when Kentucky's brass did sit down with him, they were simply blown away. For one, he was coming off an unprecedented run at Memphis; one that included four Sweet 16's, three Elite Eight's and a National Championship game appearance in the previous four seasons. Considering that the Wildcats had missed the NCAA Tournament altogether in 2009, and hadn't made the second weekend of the tournament since 2005, Calipari's recent high-level NCAA Tournament success wasn't just a selling point. It was a necessity.

To add a little icing to the cake (ok, a lot of icing to the cake), Calipari also sold the ability to field a competitive team right away. Two of the top high school players in the country --- DeMarcus Cousins and Xavier Henry --- had already committed to Memphis. Two of the nation's top uncommitted players --- John Wall and Eric Bledsoe --- were seriously considering Memphis as well.

To Kentucky, Calipari was the perfect candidate. Not only had he built the Memphis program from the ground up, and turned the school into a perennial National Championship contender (two things that undoubtedly appealed to the Kentucky brass), but he also had another National Championship contender lined up for the next season as well.

Meaning, that if he did take the Kentucky job, and if he was able to pair up a few of those recruits with Jodie Meeks and Patrick Patterson, the Wildcats could in theory, be good right away. Like, really, really good.

What more could Kentucky possibly want to hear?

"I think Cal sold to UK, 'We will be good next year," Jones said. "'This won't be a rebuilding project, we will be good next year.' And only Calipari could've done that. Izzo could've succeeded here, but it would've taken some time.'"

For Kentucky, the whole situation seemed too good to be true. They had found a coach who was successful on the court, but also had the ability to bring in big-time players off of it.

Kentucky had their next coach.

Or at least they thought they did.

But after getting back to Memphis, and after really thinking about it, John Calipari realized something: He wasn't totally sure if he wanted the job after all.

* * *

The news trucks lined the streets of Galloway Avenue, their cameras transfixed on the gated home of the head basketball coach. Fans stood on the front lawn, some chanting "Stay" others holding up signs, and all hoping they could somehow convince a once-in-a-lifetime coach to pass up the tradition and riches of another school, to stay and deliver the city a National Championship.

Would John Calipari stay in Memphis? Or would he go to Kentucky? It was Tuesday afternoon, roughly 36 hours after Calipari had returned from an interview with the UK administration, and the whole city of Memphis needed an answer. News trucks followed his every move. Reporters vigorously made phone calls and sent texts trying to get the scoop.

"It was hectic, it was crazy," former Memphis and Kentucky assistant Orlando Antigua said. "I have never been a part of anything like that. They were filming our office doors, fans were camping outside of Cal's house. I remember helicopters, police barricades. It was wild."

The biggest decision of Calipari's coaching career loomed, and he left no stone unturned. He met with players early Monday to discuss what was going on, and by that night he had a separate meeting with prominent Memphis boosters, who were offering him everything short of the keys to the city to stay. Later that evening, Calipari had his assistant coaches at his house, discussing the pros and cons of a move.

Again, Calipari looked at the decision from every angle possible, all as the entire city reacted to his every move. Calipari had promised an answer by Tuesday evening, and as the sun rose Tuesday morning everyone was looking for any information, anywhere they could find it. One newspaper went so far as to interview customers at a donut shop, after Calipari had briefly been seen there that morning.

Yes, that really happened. And it shows just how dire the situation had become. Everybody wanted to know… no, *they needed* to know what was next for Calipari.

The problem was that Calipari himself was having as much trouble finding that answer as anyone. Sure, he was weighing an offer from Kentucky. But he was also in a city that not only loved basketball, but loved college basketball, and his Memphis Tigers were the biggest game in town. While in Memphis, he had built the program into a national powerhouse, and frankly, there were no signs of slowing down. Another top ranked recruiting class was coming to town, and maybe, just maybe, Calipari could get Memphis that National Championship they'd just barely missed out on a season before.

As easy as it would be to go to Kentucky, it would've been just as easy to stay in Memphis.

"I don't know if people knew how hard it was for him to make that decision," Rod Strickland, a former assistant coach at both Memphis and Kentucky said. "He was torn. He had built something in Memphis, we were just coming off a Finals appearance and then the next year it was a Sweet 16. But he was building that program."

More than just building a program though, he was building a life too.

"He was in the community," Strickland said. "He had roots there that he was laying. It wasn't an easy decision."

For Calipari, it wasn't just about leaving a basketball team, but everything that he'd created. After some rough early years at the school, he finally had the program at the place he wanted it. His players were active in the community. His own daughter was set to attend the school. He'd gotten the program to the brink of a National Championship. How could he leave it all behind, including the players he'd convinced to come to the school in the first place?

"I do remember how hard it was for Cal to actually pull the trigger, actually make the decision, because of the kids we had at Memphis," Antigua said. "With the kids who were seniors, the guys he recruited there."

Ironically however, Memphis' players may have been the ones who gave Calipari the final nudge that convinced him to take the Kentucky job.

"They were the ones who actually gave the blessing for him to move on when we met with them," Antigua said. "That had always been the case with Cal and his players, 'You have to do what's best for you.' And when those opportunities came for them, to jump to the NBA or to play professionally (he told them to do it). Actually, Antonio Anderson was the one who said 'Coach, chase your dreams. If you said that (Kentucky) is the one place (you'd be willing to leave Memphis for), and you wouldn't leave for any one place but that (then do it). You told us to chase our dreams, go chase your dreams.'"

Calipari had promised to have an answer for both Memphis and Kentucky by the end of the day on Tuesday, and by mid-afternoon that answer started to come. A three-car motorcade left Calipari's house at 4:22 p.m. central time, and within an hour the news began to leak that he had in fact accepted the Wildcats' head coaching position.

At 6:27 p.m., it became official. Calipari sent a text to a writer for the *Memphis Commercial Appeal*, confirming the rumors.

He was the new head coach at the University of Kentucky.

"I am accepting the uk job," the text message read. "Go Big Blue."

And just like that, college basketball history changed forever. Kentucky had its next head basketball coach, and at the same time, the door slammed shut on the most successful era in the history of Memphis basketball.

In an interview with FoxSports.com this past January, Calipari explained the decision in detail. In the process, he confirmed what his assistant coaches said: It wasn't easy.

"I loved my time at Memphis," Calipari said. "I loved what we had rolling."

"Rolling" would be an understatement. The school had made the second weekend of the NCAA Tournament in Calipari's final four years, including that championship game run in 2008. With recruiting picking up, there was no reason to think that Calipari couldn't have had the Tigers competing for championships as long as he was there.

So why then, would he leave in the first place?

The answer was simple.

"It was Kentucky," Calipari said. "I just looked at, either I was going to do this, or I was going to finish my career at Memphis. At my age, the opportunity kind of came up and I was like 'I'm doing this.'"

Simply put, Calipari had spent the previous nine seasons building up Memphis, turning them from a middle of the pack Conference USA school, into one that could stand up to all of college basketball's biggest bullies. More often than not, Memphis not only looked the bully in the eye, but knocked them out cold.

But after years --- a career really --- of having to stand up to the bully, for once, Calipari was ready to see what it was like to actually be the bully.

"I had never coached at a school like this," Calipari said. "And before my career ended, I wanted to see how I would do."

He continued.

"Now I wanted to sit at the table with them, rather than the little table on the side," he said. "That was my thinking, look, before I retire, let me sit with these guys at the table and see how I do."

As the world would eventually find out, Calipari would be just fine.

But that was still a long way away.

In the meantime, John Calipari was coming to Kentucky.

And the school had less than 24 hours to prepare.

You Can Call Me Cal

I T WAS THE day Kentucky basketball fans had waited for, the moment their savior was set to arrive, and revive Kentucky from the dead. But while all of Big Blue Nation grew restless waiting for John Calipari to be introduced as the school's new head coach, the people actually working for Kentucky needed every moment they could get. Calipari had accepted Kentucky's offer late Tuesday night, and his introductory press conference was at the ungodly hour of 9:30 a.m. the following day. That meant the staff in Lexington had just a brief few hours to prepare the team's practice facility for the introduction on the morning of April 1, 2009.

With the Billy Gillispie era now over, things were going to be different in Lexington, and it started with that very first press conference. Unlike two years earlier, when Gillispie's opening press conference was held at Memorial Coliseum, allowing every wackadoo with a half tank of gas and passion for Kentucky hoops to show up and sit a few feet from the Wildcats' new head coach, this time the UK administration was more cautious. The event was held in the team's practice facility, meaning that everyone who attended had to be approved by the school itself, and be physically let into the building by a Kentucky staff member. The decision to change venues helped keep the wackadoos away (or at least, at a distance), but it also created a whole new set of problems.

"The logistics were kind of a nightmare," former Kentucky Sports Information Director, DeWayne Peevy said. "We were hiring John Calipari and it was less than 24 hours (we had to prepare the gym)."

Twenty-four hours, forget that. Maybe 12, if they were lucky. And there was a lot of work to be done.

A basketball hoop had to be moved from one of the gyms to another, so that a podium could be put in its place. The building --- which again, had only served as a practice facility in every other day of its existence --- had to be equipped for both local and national news stations to go on live television, before, during and after the event. And even though fans wouldn't be allowed into this press conference, the media would...and they began arriving by the hundreds.

Add it all up, and by the time Calipari prepared to take the podium, the number of people in the crowd seemed inconceivable.

"The press conference appeared to have over 1,000 people there," Calipari said to Fox Sports last winter, when asked about his arrival in Lexington.

But while the moment --- and the cameras that came with it --- would have overwhelmed a lot of coaches, it actually invigorated Calipari.

The Kentucky job had first come onto Calipari's radar in the early 1990's, when he was coaching at UMass, and brought his club to Lexington for a regular season game. And even in the two decades that followed, which included stops in the NBA and at Memphis, Kentucky never really left Calipari's radar; he would later admit that he was disappointed the school didn't call him back in 2007, when Tubby Smith resigned and Billy Gillispie got the job. As he explained to reporters, he called his wife Ellen several times a day during that stretch, asking if Kentucky had reached out. It took him several days to realize that the call wasn't coming at all.

But for whatever disappointment 2007 brought, Kentucky did reach out in 2009, and this time Calipari would leave no stone unturned. After interviewing for the job in Chicago that March weekend, Calipari actually went so far as to call former Kentucky coaches to pick their brains. What would the job entail? What kind of responsibilities would he have off the court? If Calipari did accept the job (which he obviously later did), he wanted to make sure that he was as prepared as possible.

From those conversations Calipari began to understand the scope of what he was getting into, and just how much basketball and the Kentucky program, meant to the people of the state. That's why even after accepting the job, the work didn't stop; Calipari spent the final few hours before his introductory press conference brushing up on Kentucky basketball history, trying to cram every little nugget and detail into his head.

That decision by Calipari left DeWayne Peevy shocked the first time he met his new boss. Peevy had written down a few final notes to give to Calipari before the press conference.

To Peevy's surprise, Calipari barely needed them at all.

"We went over some different bullet points and some notes to make sure he knew enough about Kentucky," Peevy said. "But you could tell he had really done a lot on his own. I didn't add much."

Not that there was time to go over the fine print anyway. It was 9:30 a.m., and the press conference was about to begin.

Athletic Director Mitch Barnhart opened the festivities with some quick comments, including the announcement that Calipari had already agreed to, and signed an eight-year contract worth over $31 million. The deal became significant for two reasons; one, it made Calipari the highest paid coach in college basketball. Two, Calipari had actually *signed* the deal, which was no small feat; believe it or not, Gillispie had refused to sign a contract during his two seasons at the school.

With Calipari's signature officially on paper, Barnhart introduced the new Kentucky head coach and his family. Calipari then slowly walked his way through the crowd and to the podium. Once on-stage, Barnhart and President Lee Todd greeted him.

And from there, Cal was…. well, he was Cal. He mentioned his trip to Lexington with UMass some two decades before. He discussed the conversations he had about the job with Rick Pitino, Tubby Smith and Joe B. Hall. He talked about his graduation rates at Memphis and his decision to leave the school, not to mention his family history, and his grandfather's time working in the coal mines. Basically, he discussed it all.

Most importantly though, he discussed who he was, and what fans should expect from his team.

"I'm a regular guy folks, I do not walk on water," Calipari said. "I do not have a magic wand, I'm day-to-day. I told Dr. Todd and Mitch 'If you want something to happen in a year, do not hire me. That's not how I do things.'"

Not that he was shying away from expectations, either.

"When we get it right, you notice we're No. 1 in the country, we're No. 1 seeds and we're playing in Final Fours," Calipari said, pausing for emphasis. "When you get it right."

And from there, he slowly began to explain how he planned to build a National Championship contender, one that would be a constant threat in March. He discussed the origins of his famed "dribble drive" offense, which he had picked up from friend Vance Walberg, who was the head coach at Pepperdine at the time. He talked about the assistants he planned to bring with him from Memphis. But mostly he talked about the players. Long before Calipari ever coined the term a "Players First Program" he readily admitted that it was the players on the court, not the guy on the sideline, who would be the ultimate difference between success and failure.

"The key to winning, and winning in the NCAA Tournament," Calipari began. "This is the key; there are three keys to winning and winning championships. The first thing is have really good players. The second thing is, have really good players. And I hate to tell you, that's the third thing."

The crowd laughed, but Calipari was dead serious. He had already gotten a reputation at Memphis as the best recruiter in college basketball, and everyone in the audience knew that he had another top class lined up. In the short-term, the hope was that he'd be able to bring some of those guys with him to Kentucky. In the long-term Calipari made a promise, and it's a promise that he hasn't broken yet, six years later.

"I'm here because I can recruit the best...of the best," Calipari said.

It was music to the ears of Kentucky fans, and also seemed to point to a bigger picture point on Calipari: He seemed to "get it." He didn't shy from expectations of winning big, or recruiting the best players in the country. Instead, he embraced it.

He also understood just how much the team, and its players meant to the entire state of Kentucky. One quote particularly summed that up. Calipari may have been trying to make a joke, but that joke ultimately endeared him to the Wildcat faithful everywhere.

"I saw Jeff Sheppard doing commercials on TV. They tell me Richie Farmer, who scored against us, is like the Secretary of Agriculture," Calipari said, before the laughter from the audience caught him off guard.

He stopped in his tracks, before then continuing.

"They take care of these kids. Is that right? That guy scored baskets; he's going to be governor. That's crazy."

Crazy indeed. But to those who were paying close attention to the comment, it pointed to a larger, big picture point on Calipari.

"He referenced Richie Farmer," Jones said. "Now Richie Farmer is in jail so it's not as easy to reference him, but at the time, he referenced this idol of Kentucky basketball. He just 'got it.' You could tell he just 'got it.'"

Peevy agreed.

"I was just as blown away from that press conference," he said. "It just felt like 'This was something different.'"

Eventually the press conference wrapped up, but the excitement stayed in the air for much longer. After two long years --- a decade, really --- it seemed like the dark cloud had been lifted from above Kentucky. The Billy Gillispie era felt like something from a past lifetime, a chapter from a book that had been put on a shelf and long since forgotten about. John Calipari had arrived, and with him, real expectations for the future of the program arrived as well. There would be no disappointing NCAA Tournament runs, or even worse, no worries about missing the NCAA Tournament altogether. There would be no more second-tier players; good kids with great personalities, but also guys who simply weren't talented enough to compete at the highest level.

No, no, no. There would be star players, and big games and deep tournament runs.

Simply put, Kentucky was "Kentucky" again.

"Kentucky had stopped being what every fan wants it to be," former Kentucky star Scott Padgett said.

Padgett should know. He spent five years playing for the school at the height of its success in the late 1990's (making two Final Fours, and winning a National Championship in 1998), and would later join Calipari's first staff as an assistant strength coach. But in the spring of 2009 he was working as a radio host, in the final dark years of the Gillispie era.

"At the end of the day, Kentucky fans want Kentucky to be on the end of everybody's tongue when it's basketball season," Padgett said. "At all times they have to be relevant. At all times."

Well, for the first time in a long time that's exactly what the team was: Relevant. Fans were talking about the team. Students on campus had forgotten about the NIT debacle of just a few weeks earlier, and were thinking about championships. Everyone was thinking big, and talking about the future.

"That first press conference he had, you could tell all the buzz around campus," Mark Krebs said. "For me as a player, you could tell the buzz around campus was a microcosm for what the buzz was like around the state. You could just tell people were really excited."

But as excited as the fans were, no one was more excited than the players themselves. Before Calipari had met with the media, he had briefly met with the players at the Wildcat Lodge. There, he had laid out his vision for where the program was, and where it was going.

And what a moment it was for the players. Understand that for those in attendance, the final days of the 2009 season were about as bad it gets, for any Kentucky player, pretty much ever. Part of it was that they had just gone to the NIT, and no college basketball player, at any program in the country is excited about going to the NIT.

At the same time, it was even bigger than that. It was the fact that they went to the NIT…. at Kentucky. Simply put, you come to Kentucky to play for National Championships. You come to Kentucky to play in front of 24,000 fans at every home game. You don't, even in your worst night-mare, come to Kentucky with an expectation of playing in the NIT.

Only that's exactly where Kentucky's players were coming from, meaning that Calipari's arrival not only meant a fresh start for the pro-gram as a whole, but also his players individually. And when Calipari did gather the team for their first meeting at the Wildcat Lodge, well, it was better than any of those players could've ever imagined. The nightmare of the NIT had been replaced by the dream of getting back to the tourna-ment, and winning big.

"He came in with the idea of 'here's what needs to change around here,'" Krebs said. "And it wasn't like he was pointing at us and saying we were bad kids and bad athletes, and we needed to change things around here. He was excited to take his dream job, and he seemed like he was excited to take this journey, and it felt like man, his energy was really fun to build off of."

From there, Calipari laid out how things would be different.

After years of unspeakably grueling practices under Gillispie, practice would be used instead to… umm, actually practice. It wasn't about run-ning stairs at Rupp Arena, or 6:00 a.m. sprints all summer and fall that left players broken down by the time the games began in October. It wasn't about psychological warfare and turning "boys to men." Instead, it was about basketball, and basketball concepts. It was about the dribble drive offense, beating your man off the dribble, and putting all of Kentucky's players in the best position to succeed as possible.

To quote the old episode of *Seinfeld*, it was basically about doing the exact opposite of everything they had done under Gillispie. And as Calipari spoke, it was music to the ears of his future players.

"We're sitting there as players, and he's telling us, it seems too good to be true," Krebs said. "It seemed like all the stuff we had problems with under Gillispie --- as players, you always have problems with coaches, and things they do --- it's natural… But for us, who had been through two years of a different style, we're like 'Oh, this is going to be good.'

It truly was a fresh start for Kentucky basketball, and after a wild few days, it seemed like the storm had finally calmed.

Kentucky had gone out searching for a new head coach, and gotten the man they wanted. They introduced him to the world and the team, and in his first test in front of the state, Calipari passed with flying colors.

Finally, after a whirlwind few days, things began to calm. The pomp and circumstance was complete, and Calipari was set to fly back to Memphis that afternoon, to meet with the media for one final time to tie up loose ends.

But before he left, Calipari finally got a moment to himself, where he took just a few brief moments to sit alone in his new office and reflect. Reflect on the whirlwind 24 hours that had just gone down, and what was ahead at his new job.

And it was in those few brief moments that Calipari looked outside his office window, onto the practice floor, and noticed something. It was something that was easy to overlook at first glance, but impossible to miss when he had a moment to really sit back and let everything sink in.

"You get up in an office, in a practice facility and you look out, and there's the words 'Kentucky' in glitter," Calipari said. "And there's seven National Championship banners. There's no Final Four banners, there's no league championship banners. It's national titles. And you kinda know 'Uh oh, I'm in a little bit of a different place now.'"

Indeed he was, and it was time to get to work. Calipari had been on the job for just a few hours, but the clock was already ticking on the way to title No. 8.

Little did Calipari know that there was a lot of work to be done, not just to be a championship contender, but to put a competitive team on the court.

He found that out the hard way, at his first practice the next day.

'I Was Just About Physically Ill': Cal Holds His First Practice

W HEN YOU THINK about the most important moments in Kentucky basketball history, a few obvious ones immediately come to mind: There are the NCAA titles, deep tournament runs, and of course, draft nights in 2010, 2012 and 2015.

What you might not consider though, is that one of the most important moments in recent Kentucky history came the second that John Calipari put pen to paper, and officially signed on to be the school's head basketball coach. Because had he not signed that contract binding him to Kentucky...well, he might've fled town after working his team out for the first time.

Ok, that might be a bit of an exaggeration. But not by much.

Following his introductory press conference, Calipari made a brief return to Memphis to tie up loose ends, and then the following day he was back in Kentucky for that first workout.

The workout --- which was allowed because the NCAA Tournament was still going on --- provided a fresh start for everyone; the players got a chance to exorcise the demons of the Billy Gillispie era, while Calipari had a chance to evaluate his new team.

So what did he see when he worked them out for the first time? Well, it wasn't pretty. At all.

"My job at the time was to make sure he didn't run away," DeWayne Peevy said of his initial reaction to seeing it up close and in person.

Yes, it was *that* bad. But before we get into the gruesome details, first, a little background.

For starters, it's worth noting that Calipari had no preconceptions --- good or bad --- heading into that first practice. At his opening press conference the day before, Calipari openly admitted that he wasn't too familiar with his new team. Sure, he knew the name Patrick Patterson. And yes, he'd seen Jodie Meeks score 54 points the previous season against Tennessee because, well, everyone saw Jodie Meeks score 54 points against Tennessee. For a brief, 24 hour window, it was the talk of the sports world.

But other than that, Cal didn't know all too much about his new squad. He didn't know his new player's names. He didn't know their strengths and weaknesses. And maybe most importantly he didn't know just how many of them there were. While Calipari is a coach who likes to keep his bench short, and his roster relatively thin, Gillispie was a coach who preferred to use every scholarship available to him, plus keep a healthy number of walk-ons as well (Kentucky had six non-scholarship players during Gillispie's last season in Lexington).

So you can imagine Calipari's surprise when several of his new players walked into the gym for the first time…and then several more walked in after them….and even a few more after that.

It was a sight to be seen. And the first sign that maybe, Calipari wasn't fully aware of exactly what he'd gotten into.

"I think we had 19 guys at his first practice," Mark Krebs said. "He said it felt like he was coaching a football team."

Safe to say it was a shocking moment for Calipari, and when the balls were actually rolled out onto the court, it was a shock for the players too. At the first team meeting the day before, Calipari had promised the team that practice time would actually be used to… surprise, surprise… practice, but it was one thing for the players to hear it, and another thing to experience it first-hand. It was a far cry from the treacherous, grueling, exhausting practices that Gillispie had put the team through over the previous two seasons.

"Under Gillispie, (it was) let's work on running up and down the court," Krebs said. "'We're going to run here, run there, then we're going to be really tired and then we're going to go get the basketballs and we're going to do passing drills, where you're constantly passing and running, and passing and running.'"

That doesn't sound too bad, until you realize that that was pretty much how practice was, every day, even late in the season, even on the day of games, and even after a rigorous off-season of conditioning. Often, it left players beaten up by mid-season, and just plain broken down by the time March rolled around.

So you can imagine their surprise when Calipari began speaking at that first practice. Instead of focusing on a balls-to-the-wall conditioning approach, he wanted his players to be in shape, but let their bodies evolve as the season did. They shouldn't be peaking physically in October, but be rounding into mid-season form in, well, mid-season.

More importantly, to Cal, basketball wasn't a sport of drills; instead he emphasized basketball moves, and basketball concepts. Understand that at its core, basketball really is pretty simple: It's about skills and fundamentals yes, but it also helps when you have athleticism to go along with those skills and fundamentals. Sure, bounce passes are great, and the triple-threat position is wonderful, but it also doesn't hurt when you can run faster, jump higher and move your feet quicker than the opponent. Simply put, you can teach fundamentals. You can't teach athleticism.

Well sort of.

Because even though Calipari couldn't technically teach athleticism he sure was going to try. At the very least, he was going to extract every ounce of athleticism, out of every one of his players that he possibly could.

And in essence, that was at the core of everything he taught on that first day.

"Essentially, he wanted you to play more athletic than you've ever played," Krebs said. "We did a lay-up drill, he wanted you to try to dunk it, he wanted you to get up as high as you can and try to dunk it. He wanted you to jump from as far out as you can in a lay-up drill, because that way, if you're in motion going in, and you're on a fast break, and you jump before the other guy, there's no way they can block you."

It was all so new to the players, so exciting, and so different than what they'd experienced when Gillispie was the head coach. Not just the drills themselves, but the concept of what basketball is all about. Even though it's a sport that is ultimately about scoring more points than your opponent, that was never the emphasis under the previous regime. For Gillispie, his practices were about defense, defense and more defense, and when they were done with defensive drills, well, they did one more just to be safe.

Not so much for Calipari, however.

For Cal, the emphasis was on offense. It was on putting the ball in the bucket. It was about playing ball.

"You go from a coach who was all about defense," guard Ramon Harris said. "*All* about defense. Ninety-five percent of practice is defense. And then your first workout with a coach it's all offense. Nothing defensive, all offensive moves."

The players couldn't believe it. Literally.

"You're kind of like, shocked," he said. "Like 'we're not going to go over defense? We're not going to work on defense? You're not going to even mention defense in this workout right now?'"

Eventually, for a very brief moment the focus did turn to defense, but even that was different. Once again, Calipari put the emphasis on athleticism, and using athleticism to your advantage. To use a bad pun, it was about making the offensive player, well, defensive.

"When you're guarding somebody, the first lunge you take, or the second lunge, is what stops a guy," Krebs said. "It's not about moving your feet, but instead, taking really aggressive lunges, and being lighter on your feet."

The concepts were new to the players on the floor that day, but they were something else as well: They were fun. For the first time in a long time, the Wildcats' basketball players were actually enjoying being on the court. There was no yelling and screaming, no hours of monotonous drills that didn't translate when the games actually tipped off.

Instead, the players could actually *feel* themselves getting better.

Unfortunately while the players could feel themselves getting better, it didn't necessarily translate that first practice. That's because, while the concepts might sound great on paper, watching them acted out in real time was another thing altogether.

Now in defense of the players, it's important to remember something: This was all new to them. They were being asked to process and act out entirely new concepts, to do it at a fast pace, for a coach who they'd just met the day before.

At the same time, there's no arguing something else altogether: It was ugly. Very ugly.

Like worse than words can even describe.

"I've never seen so many missed layups in my life," team manager Chad Sanders said with a laugh.

For Calipari, that first practice was about teaching his offense, and if there's one overall concept you need to understand about the dribble drive, it's that if it's executed correctly, it should lead to one thing: Easy buckets at the rim.

Unfortunately, to fully hammer that point home, Calipari had to teach his players how to score at the rim, under pretty much any circumstance. It wasn't just about easy buckets at the rim, but about preparing the players for everything they could possibly encounter once they got there. That meant that the first practice was spent practicing every type of layup known to man, and then creating a few more that hadn't been invented yet. It meant practicing jumping off the wrong foot. It meant attacking the rim with the wrong hand. It meant jump stops and drop steps and Euro moves.

And at least on the first day of practice, it also meant missed layups. Lots and lots and lots of them.

"That's what Cal kept preaching," Sanders said. "'You're going to get layups (in this offense).' It was funny to see the guys struggling to make layups and do things that were so simple."

Finally, mercifully, after several hours the workout ended. Players trudged off the court, mentally exhausted from processing so much new information, but also physically exhausted as well. Although they had just finished a season full of grueling practices, Calipari's workout was different.

"The biggest indicator for me, was that our hip-flexors --- from getting out and running, and doing different things --- I was so sore," Krebs said. "And I had played an entire season of basketball. But for some reason, after Coach Cal's practice, my lungs weren't necessarily sore, and I wasn't winded, but my body ached, because I was using longer strides, doing defensive drills that we've never done before."

Calipari on the other hand felt a different kind of pain; one in the pit of his stomach. What the heck had he just seen?

"When we went through that first practice, I was just about physically ill," Calipari said, wondering what exactly he had gotten himself into.

Understand that Calipari had spent years, his entire career really building up to that exact moment. All the long days grinding as an assistant coach, building up programs at UMass, in the NBA and at Memphis, had all led him to Kentucky. It was his dream job, the place he had spent decades hoping to one day coach.

Only now he was here, and _this_ was what he had? It just couldn't be.

"I'm pretty sure that he had some perceptions of the talent he had," DeWayne Peevy said. "In coming in, he seemed a little disappointed with the depth of the talent. Not the front end, but the depth."

Understand that it wasn't the player's fault --- as Calipari explained to Fox Sports, they were simply coached to play a different style of basketball --- and it certainly wasn't Calipari's fault, but this also wasn't going to be acceptable going forward.

Something had to change, and something would change immediately.

"He realized, 'You know what? I've got to get some players," Matt Jones said. "This was not the standard they were going to have."

In his introductory press conference, Calipari said he would recruit "the best of the best."

Now it was time to deliver on the promise.

The Waiting Is the Hardest Part

O**N THE SAME** night that John Calipari met with Kentucky officials to discuss their head coaching vacancy, an equally important meeting took place about 800 miles away in Durham, North Carolina.

For months --- a full year, really --- the Duke basketball program had been courting the top high school player in the country, calling John Wall, doing whatever they could to convince him to become a Blue Devil. And finally, after all those months of calls, texts, back-and-forth conversations, they finally got their chance to meet him face-to-face.

On the night of Sunday, March 29th, 2009 --- the same evening that John Calipari was meeting with Kentucky --- Wall was having his own meeting. The top ranked player in the country met with Duke's coaching staff, joined by his mother, and advisor Brian Clifton on an official visit to the school.

There, John Wall got to see it all. He got to see the campus, located just a few miles from his house in Raleigh, North Carolina. He got to see the school's basketball facilities, the building where he'd fine-tune his game, and hopefully become the first pick in the next year's draft. And it's where he got to meet Duke head coach Mike Krzyzewski for the first time in a face-to-face setting.

Krzyzewski had made hundreds of recruiting pitches before, hosted dozens of high school All-Americans in his palatial office, but this one was different. In the past, Krzyzewski had centered his pitch around the virtues of Duke academically, as a school where players could succeed academically and in basketball. He'd then explain the value of getting a degree from the school, of spending your four-year college experience on the pristine Durham campus.

But again, this was different. For the first time, maybe ever, Krzyzewski wasn't selling the four-year experience at Duke, because it was no secret that John Wall was *too good* to stay in college for four years. Wall was a player tabbed as a "one-and-done" prospect long before he ever stepped foot on a college campus, and finally Krzyzewski had come around on the idea that he'd have to go after the best players, even if he knew they wouldn't be on campus for more than a year or two. And if he were going to start anywhere, Wall seemed like the logical fit; Wall was a local kid who just so happened to be the top-ranked player in the country. In other words, he was a guy who could help Duke immediately on the court, and just so happened to be a really good student off of it as well.

So when Wall, his team and Krzyzewski met in his office that night, there was no old-school recruiting pitch about the four-year college experience, or the value of a Duke education. Sure, elements of it were there, but it was replaced with more of a new-school approach that fit Wall specifically.

Duke sold the nation's top ranked high school player on the opportunity to play just minutes from his childhood home; which was no small sell for Wall, who was especially close with his mother. They sold Wall on his skill-set fitting in seamlessly with the players Duke already had; the blazing 6'4 point guard with brilliant court vision would be surrounded by capable shooters on the perimeter and big guys who could run the floor and play on the block. And in essence, they sold Wall on being _the guy_; the last piece of a championship puzzle. While other schools were offering guarantees of playing time or a starting spot, Duke was offering Wall the keys to a powerful and highly efficient offense. They were offering him the chance to do something extra special in his one season of college basketball. They were offering him the chance to potentially win a title.

The pitch stuck with Wall, who for weeks --- and years really --- had considered Memphis his favorite. For nearly two seasons he had envisioned himself in John Calipari's dribble-drive offense, as the player who could follow in the footsteps of Derrick Rose and Tyreke Evans at the point guard position.

But after the visit from Duke he had no choice but to reconsider.

"They have given me a lot to think about," Wall told Scout.com following the trip.

Indeed they had, and with that trip complete, it added another layer to the recruiting drama of the top high school player in the country. It also set off a wild, six-week odyssey that centered around one question: Where would John Wall go to college?

It was a question which gripped the entire college basketball world.

And it left Kentucky in a frenzy.

*   *   *

While Wall's recruitment was heating up, things were just getting started in Lexington. John Calipari had arrived and worked out his team. Now it was time to see which, if any of his highly-ranked recruits would join him at Kentucky.

"When Coach Cal came," Josh Harrellson explained. "That's all you heard about, was the new guys coming in. All the excitement about them."

The excitement was justified as Calipari had put together one of the top recruiting classes in the country at Memphis; a perfect blend of size and athleticism, players who were considered "one and done's" and others who could help build the program for the long-term.

The top-ranked player headed to Memphis, was the top-ranked power forward in the class, DeMarcus Cousins, a bruising 6'11 big man out of Alabama, who had once committed to UAB before changing his mind and pledging to go to Memphis just weeks before. Because Cousins had yet to sign a Letter of Intent, and because Calipari had been the biggest reason he chose the school, there was good reason to believe he might come to Lexington.

The other big name in the class was the top wing player in the country, forward Xavier Henry. Henry's situation was a little more complicated; he had already signed a Letter of Intent at Memphis, but had a clause to get out of it, if Calipari left. However the bigger issue with Henry was his family; he had an older brother who was a walk-on at Memphis, and he'd likely end up wherever his big brother did.

Memphis' class was rounded out by another wing, Nolan Dennis, and a pair of junior college forwards, Darnell Dodson and Will Coleman. Kentucky would also recruit two uncommitted players who Memphis had been chasing under Calipari as well; Wall, and Eric Bledsoe, a player that most perceived to be a back-up plan in case Wall went elsewhere.

But while the entire world --- including Calipari's own players at Kentucky --- seemed to be intrigued by who he was bringing with him from Memphis, the new coach's first order of business was to actually figure out which, if any of Gillispie's recruits might be a good fit for him in Lexington.

With Calipari targeting Wall and Bledsoe, he immediately released Gillispie signee G.J. Vilarino from his scholarship. The point guard eventually signed with Gonzaga, before later transferring to Appalachian State. Gillispie had also received verbal commitments from younger players, all of whom began to look elsewhere as well.

At the same time, there were players who Calipari felt could help the team and he immediately began focusing on them.

It started with Daniel Orton, a 6'11 center from Oklahoma City who had been the crown jewel of Gillispie's final class at Kentucky. Calipari had been following Orton since seeing him play with Xavier Henry on a summer league team, and was intrigued by his size and mobility.

Visiting Orton, and convincing him to stick with his commitment to Kentucky was Calipari's first order of recruiting business after he got to Kentucky.

"Literally right after they got the job, the next day or two they came out to visit me at my house," Orton said. "That's what they said, that I was one of their main priorities. That they knew they had to come recruit me. That was really impressive to me that they did that."

For Orton and his family, the meeting was designed as more of a feeling out process than anything else. Understand that Orton had committed to Kentucky months earlier, and wanted more than anything to play his college ball in Lexington. At the same time, he had also committed to play in Billy Gillispie's high-low offense, an offense that was perfectly tailored for his game in the low-post. The dribble drive offense was a different story altogether. Considering that he had only really watched Kentucky games the previous season, he had no idea what to expect.

It also led to a slew of questions when Calipari first arrived. How would he fit? How would his skills translate? Would he still be able to have an impact?

"I wasn't really familiar with the dribble-drive offense," Orton said. "I hadn't watched Memphis play at all. I just didn't really know what to expect."

In the end, Calipari was able to convince Orton and his family that the dribble-drive offense could work for him. In turn, Orton recommitted to Kentucky, giving Calipari his first big recruiting victory in Lexington. Shortly thereafter, Jon Hood --- Kentucky's high school player of the year --- gave the Wildcats their second big recruiting coup of the Calipari era.

Next up, the attention turned to Calipari's Memphis recruits. It started with Cousins, a player with a unique and winding recruitment, which dated back several years and tied in multiple schools.

Cousins had been tabbed as one of the top players in the class of 2009, dating back to his freshman year in high school. And by his junior year, Cousins had narrowed down his list of schools to just one; he committed to UAB in the fall of 2008. Part of the decision was due to the school's proximity to his home in Mobile, and part of it was because of his relationship with head coach Mike Davis.

The problem was however, that while Cousins' relationship with Davis was airtight, his relationship with the school eventually grew sour;

Cousins wanted a clause in his Letter of Intent that said he wouldn't be forced to attend UAB if Davis left. But the school balked, and so did the All-American forward. Without it, he wasn't going to UAB.

From there, Cousins reopened his recruitment, with Kansas State, Washington and Memphis amongst the many schools who tried to get in the mix. Eventually though, Calipari convinced Cousins to come visit Memphis, and when he did, he reeled in a commitment. Cousins pledged to join Memphis before leaving campus that weekend.

Of course nothing is set in recruiting until the Letter of Intent is signed, and while Cousins was committed, he had not yet actually signed with Memphis when Calipari left for Kentucky. The news of Calipari's departure broke when Cousins was at the McDonald's All-American game, and left him in a state of shock. Unsure of what his next move was, Cousins told reporters all weekend that he wouldn't make any kind of decision until he got home and spoke with his family.

But after getting home, it really wasn't a tough choice at all. Cousins had committed to Memphis because of Calipari, and when Calipari left, Cousins decided to follow him. He would be coming to Kentucky.

"Basically I went home and tried to figure out which coaches were going to get me to the next level," Cousins told Rivals.com. "The answer was Coach Cal. Then I asked what school was the best fit for me. And what school is better than Kentucky?"

In Cousins' eyes, the answer was apparently "none." And in addition to committing to the school, he sent out a cryptic note to the rest of the basketball world: He wanted more guys to come with him.

"I'm working on John Wall and Xavier Henry right now," he said. "I think we have a chance to get them."

Henry was the next domino to fall, but it wouldn't be nearly as easy to get him to Kentucky. That's because while Cousins was essentially committed to going wherever Calipari did, Henry had other things to consider; mainly his family. The 6'6 forward, who was Calipari's first big recruit in the 2009 class for Memphis, had chosen the school in part because his brother was already there. C.J. Henry was a former minor league baseball player, who'd quit, and joined Memphis the past fall as a walk-on basketball player. He had spent the previous season redshirting.

But with Calipari gone, Xavier Henry had to not only consider which school was the best for him, but also the best for his brother. Because C.J. Henry was a walk-on, he was free to transfer, and wherever the two ended up, they'd end up there together.

Kentucky seemed to be a logical choice, but again, family history came in to play. Henry's parents had met at Kansas, where his father played on the basketball team in the 1980's. Xavier Henry admitted --- even after committing to Memphis --- that he nearly chose Kansas the first time around. And the second time, with the opportunity for his brother to join him, it proved to be too much.

He was going to be a Jayhawk.

"With my parents going there and all that, when I grew up, all I was watching was Kansas," Henry told reporters. "I switched a little bit because of my brother, and then somehow it got switched back."

Next, the attention turned to Eric Bledsoe, maybe the most interesting player Kentucky was recruiting in the spring of 2009.

The 6'0 guard from Alabama actually had a somewhat lengthy history with the Wildcats even before Calipari got there; he had actually been one of the focal points of Gillispie's recruiting efforts throughout that season. He'd also been recruited by Calipari at Memphis, but under much different circumstances: Most viewed Bledsoe as a back-up plan at Memphis, a contingency in case they didn't get John Wall.

That was the perception anyway.

But while most viewed Bledsoe as a back-up plan, what few knew was that Bledsoe wasn't planning on taking a back-seat to anyone. And once he got on campus for his official visit one thing became clear: While Kentucky would've loved to get John Wall, Eric Bledsoe was pretty darn talented himself.

"John had taken a couple unofficial visits so we knew about John," guard Ramon Harris said. "But when coach had gotten established and

Eric Bledsoe came on his official visit and he played with us, we were like 'Wow, he's good.'"

Indeed he was, but whether viewed as a back-up plan, starter or something in-between none of it really mattered to Bledsoe himself. While the world was focused on where exactly he fit in Kentucky's recruiting efforts, the truth was, all Bledsoe really wanted was a chance. Other schools offered playing time and starting spots, and most of the experts assumed that he'd much rather have guarantees at other schools, than risk potentially not starting at Kentucky.

The thing is though, that no one took the time to ask Eric Bledsoe what he wanted. When they did, they realized that all he wanted was a chance. If he was given that, he would take care of the rest.

"He (Calipari) never promised me anything," Bledsoe said. "That's what he told me when he came and recruited me. There were a lot of teams that were promising me playing time."

As for the idea of playing with Wall? What was wrong with that?

"They knew there was going to be competition and a challenge as well," assistant coach Rod Strickland said. "But Eric Bledsoe, he *embraced* that. He had no problems with that. There was no hesitation, none of that."

Oh, and there was one other thing. While the media was playing up the idea of one backing up the other, what no one considered was that John Calipari was trying to figure out a way to play them both *at the same time.* Maybe John Wall would come, and maybe he wouldn't, but if he did, and if Bledsoe joined him, who's to say they couldn't work together? Remember, the dribble-drive offense is at its core, about beating guys off the dribble and finishing at the rim. If you can have one guy that can do that, great. But if you have more than one, well, that's even better.

And it's an idea that Calipari raised during the recruiting process. Why couldn't both be on the court at the same time? Why did it have to be one or the other?

"He (Coach Calipari) felt like those two guys could play well together," Strickland said.

And it was something that Bledsoe embraced. Again, he wasn't going to take a backseat to anybody, and he wasn't going to back down from anyone either. But he also wasn't opposed to sharing the ball and sharing the spotlight.

If anything, he was intrigued by the idea of playing with John Wall. He was excited about it. And told John Calipari as much when the two met face-to-face.

"He wanted us both to come in and play," Bledsoe said. "He definitely told me that. That made me want to come even more."

In the end, Bledsoe's recruitment *technically* came down to Kentucky and Memphis but in Bledsoe's mind, it really wasn't that close at all. Bledsoe took official visits to both schools in the same weekend in early May. But by the time he left Memphis to go to Kentucky, his mind was already made up.

Ironically, Josh Pastner --- Calipari's former assistant who'd taken over at Memphis when he left --- knew where Bledsoe was going before Kentucky's staff ever did.

"I had recruited Eric Bledsoe for Coach Cal when I was here at Memphis," Pastner said. "When I got the (Memphis head coaching) job I was trying to recruit Eric Bledsoe to Memphis, to come here and play for me."

He paused, before explaining the final moments of what turned out to be his final meeting with Bledsoe.

"I remember Eric Bledsoe sat across from me and said, 'Coach, I have a question for you.' And I said 'What's that?' And he said, 'Is everything you said about Coach Calipari during the recruiting process at Memphis, was that true?'"

Pastner didn't even hesitate in answering the question.

"I told him 'Everything I said was true,'" Pastner said. "'And he said 'Thanks, that's all I wanted to know.'"

It would be three days before Bledsoe officially committed to Kentucky. But at that point, Pastner knew the recruitment was over.

"I knew right then we weren't getting him," Pastner said.

Bledsoe was committed, which meant it was finally time for Kentucky to turn its full attention to John Wall.

Ok, well that's sort of incorrect since, well, the attention had never technically left John Wall. But with Bledsoe signed, sealed and delivered, Wall's recruitment picked up full-steam ahead. He was the last big star still unsigned, the final piece of what would be a dream first recruiting class for the Wildcats.

And all of Kentucky was dying to know what he was going to do.

"I do remember the build-up for Wall," Matt Jones said. "It was 'Is Wall going to come?'"

For Calipari, the chase for Wall had actually begun years earlier, and had really picked up steam just weeks before he'd left to take the Kentucky job; Wall had actually named Memphis his leader on the same weekend that DeMarcus Cousins had committed to the school.

The truth was, however, that although Wall had named Memphis his leader, his love affair with the school --- and more specifically Calipari's offense --- dated back a bit longer than that. It had actually begun two years earlier, when Wall first saw Calipari's dribble-drive offense firing on all cylinders, during Memphis' run to the 2008 title game. After watching Derrick Rose lead the Tigers' to a near-championship, Wall wondered why he couldn't do the same.

"I turned on the TV and I saw Derrick (Rose) playing," Wall said. "I was like 'Shoot, I could play here.' I loved how they were playing."

It made Memphis the very early front-runners for Wall, right up until he officially named them his leader in March of his senior year.

Of course just because they were his leader, didn't mean there weren't others in hot pursuit.

There was the aforementioned trip to Duke, where Mike Krzyzewski told Wall that he was the final piece of the Blue Devils' championship puzzle. There was a trip to Baylor a week later, where one of his advisors --- Brian Clifton's brother Dwon --- had recently been hired. Following the trip to Baylor was a visit to Miami, the surprise finalist in Wall's recruitment, and a place that Wall said "really opened my eyes up." Even Wall's home-state school of North Carolina tried to get into the mix after their National Championship run that year. Unfortunately for Roy Williams, he was a little late to the party (much more on that coming later).

As the visits piled up the rumors began to swirl, with every one of Wall's moves analyzed and dissected. What did Bledsoe's signing mean for his recruitment? Why didn't Wall end up taking an official visit to Kentucky? Did that mean something?

It was all too much to take, and finally in late May, the whole college basketball world got their answers.

"It's been a really tough process," Wall told reporters at a press conference at his high school. "But I have decided to attend the University of Kentucky."

Wall breathed a sigh of relief (as cheers undoubtedly went up across the state), before he laid out the reasons for his decision. Wall went one by one, but in the end, it all came down to seeing Calipari's club on TV two years earlier. It was all about the coach. And it was all about the system that could make him a star.

"I kind of already knew where I was going to go," Wall told FoxSports.com in January 2015. "But I wanted to give every school an opportunity in case I switched my mind up. But in the back of my mind I knew I wanted to go play for Coach Cal, just because of the style of play he played, plus how I saw Derrick play."

Wall's commitment had the Bluegrass buzzing, and with Wall, Bledsoe and Cousins joining a team that potentially included Patrick Patterson and Jodie Meeks, it was quickly apparent that Kentucky wasn't just going to be good in Calipari's first year, but really good.

For John Calipari, there would be no "three year plan," no "wait until next year." Next year was now. Not bad for a team which had just played in the NIT a few months before.

"It wasn't the expectation that people have right now that freshmen can come in and immediately put up numbers," DeWayne Peevy said. "Back then it was 'Hey, we're going to be better and it's going to be a lot of fun.' But nobody was talking about 'we're going to win the National Championship.'"

Maybe not, but hey, at least people were going to be talking about Kentucky....period.

More importantly it showed fans, administration and Calipari's own players that the new coach could deliver. After promising to field a competitive team immediately in his interview with Kentucky, and after promising to recruit "the best of the best" at his first press conference, Calipari had backed it all up.

"That was one of the things that struck me about Coach Cal," Mark Krebs said. "It was the John Wall signing. Him deciding to come to Kentucky, after Eric Bledsoe had just decided, it just showed me that guys really do want to play for him."

Krebs continued.

"Call me old-school," Krebs said with a laugh. "But when you have a point guard who just committed, who's highly-touted and highly-talented, the other guy will probably go somewhere else. And that wasn't the case."

No it wasn't, and as spring turned to summer, the freshmen were set to arrive.

Kentucky basketball would never be the same.

They Were As Good As Advertised: The Freshmen Arrive

I T WAS A late night in the summer of 2009, not all that different from a bunch of other late nights in June and July of that year. The University of Kentucky's campus was quiet; most students had returned home for the summer, and the ones who remained on campus had long since retreated to their dorms.

But inside the Joe Craft Center, things were just starting to heat up. A hotly contested two-on-two game had just broken out and the winner wouldn't be decided for hours.

On one side of the court were "The John's" Wall and Hood. Both of the freshmen had recently arrived on campus; one as the top-ranked high school player in the country, the other, the top-ranked player in the state of Kentucky. On the other side were "The 'Bama boys" DeMarcus Cousins and Eric Bledsoe. The pair had grown up about four hours apart in Alabama, but through basketball had known each other for years. The two had even gone head-to-head in Alabama's high school state championship tournament just a few months before, with Bledsoe's Parker High School squad taking down Cousins' LeFlore High School team.

But on this night --- and most every night that summer --- the pair were on the same team, going head-to-head with Wall and Hood. The four had arrived on campus as freshmen just a few weeks before, but had already made a habit of playing late-night, two-on-two games against each other.

"That's when you have the most fun," Hood said. "Not playing in games, but playing in the pick-up games against your brothers, because you have to invent new stuff. After three weeks, after a month, we already know everything you're going to do. We can predict what you're going to do, before you do it, because we play every day, multiple times a day."

It may have only been the summer, and the season may have still been months away, but the freshmen were quickly bonding.

Well, sometimes.

Other times they were simply getting under each other's skin, and poor Hood might've gotten the worst of it. Hood stood at 6'7, meaning that he was forced to guard the 6'11 Cousins, a player who may have only been 18-years-old, but was built like an NBA power forward.

So how did Hood handle Cousins in the post?

Well...

"I was fouling the living crap out of DeMarcus, and he was getting frustrated," Hood said with a laugh. "After a while he gets tired of calling fouls on every play, so he just powers through you."

It left Hood beat up. And with memories that are impossible to forget.

"My memories were, after they were over, after those pick-up games were over, it was going into the locker room and counting the number of bruises from DeMarcus," Hood said.

Despite the black and blues, Hood readily admitted that those late-night pick-up games were some of the best memories he had during his freshman year at Kentucky.

Those games also set the tone for the entire season ahead.

* * *

That's right, the freshman had arrived in Lexington, and things were immediately different around Kentucky basketball. Overnight, the talent level had risen. So too had the intensity.

"Playing pick-up games, you could just tell the competition was stiff," Mark Krebs said. "You could tell the way that the guys were playing, the things that were happening in the pick-up games, that things were just different. The alley-oops, the fast-break dunks were phenomenal."

The new players were also phenomenal.

It's interesting, because at times recruiting can be a bit of an inexact science. Kids can look good in a highlight tape or on the summer circuit, but that doesn't mean it'll translate to on the court success once they arrive on campus. Any number of factors could lead to a potential recruiting bust; maybe the kid isn't mentally ready to handle college. Maybe he peaked physically at a young age and all his peers have caught up. Maybe he didn't mesh with his teammates. Or maybe he just wasn't as good as everyone expected.

They're all legitimate concerns for college basketball coaches all across the country.

Fortunately for John Calipari and his staff, none of those concerns applied to Kentucky's new freshmen. The trio of Wall, Bledsoe and Cousins weren't just as good as advertised. They were better.

"I was there the first day he (John Calipari) worked them all out (in April), the players who had stayed," assistant strength coach Scott Padgett said. "And I was like 'Ooo, this is bad.' And then you bring in the new class of six and you're like 'Ooo, we've got some talent here.'"

Indeed they did. And it all started with Wall.

Wall of course had come to Kentucky as the nation's top-ranked recruit, hoping to have the same success that Derrick Rose and Tyreke Evans had in John Calipari's dribble-drive offense at Memphis. But while Wall was hoping to match their success on the court, what the coaching staff quickly found out was that as good as those guys had been, Wall might've actually been just a little bit better than either.

"We've had obviously some great guards come in," Rod Strickland said, the former Memphis assistant who'd come to Kentucky with Calipari. "But he (Wall) was probably the one guard that came in from the beginning, walking in the door that didn't struggle. There was no adjustment period for him."

Fellow assistant Orlando Antigua put it in another, much simpler way.

"John, out of all the guards that we've had, picked up the dribble-drive concept as fast as anybody has ever picked it up," Antigua said.

Then there was Bledsoe.

Remember that during the recruiting process Bledsoe was seen as a back-up plan, the guy that Kentucky was recruiting just in case Wall decided to go to college somewhere else.

And even when he got to Lexington, Bledsoe wasn't seen as a golden child, or program saver, let alone a potential "one-and-done" star like Wall. Instead, Bledsoe was viewed as a project; someone who could play a role, and become part of the foundation of the program long-term. After a year or two, maybe Bledsoe could earn a starting spot. After three or four years, maybe he could land in the NBA.

Maybe.

At least that was the thought. Right up until Bledsoe arrived at Kentucky and blew everyone's expectations away.

"What we realized was that Eric was better than we could've ever imagined," Antigua said. "His quickness, his speed, his athleticism and his toughness was...if John was 1A, then Eric was 1B."

Finally, there was Cousins, a player unlike any that Calipari and his staff had ever recruited.

And that was in more ways than one.

In high school, Cousins had gotten a little bit of a reputation for his attitude; as Hood alluded to, he was a player who could at times, have a bit of a temper. Cousins was by no means a "bad" kid, but definitely a player that the staff had to handle in a different way.

"DeMarcus was as skilled a big guy as we'd ever worked with," Antigua admitted. "We knew we just had to get him in great shape, and we had to build a relationship, and continue to build a relationship with him, where he respected us one, and trusted us two."

Cousins' maturity improved throughout the year (more on that later), but one thing that was undeniable right away was his talent. As Antigua mentioned, the Kentucky staff had never worked with a big guy quite like him to that point. Strickland --- who spent nearly two decades in the NBA --- had never seen a big guy like him, period.

"I remember the first thing with him was, I'm looking at this big dude, I mean this big body dude, who's agile," Strickland said. "I'm watching him bring the ball up court, put the ball between his legs, make plays, and it wasn't made up. I've been around big guys that are trying, they're trying to be the Magic Johnson type and it feels forced. Well DeMarcus, I watched him and I was like 'I've never seen anything like this.'"

Cousins' game was so unique that when Kentucky Sports Radio ran a contest later that fall to find him a nickname, Strickland had the perfect answer. Strickland said Cousins should be called "Boogie" because "he had some 'Boog' in his game." The nickname has stuck with Cousins to this day.

Safe to say that it was a fun time to be at Kentucky, and not just for the new players but the coaches who joined them as well. In the same way Calipari had spent the previous few months filling out his roster, he rounded out his coaching staff as well.

As you might've guessed by now, Antigua and Strickland followed Calipari from Memphis, one staying in the same role he'd been in previously, the other taking on a new role altogether.

Let's start with Antigua, who might've had one of the most unique backgrounds of any assistant coach, anywhere in college basketball. Antigua starred as a player for Pittsburgh in the early and mid-1990's, before a professional career that included a brief stint with the Harlem Globetrotters (he actually became the first Hispanic to ever play for the team during that stretch).

Following his playing days, Antigua quickly transitioned to coaching, where he began as a high school assistant, before returning to Pitt as the Director of Basketball Operations in 2003. After several years with the Panthers, Antigua would move to Memphis for a season before following Calipari to Kentucky. In Lexington, he would be in charge of coaching the team's big men, and would also be the Wildcats' primary recruiter.

Strickland had a similar, albeit completely different story altogether. He had a very productive professional career, playing 17 years in the NBA before transitioning to coaching upon retirement. He ended up as the Director of Basketball Operations at Memphis, and at Kentucky he would get his first shot at being a full-time assistant, filling Josh Pastner's role on the staff. Pastner had intended to come to Kentucky with his former boss, right up until the point that Memphis offered him the job that Calipari had just vacated. At that point, Pastner had no choice but to take the job at Memphis…literally. Calipari jokingly told Pastner that he'd be fired if he tried to come to Kentucky, rather than staying at Memphis.

The third coach on the bench was a face that would become familiar to Kentucky fans throughout the Calipari years. It was the face of John Robic.

Robic had known Calipari for decades; the two had been friends long before Calipari got his first head coaching job in 1988, and when Calipari was eventually hired at UMass, one of the first calls he made was to Robic. Robic stayed with Calipari through the end of his time at UMass and briefly considered joining the coach when he left for the NBA, before deciding to stay in Massachusetts, where he was elevated to associate head coach. Robic later became the head coach at Youngstown State for six years… and even when he was let go, well, you can probably guess who one of the first people to call him was. Yup, it was John Calipari who offered him an assistant coaching job at Memphis. The two have been together since, with Robic serving as the coach's right-hand man, preparing scouting reports, breaking down film, and things of that nature.

With the assistant coaching roles filled, Calipari next turned his attention to the administrative ones. There, Calipari decided to dip into Kentucky's past and hire a pair of former Wildcat hoop stars. On the one hand, Calipari hoped to give each of them their first big break in coaching. On the other hand, he also hoped they could serve as mentors for the younger players who were just arriving in Lexington.

Calipari's first call wasn't actually a call at all.

Scott Padgett was a Kentucky legend, a forward who had played at the height of the Rick Pitino and Tubby Smith eras, making two Final Fours and winning the 1998 National Championship during his five years at the school. The Louisville native was about as "Kentucky" as Kentucky basketball could get, a native of the state, who'd played (and won a championship for the Wildcats) and who'd recently returned to the state after a long NBA career. Padgett had worked in radio during the 2008-2009 season, but by the time it wrapped up, he was getting the itch to get into coaching.

By the time Billy Gillispie was fired, that itch became a rash; simply put, he wanted a job with the new coaching staff, regardless of what he had to do.

"I started hearing the rumors that Calipari was going to get the job," Padgett said. "I started calling anyone I knew who might have a connection to Cal to put in a good word for me, to where at least I could sit down in front of him and talk. I had about 10 people call on my behalf."

Once Calipari was hired, he took things one step further.

"On the day he got the job I wasn't going to take any chances," Padgett said. "I literally showed up at the press conference and sat in the back. And I was like 'Can I get five minutes with you, blah, blah, blah, blah.'"

Padgett was offered the position of "assistant strength coach" while fellow UK legend Tony Delk was named assistant Director of Basketball Operations. On paper the two had received entry level coaching jobs, but their titles gave them plenty of flexibility to do what they wanted with the opportunity. The position was a "jack of all trades" kind of deal; one day Padgett might help Antigua send out mailings to recruits, an hour after that, he'd break down tape with Robic.

But more than anything, Padgett --- who again, had been part of Kentucky's program for five years --- was there to provide an ear for Kentucky's current players. He had lived through the whirlwind of being a UK basketball player, and the hope was that by having him around the program, he would be able to dish out advice to whoever needed it.

"If you go to Kentucky now it's because you want to be in the NBA, and you want to be a part of winning a championship," Padgett said. "As a guy who has been there to the NBA who has done it, you can give those guys pointers and little tips here and there, to where you can have an influence that way."

The final spot on the staff was the Director of Basketball Operations, which opened up when Pastner stayed in Memphis, and Strickland took his spot as a full-time assistant coach. The position ultimately went to one of the most unlikely candidates anyone could have ever imagined.

Before we get to just how unlikely that candidate was, you first need to know exactly what the role of "Director of Basketball Operations" entails.

For starters, it isn't actually a coaching position, but instead much more of a "grunt work" type gig. The Director of Basketball Operations handles all the stuff that none of the coaches actually want to do, things like hotel reservations, dinner plans and booking flights. At most schools, the job is understandably given to young, up-and-comers, the type of 20-somethings who are willing to do whatever it takes to get into coaching. If that means working 20-hours a day, so be it. If it means giving up any social life outside the basketball office, well, too bad.

That's just what the Director of Basketball Operations does at most schools.

But in Calipari's eyes, Kentucky isn't "most" schools, and he couldn't hire the typical candidate. Kentucky is a big-time job, with big-time expectations, and the idea of giving the gig to a 20-something was disconcerting to Calipari. Could he really trust some kid just out of college to handle all the day-to-day matters that came with Kentucky basketball?

It was a risk he simply wasn't willing to take. Which is why when the job opened up, he took the opposite approach to filling the position that most do. He went with someone a bit older, who was not only a personal friend of his, but also someone very familiar with Kentucky in general.

That man was Martin Newton, who at the time was a Nike executive living in Lexington, and who'd also known Calipari for close to 20 years.

Newton had no intention of leaving the corporate world, at least until Calipari was hired.

And once Newton did make the decision to leave, he seemed like the perfect fit. He was a man who knew the business of college athletics from his time at Nike, but also knew the responsibilities that came with Kentucky basketball specifically. After all, UK basketball was in his blood...literally. Newton was the son of C.M. Newton, who had served as Kentucky's Athletic Director from 1989-2000, meaning the younger Newton had seen the inner-workings of Kentucky basketball first-hand. Ironically, he'd also seen the inner workings of arguably the top program in all of *college football* as well.

"I grew up in Tuscaloosa, Alabama during the Bear Bryant era around Alabama football when my dad coached basketball there," Martin Newton said. "Then living in Lexington, Kentucky, and being around the fanaticism of Kentucky basketball, there are no two programs that are anywhere close to that passion, that fanaticism that those two programs have."

So who better to help Calipari in that first season, than a man who had lived through it all first-hand already? In Newton's mind, the answer was "no one."

Which is why, it was actually Newton who reached out to Calipari about a potential job when he was hired, not the other way around. Newton didn't care if he had to take an administrative role. He didn't care if he had to take a pay-cut. He just wanted to be part of it all.

"It was probably me making a bigger pitch to him," Newton said. "Like 'I want to be part of what you're going to build.'"

The question of course was, why exactly did Newton want in so bad? Especially considering that he had a great job, with a great company and had no experience working in college basketball before (other than on the opposite side of the business, with Nike).

Well, the answer was simple really: He knew Calipari, and he knew Kentucky. And he knew that the pairing of the two would be huge...

potentially Earth shattering. He had one of those feelings in the pit of his stomach; that something truly amazing was about to happen in Lexington.

And he knew he had to be a part of it.

"You know, you get very few chances in this life to do something special," Newton said. "I just felt like he was going to do something special."

That's right, something special was about to happen in Lexington, and the pieces were now in place to make it happen.

The freshmen had arrived, the coaching staff had been filled out, and everyone was ready to get the 2009-2010 season underway.

Well, sort of.

That's because while everyone had arrived, there were still a few months left before the season started.

And not everyone would end up staying.

I'm Ready When You Need Me

IT HAD NOW been a few months since John Calipari had held his first practice, the day he had a basketball workout, and a "football team" showed up instead. But with the freshmen arriving and the season inching closer, not every member of that "football team" would stay. Simply put, there were too many players, and not enough roster spots and scholarships for everyone.

Somebody (well actually a lot of people) wouldn't be around for long.

The first order of business wasn't a bad one, but actually quite good. The NBA Draft was inching closer, and after putting up solid numbers during the 2008-2009 season, both Jodie Meeks and Patrick Patterson were both seen as potential early entrants into the draft.

In the end, only one would stay. But ironically it wasn't necessarily who everyone expected.

"We didn't think Jodie would leave," DeWayne Peevy said. "We thought he was just going to test the waters. Back then you could test the waters, work out for teams, and Jodie was going to go through that process and see what he had to work on."

Again, that was the plan, and the full anticipation was that Meeks would end up back at Kentucky. The simple truth was that at that point in time, Meeks wasn't viewed as much of an NBA prospect. Calipari and his staff even reached out to NBA personnel on Meeks' behalf to gauge his draft buzz.

The answers they got back weren't pretty.

"The information we had gathered on him was that he could be a second rounder," Orlando Antigua said. "Potentially not even get drafted."

But while the information they gathered was 100 percent correct at the time, what no one could have predicted was that in the process of "testing the waters," Meeks would blow everyone out of the water with how well he performed. The 6'4 guard could always shoot the ball, and when he got a chance to work out in front of NBA personnel, he shot about as well as he ever had in his life.

The workouts put Meeks on the NBA's radar, and also made his choice pretty clear. With the prospect of playing for another coach, in another system, with a bunch of new freshmen coming in, there was just too much uncertainty about what his senior season would be like at Kentucky. He had to go.

"Jodie went out and had such great workouts for teams, shot so well, that he figured 'I don't want a third coach in four years," Peevy said. "I'm probably shooting as well as I'm going to shoot, let me try this.'"

With that, Jodie Meeks was off to the NBA, and despite the uncertainty of his draft position there's little doubt that in the long run he got the last laugh. Meeks did in fact fall into the second round, but in the big picture it didn't seem to hurt him too much. He has been in the NBA since the fall of 2009, and in the summer of 2014 signed a three-year, $19.5 million contract. Not too bad for a guy who many thought would go undrafted.

Patterson's decision was next, and while it appeared a little more cut-and-dried on paper, that also made it much more complicated in real life.

For starters, no one was concerned about Patterson's draft position; if the chiseled, 6'9 power forward entered the NBA Draft he would've been a lottery pick. No doubt about it, no questions asked.

So the question became "why wouldn't Patrick Patterson go pro?"

It wasn't just a question that NBA pundits wondered, but also the Kentucky coaching staff as well. Before they allowed Patrick Patterson to return to school, or even entertain the thought of it, they asked him point blank: Why was he coming back?

No, seriously. They actually asked him that.

"Patrick Patterson after meeting us had to explain to us why he wanted to come back to school," Antigua said.

It's hard to believe, but it really did happen: Patrick Patterson, a good player, with really good grades, and great leadership qualities ---- someone that any coach would've practically begged to have on their roster --- was practically being forced out the door by Kentucky's new coaching staff.

Ultimately, it wasn't because they *didn't* want him to stay; but they did know just how much he could risk by returning. In hindsight it's funny to think about, although Patterson was still a little surprised by the whole situation.

"Yeah it was funny, normally a coach would try to convince you to stay," Patterson said. "Or even try to sell a few things whether it be playing time or getting you more touches or revolving the system around you."

Again, that's what a normal coach would do. But there's nothing normal about John Calipari.

"Cal did none of that," Patterson said. "All he basically said was 'I'd love to get the opportunity to coach you, but you have to do what's best for you and your family. You will be a first round draft pick.' And that was basically it."

In the end, if Patterson insisted on returning, Calipari at least wanted a good explanation why. Thankfully, Patterson had more than one lined up.

For starters, he had never played in an NCAA Tournament game; the team had missed the Big Dance his sophomore year, and he had been injured when they lost to Marquette when he was a freshman. So that was one experience that Patterson wanted before he left college. He also wanted to improve his outside game; at 6'9 he was probably going to have to develop his jump shot further if he wanted to make it in the NBA. And most importantly, he wanted his degree. Patterson was on pace to graduate by the end of his junior year.

Add it all up, and the explanation made sense to Calipari. Patrick Patterson would stay another year at Kentucky.

So one player was in, one player was out, and with the freshmen in place, it was now time for Calipari to decide who would stay with them.

Josh Harrellson, who made the cut described the tension around the program at the time.

"I didn't know what was going to happen," Harrellson said. "If he was going to keep me, or let me go."

Few players did, and over the summer months, Calipari was left with the difficult task of figuring it all out.

Whether the players fully understood it or not (and most of them did) from the moment that John Calipari had arrived in the spring, they were, in essence, auditioning to stay at Kentucky. When the first practice was held, and "a football team" showed up, that was an audition. Summer workouts were an audition. Lifting sessions with the strength and conditioning staff were an audition. Going to class, and acting like an adult while you were there, was an audition as well.

Ironically, that may have been the part that few players considered: They were constantly being evaluated. Not just for their on the court performance, but also off the court too. Calipari and his staff were doing their due diligence to not only figure out what kind of basketball players they had on their team, but what kind of *people* they had as well. Calipari had been preaching a "culture change" since the day he arrived. And he was sticking to his word.

"Coach Cal came in and really did his homework," Mark Krebs said. "And talked to people all over campus on a daily basis, and he got a good sense of who were the good teammates."

And that last part may have been the most important: Who would make a *good teammate.*

The simple truth was that with a new coach, a new system and so many talented freshmen, things would be different for the returning players. Everybody's roles would be changing in some capacity. Starters would have to come off the bench. Bench players might not play at all. Veterans would have to take a back seat to younger players. Minutes and stats might not be there for everyone.

Calipari had been around basketball long enough to know that not everyone would be happy with the new setup. And that's why he spent his first few months on campus closely evaluating his players; not just their basketball skills, but also their ability to fit in with the team he was building as well. Simply put, Calipari wanted to know who might have a problem with a new role. He also wanted to know who might cause trouble in the locker room if their minutes were reduced, or taken away altogether.

In other words, who was about the team? And who was about themselves?

"That was all part of the culture change that Coach Cal always talked about," Krebs said. "It was about having new guys coming in, and the older guys accepting them. One of the reasons you had Perry Stevenson, Ramon Harris, their skill on the court, they could play, they could hold their own. (But) they weren't going to be a distraction off the court (either)."

In the end, Calipari had some tough decisions to make, and not everyone was going to be happy. But he stayed true to his word, stuck to his guns and really did evaluate all facets of a player's game and personality. It wasn't just about on the court skill, but what kind of headaches --- or lack thereof --- they might bring off the court too.

Calipari proved it when he made his final cut.

"His 13th spot came down to Josh Harrellson or Matt Pilgrim," Kentucky Sports Radio's Matt Jones explained. "And it was interesting when he did that. Matt Pilgrim was considered a much better talent, but he was a troublemaker. He went to Oklahoma State, and got in trouble."

The decision was a turning point for Kentucky's program. It also pointed to something much bigger, according to Jones.

"Cal chose Josh Harrellson at the time and a lot of people were surprised by that," Jones said. "But that sent a signal to me that Cal realized he didn't have to worry about questionable character guys anymore. That he was at Kentucky and he didn't have to take chances on kids."

In the end, 13 players left Kentucky between the time that Calipari arrived, and the start of his first season (including Meeks who went pro). Granted, six were walk-ons, and as mentioned earlier, Calipari never intended to keep around as many walk-ons as his predecessor did.

But the others were scholarship players, and when they did leave, well, a narrative quickly formed. The national media jumped on Calipari, for what they believed to be unfair treatment of those players. Most assumed that they had done nothing wrong, and this was simply a matter of a big-time coach pushing out players, to bring in more talented replacements. In this case, those talented replacements were John Wall, DeMarcus Cousins and the entire freshman class.

While that was true to a degree, it wasn't the full narrative either. What few in the media knew at the time was what was already discussed above: Calipari had done his homework, and he had no patience for players who were going to create problems off the court.

And reflecting back now (with a few years of hindsight under our belts) two things are clear: One, the guys who stayed (guys like Perry Stevenson, Ramon Harris and Patrick Patterson) did in fact stay out of trouble, and proved to be both model citizens off the court, and valuable members of Kentucky's team on it. And two, virtually every single one of the guys who Calipari sent packing, did in fact find trouble after they left Kentucky. Several were kicked off the team at their next stop, a few got in trouble with the law, and one was even sentenced to prison time.

Again, it's all hindsight now, but it is important to point out. It's also important to point out that while the national media buried Calipari for the decision, what few people ever bothered to do, was ask the players who stayed about how Calipari handled everything.

Do that, and they would've found an entirely different picture altogether. Veterans weren't treated as commodities, or as barriers between

Calipari and his new star-studded freshmen class. Instead, they were treated like anyone else, like members of the team, like people who belonged at Kentucky.

"When he came in, he treated me like I wasn't a dude that was already there that he has to 'put up with,'" Ramon Harris said. "He didn't treat me like that. He treated me like 'Hey, you're a part of this team, and I'm going to treat you like I treat everyone else.'"

Harris was one of the veterans who did stick around, but he was also one of the veterans who might have his role reduced because of the freshmen. Not that it bothered him one bit.

The truth was that while the media was pushing the narrative that the "veterans" were forced out, it actually wasn't the case at all. Instead, Calipari had a tough list of requirements for his players; it was up to them whether they wanted to abide by them or not.

As they say, sometimes "the truth hurts." And Calipari was brutally honest.

"He was very honest with me," Harris said. "He said to me 'Ramon, I know you've started for the past two years. I don't know if I'm going to start you this year, but I don't want you to take that personally like I don't like you, or that I don't think that you're good enough. I just think that your role might change.'"

Calipari had similar conversations with a lot of his players. And while some players couldn't handle the truth, Harris took it in stride. Actually, he more than took it in stride. In a weird way he was flattered that the coach had been so truthful, and so willing to tell him exactly how things would be. The truth might hurt. But it's better than beating around the bush, or being outright lied to.

"I just said 'Coach, I appreciate you bringing me into your office and telling me that. Because you really didn't have to,'" Harris explained, recounting his conversation with Calipari. "You could've just been like 'I'm going with this, this is what I'm going with.' But you really didn't have to explain nothing to me. But I really appreciate you telling me."

But Calipari actually felt guilty for the honesty. He kept going.

"He was like, 'Ramon I really want you to be part of this team, I just want you to know that your role might change a little bit,'" Harris said. "And I said 'Ok coach, I'm ready when you need me.'"

The comment was music to the coach's ears, the exact kind of veteran presence he needed on his team. And Harris wasn't the only one willing to sacrifice whatever it took --- minutes, shots, stats --- to help the team.

"It's the same thing for Perry Stevenson," Harris explained. "He said 'Coach, I'd rather be coming off the bench for a Top 5 team than starting for an NIT team.'"

The Wildcats were slowly coming together, the culture change that Calipari had wanted was coming to life. The roles hadn't yet been defined, but the attitude of the team had been. A year after missing the NCAA Tournament, the sole focus became getting back into the Big Dance. Sure, everyone would have to sacrifice stats, but the team as a whole would start compiling the most important stat: Wins.

It was an attitude that started permeating across the team, and it began at the top.

"Patrick Patterson, he was a roommate of mine, and that kid just wanted to win," Chad Sanders said. "And he was the one who always kind of brought them together, to play pick-up or whatever."

But for Patterson it wasn't just about uniting the team. It was also about being a leader, and leading by example. It was about putting Calipari's vision --- to sacrifice for the good of the team --- into practice, and showing that if you stop worrying about yourself, and instead start worrying about getting better every day, than the rest would take care of itself.

"Patrick Patterson set the tone," Martin Newton said. "Patrick was a blue-collar, take your lunch pale, put your hat on, come to work kind of guy. His ego was not such that he had to have the ball all the time. He was just going to work. He set the tone for everyone else, because if Patrick could do it, if he was going to be the hardest working guy on the court, the rest of the guys could do it."

It was an attitude that trickled down to the entire team, and also set the tone for the entire season. With some of the trouble makers gone, the focus shifted to coming together as a group. Players began bonding; the older players showing the younger players the ropes, answering their questions and teaching them what life in Lexington was like. They took them to the mall and movies, told them not to be bothered by what fans or the media were saying.

"Yeah they did (embrace us younger guys)," Bledsoe said. "There wasn't any animosity. They could've easily been like 'you're the young guys of the team, you've got to fall in line.' But they let us come in and pretty much run the show."

Harris, who had been through the transition from both Tubby Smith to Billy Gillispie, and Gillispie to Calipari, agreed.

"It was never an issue of territorial, like 'I've been here three years. You're not just going to come in here and take mine,'" Harris said. "No, it was never like that."

The veterans were sacrificing, but it's also important to remember that the younger players were as well. Remember, they had all been the biggest stars pretty much everywhere they had played, their entire careers. Now they were entering college where their roles changed, and where they were playing with guys who were equal to or better than them, sometimes in their own class.

But like the veterans, they were quickly learning not only to live with it, but to actually embrace it as well.

"All those guys sacrificed something," Harrellson said. "When Daniel (Orton) found out DeMarcus (Cousins) was coming, Daniel could've gone anywhere in the country and started at center. Eric Bledsoe could've gone anywhere and started at point guard rather than playing two guard."

The 2009-2010 Kentucky Wildcats were not only together, but now coming together as well.

And after a summer together, it was time to show the world just how much they'd learned, and just how good they could be.

They got that chance in early October at Big Blue Madness.

It was a night that no one would ever forget.

It was also a night that would reveal a phenomenon no one was prepared for.

THE JOHN WALL DANCE

I T WAS A cool evening in Kentucky in October 2009, and the scene wasn't all that different than the scene in any other year, on any other October night in Lexington. Class had been in session for several weeks; add in summer school, and Kentucky's freshmen basketball players had already spent several months on campus to that point.

But despite quickly becoming accustomed to all the quirks of life on campus --- class, workouts, random autograph seekers who seemed to stop them every time they left the dorms --- the freshmen could have never been prepared for what they'd see upon passing Memorial Coliseum on that October evening: There were tents everywhere they looked. Tents filled with Kentucky fans, all hoping to score tickets to Big Blue Madness that year.

Ah, "Big Blue Madness," Kentucky's version of Midnight Madness, the annual event where college basketball programs turn their first "official" practice into an open event for the public. But while Midnight Madness is in fact an event for a lot of schools, it is something entirely different altogether at Kentucky. In Lexington, it's an event that fans wait weeks just to attend. Hundreds camp out on campus, all hoping to get tickets to what essentially amounts to a glorified scrimmage.

Yes, it's safe to say that Big Blue Madness is indeed a big deal in Kentucky. Yet with John Calipari in charge for the first time in 2009, it felt even *bigger*.

"The atmosphere was way better (than in previous years)," Mark Krebs said. "You had the energy in the tent area where people were hanging out. It seemed like it was a party, a festivity, and not 'Man, we're camping out to go to a practice.' It was lively. They made the most of it."

Part of the excitement was the newness of it all; a new coach taking over and bringing in a bunch of new players is going to get any fan base fired up. But what can't be underappreciated about 2009 specifically, was the fact that Calipari was the first coach in a long time who actually embraced the event. His predecessors had always viewed Big Blue Madness as a nuisance, something they *had* to do for the fans, before the work of the preseason really began.

But with Calipari in charge, an important distinction was made: Yes, the practices after Big Blue Madness were important. But for this one night, it wasn't about the team. It was about doing something for the fans; and Calipari put his money where his mouth was --- literally --- in the weeks leading up to the event. He personally delivered donuts and coffee to fans in the morning, and followed up by bringing pizzas at night. His players then followed his lead.

"Whether they were told to or did it naturally, they (the players) engaged with fans in ways they hadn't done before," Kentucky Sports Radio's Matt Jones said. "Now it's normal. Players come out and play games with fans, but that didn't used to happen before Cal. It used to be that the players stayed away from it honestly."

One player in particular may have taken Calipari's message a little too literally. If anything, he probably spent a little *too much* time amongst the fans in the tents.

That man was DeMarcus Cousins, the normally quiet and reserved 6'11 power forward, whose true personality and character came out in those weeks leading up to Big Blue Madness. For whatever temper Cousins might have occasionally shown on the court, he was equally compassionate off it and also showed a genuine love for Kentucky basketball fans during that timeframe as well.

Simply put, DeMarcus Cousins was everywhere in the weeks before Big Blue Madness. He posed for pictures with small children. He signed autographs. He played pick-up hoops with students on the blue courts near where the campout was held. And while outsiders to Kentucky basketball would spend the next few months pigeonholing Cousins as too brash, too immature or too temperamental, Wildcats' fans saw another side of DeMarcus Cousins altogether.

Sure, he may have the body of a grown man. But at 19-years-old, DeMarcus Cousins still had the heart of a kid. And even at 6'11, he had no problem "fitting in" amongst the sea of fans outside Memorial Coliseum.

"During the campout is when you got a chance to realize, 'holy moly' there was a connection of our guys and the fans," Orlando Antigua said. "You had DeMarcus going out there playing at one in the morning, two in the morning, playing out there with kids on the blacktop, and we had to say 'Guys, you can't be out there! You're going to hurt yourselves!'"

Thankfully Cousins and all his teammates made it through those 2 a.m., pick-up games unscathed, and a few weeks after the campout wrapped up, it was time to move the Big Blue Madness party into Rupp Arena.

Once there, the fans were once again reminded that Big Blue Madness was completely different than ever before, and that Calipari himself took a completely different approach than any of the coaches who'd come before him.

With John Calipari in charge, Big Blue Madness was no longer just a basketball practice, and saying it was an "event" was probably underselling it as well. With Cal calling the shots, it was now a spectacle. It was a scene. And it was a showcase, not just for fans, but also for recruits who might be in attendance as well. Several big-name prospects were in fact on-hand for Big Blue Madness in 2009, including a small forward from New Jersey who did eventually end up in Lexington. His name was Michael Kidd-Gilchrist (although he went by "Michael Gilchrist" at the time), who was accompanied by his high school teammate, Kyrie Irving.

The night truly was a spectacle, if not an outright circus. And John Calipari was the ringleader.

"You've got to remember that you're dealing with Coach Cal, who's a big 'ideas' guy," DeWayne Peevy said. "And he's used to running everything (at his previous stop in Memphis). He's kind of thinking of everything from an entertainment standpoint. 'Should we do a dunk contest? Do I need to go make some calls for some entertainment?'"

Ultimately Calipari didn't have to make too many calls --- Peevy and Jason Schlafer, who was Kentucky's assistant AD for marketing at the time, did that --- but the night itself did not disappoint. A young, up-and-coming recording artist named Drake showed up, and a slew of former Kentucky legends including Tayshaun Prince came as well. A video montage followed, and ended with a message which the fans couldn't help but love. It read: 'Envy our past. Fear our future.'

And then, John Calipari himself came out. The man who told fans at his introductory press conference that he wasn't 'The Grand Poobah' sure looked like it that night, as he walked out to roars of the adoring, screaming crowd, wearing a light grey Kentucky sweat suit and slapping hands with the fans who lined the stage. His players lined up behind him, while smoke billowed from the floor, and fireworks exploded above his head.

The moment was quintessential Calipari. While it might have overwhelmed another coach, Calipari reveled in it.

"You knew John Calipari was the perfect storm in recruiting," Scott Padgett said. "But you didn't realize how great a fit he was (as an actual coach) until Midnight Madness when he came out with that opening speech."

Oh that's right, the speech.

After the crowd finally quieted down, Calipari began to address them. He looked more like a Senator running for office than a basketball coach at that exact moment, moving from one subject to the next, pausing for effect and basking in the crowd's admiration, before immediately moving to the next point. Calipari thanked the student section ("The eRUPPtion Zone"), the band, and the (in his own words) "National Championship winning cheerleading squad." He recognized Kentucky legends like Dan Issel, Jamal Mashburn and Pat Riley, former coaches like Adolph Rupp and Joe B. Hall, and some of the school's legendary teams like "Rupp's Runts" and "The Unforgettables." But mostly he thanked the fans, beginning the speech with one simple phrase: "You all are awesome."

Padgett, the Louisville native, who'd played for two National Championships during his time as a player at the school, had never seen anything like it.

"Every single statement that he said in that speech, it hit home to everything a Kentucky fan would want to hear," Padgett said. "There were no wasted words that were the lull before (he moved onto the next point). No, it was 'we're gonna do this. And we're gonna do this.' And they're each leading to a cheer, to another cheer, to a bigger cheer, to the end, let's all 24,000 go nuts. It was like he was speaking to exactly what everybody wanted and had been missing since 1998."

Director of Basketball Operations Martin Newton, the Lexington native whose father had been the Athletic Director for over a decade at Kentucky, put things in a slightly different way.

"When he came out and gave his talk, and you watched the fan base," Newton said. "They were just in awe."

* * *

If Calipari's speech set the tone for the future of Kentucky basketball, the player introductions set the tone for the season ahead. As Kentucky fans would learn by the end of the night, their team not only had the most talent in college basketball during the 2009-2010 season. They had the most style and swag as well.

Prior to the festivities, the players hung out in the locker room, where they put the finishing touches on their own introductions. Some, like John Wall and DeMarcus Cousins had planned intricate dance moves for the occasion; others were simply excited to be introduced to the crowd.

But it's how they were introduced which quickly caught everyone's attention that night. Over the previous few months Calipari, Peevy and Schlafer had planned out every moment of the night, but nothing was bigger than the player introductions. Each player would be introduced while standing on a crane, 40 feet in the air, before slowly being brought down by the rafters.

Yes, you read that correctly: Each player began their night 40 feet in the air.

It was a crazy idea, and maybe just a tiny bit dangerous. But this was a big night, and Calipari was a big thinker.

You only get one chance to make a first impression, right?

Right?

Well, not all of Kentucky's players were thinking that way.

"We were all like 'We're going to do what? From where?'" Mark Krebs said. "And they were like 'Don't worry, you're going to be safe!'"

Eventually the players calmed down (they also received plenty of safety training) and as the moment inched closer inside Rupp Arena, the anticipation grew. Finally, the public address announcer got on the microphone and said for all the fans to hear: "Ladies and gentlemen, this is the 2009-2010 edition of your Kentucky Wildcats."

It was a surreal moment in time, as one by one the players were introduced. Some, like Patrick Patterson were familiar faces to the crowd, others like Eric Bledsoe, completely new. The Kentucky players smiled and waved, and just embraced the moment in general, as each heard their name called.

Well, actually let's take that back. Not everyone embraced the moment; one player was outright terrified by it.

"DeMarcus Cousins was the most scared person alive doing that," Peevy said with a laugh. "If you go back and watch the video on YouTube you will notice, he doesn't move, he doesn't say a word, he doesn't shake, because he was scared of heights and he did not want to do that."

At that particular moment Cousins didn't do much of anything (other than to hold onto the rails for dear life), which is a damn shame, since he had made a big promise to his teammates in the locker room that evening: DeMarcus Cousins had promised to dance.

The decision itself wasn't surprising since, well, DeMarcus Cousins, John Wall and Eric Bledsoe pretty much danced every chance they got.

The three danced in the locker room before practice. They danced in the locker room after practice. They might even sneak a quick two-step in during practice if Calipari wasn't paying particularly close attention.

But on this night, there would be no dancing for DeMarcus Cousins. Even if he and John Wall had promised teammates they'd do a dance when they were introduced at Big Blue Madness.

Yup, you read that correctly: DeMarcus Cousins --- who was introduced before John Wall --- was supposed to dance during his introduction at Big Blue Madness. Meaning that if history had turned out just a tiny bit differently, the "John Wall dance" very well might have gone down as the "DeMarcus Cousins dance."

"He was going to go first because he was before me," Wall admitted. "So he was supposed to dance before me. Then I was going to dance. But he was so scared."

Chad Sanders backed up the story.

"In the Joe Craft Center, the first person I saw do the dance was DeMarcus," Sanders said.

When Sanders says "the dance" he is of course talking about the one that Wall made famous that night.

Honestly it wasn't anything special (at least to Wall), and wasn't intended to turn into anything that anyone would remember. But when the spotlight turned to John Wall that evening at Big Blue Madness, he let loose the famed "John Wall dance."

And Kentucky basketball would never be the same.

"It's a dance, it seems stupid," Matt Jones said. "But for the first time in my lifetime, with the possible exception of Rex Chapman, Kentucky had the coolest player in the country. Now everyone thinks of Kentucky as the cool team, but that didn't used to be the case. People kind of looked at Kentucky like, they were always the good team, but they never had the cool player. Nobody had posters up of the UK players. We weren't the Fab Five, we weren't UNLV, we weren't even Duke, who wasn't cool, but at least had players everybody knew. The only player Kentucky had in

20 years that the whole country really cared about was probably (Jamal) Mashburn."

The dance truly was one of those perfect moments in time, a rare instant that can't be scripted, can't be anticipated and just kind of *happens*. To John Wall it was just a dance, but to everyone watching, it was a window into his personality. For just a few short seconds no one cared about the ancillary things that came with John Wall --- his one-and-done status, his projected draft spot, his NBA future --- but instead, fans got to see who he really was at his core. They got to see his exuberance and his excitement. And they got to remember that despite all the hype, he was in fact just a kid. A kid who really was enjoying the moment.

And speaking of "enjoying the moment" no one enjoyed that specific moment quite like Kentucky fans did.

Within days, the "John Wall dance" wasn't a dance at all. Instead, it was an outright phenomenon.

"I didn't expect for there to be that atmosphere (and excitement) behind it," Wall told me last winter. "Everybody went crazy."

Everyone did go crazy, and interestingly, it spoke to the changing world of college basketball and sports coverage in general.

Remember, 2009 was right around the time that the landscape of sports --- and how we as fans consumed those sports --- was changing. Newspapers were slowly losing their cache, with more fans turning to the internet to get information about their team. Well as we all know now, internet coverage isn't always strictly just straight "news," but all the ancillary stuff that comes with it, with box scores and game recaps supplemented by goofy pictures and videos as well. The fall of 2009 was an especially interesting time, as Twitter had just come into vogue a few months before, and YouTube was still just a few years old itself. To put things into perspective, neither John Wall nor DeMarcus Cousins had a personal Twitter account during their time at Kentucky.

So with that as context, it's safe to say that the 2009-2010 Kentucky Wildcats really were one of the first sports teams anywhere, pro or college, basketball, baseball or football to go "viral" on the internet. Unlike Michael Jordan's Chicago Bulls or the mid-90's Dallas Cowboys, the 2009-2010 Kentucky Wildcats were basically covered 24 hours a day, seven days a week. They were the perfect blend of talent and personality, and Kentucky fans simply couldn't get enough of them.

"I really believe that team is why so many Kentucky fans are on the internet," Jones said. "Kentucky fans, in my opinion, are on the internet more than any other college team. I think it was that team, and it was kind of because they (the players) all kind of were on the internet. DeMarcus Cousins asked me to help him find a nickname, and he got fans on the website to vote on it. John Wall, with the John Wall dance. They (the fans) wanted to eat up everything about the team, so the internet was there for that to happen."

And nothing personified just how much Kentucky fans loved the 2009-2010 'Cats quite like the "John Wall Dance" did. To quote Wall, everybody did "go crazy" over it, with just about everyone doing the dance itself, then recording it and posting it on the internet every chance they got. Couples did the dance at their weddings. Friends did the dance while on vacation. Kids did the dance….basically everywhere they could.

The "John Wall dance" was never intended to be a signature moment for Kentucky basketball. But that's exactly what it became.

"The moment was when John Wall danced; if you asked Kentucky fans to remember something from the Cal era, almost everyone is going to mention that," Jones said. "It was almost like a moment, where people were like 'Ok, we're back.'"

Kentucky was *back*. And it wasn't just the fans who felt it, but folks inside the program as well.

"That was the first time but from a staff standpoint it (Big Blue Madness) did what it was supposed to do," Peevy said. "It started the hype of 'This is going to be a special season.' Not just that. It was going to be a part of a new era."

That new era was just weeks from beginning, with a season opener against Morehead State.

But while everyone was excited for games to get underway, internally, the Kentucky Wildcats were nervous.

They still had a lot of work to do.

And they had to start the season with John Wall on the sidelines.

THE PERFECT STOP

T HE HYPE OF Big Blue Madness had subsided, but a different kind of buzz was in the air when the Kentucky Wildcats took the practice floor the following day. It was finally the first "real" practice of the season, a chance for players and coaches to reconnect, and put an offseason's worth of hard work to use.

It was also an opportunity for Calipari to push his squad, as if a spot in the Final Four were on the line that day.

The players lined up for a drill called "The Perfect Stop," where three teams of four players each went head-to-head. Two teams were on the court at a time (a third waiting to check in on the sidelines), with two defensive players lined up in the post, and two more at the top of the key. For the defense --- who took the brunt of pain and anguish in the drill --- the only way to get off the court was to make "The Perfect Stop."

"One (team) is on 'O' and one is on 'D' and you have to 'perfect stop' them," Jon Hood, a freshman forward in 2009-2010, explained. "You have to keep them out of the lane; the ball can't get into the lane, they can't get into the lane. They can't get an offensive rebound, and they can't score for a full 30 seconds."

Points were also awarded for attempting a charge, and by forcing a turnover, but ultimately the drill was really about the defense, and about playing defense as a team. It was about moving your feet, and communicating, and working with the other guys on the floor. If you weren't able to do that, well, it could be a long afternoon for you and your teammates.

"The object of it is if you're on defense to get out as quickly as possible," Hood said. "The objective on offense is to just bury them, because when you score, the other team comes in. The offense is fresh, and the defense is not, so it pays to get out quick. To go hard the first time."

And if you don't?

"We could spend four minutes on it," Hood said. "Or two hours."

Behind closed doors practices like these --- brutal, unrelenting, manically competitive practices --- became the norm at Kentucky. But of course, none of the national media knew just how hard this team was working, when they convened to vote in that year's preseason polls.

Now that's not to say that most media outlets didn't have the Wildcats ranked highly --- *Sports Illustrated* had them ranked No. 5 nationally, while six panelists had an ESPN poll that had them ranked anywhere from No. 2 in the country, to No. 7 --- just that most panelists assumed it was based more on the team's raw talent, than their drive and work ethic.

Few however, actually saw the Wildcats as true title contenders.

Remember, this was just a few years after the "one-and-done" rule was instituted, and the prevailing wisdom at the time was still to look at potential one-and-done players with a wary eye. Most were perceived (fairly or not) as selfish and egotistical, only in college because they had to be, and only interested in using the college basketball experience to pad their stats, on the way to the pros. Sure the players were talented, but plenty were more of a headache than they were worth.

And the idea of building your whole team around them like Kentucky was? Well, it was laughable. They were too immature and too inexperienced. Even if they did meet the hype, they'd never compete for a championship.

"It wasn't the expectation that people have right now that freshmen can come in and immediately put up numbers," said DeWayne Peevy, who has been at Kentucky for the entire Calipari era. "Back then it was 'Hey, we're going to be better and it's going to be a lot of fun.' But nobody was talking about 'we're going to win the National Championship.'"

No, they weren't. But while the focus nationally continued to be on Kentucky's surface level-talent, what few knew was that talent was only part of the equation. The Wildcats weren't only one of the most naturally gifted teams in college basketball. They also had some of the sport's hardest workers.

And it all started in the backcourt, with Wall and Bledsoe; the guard that everyone wanted, and the one that everyone overlooked were quickly turning into one dynamic duo.

"John Wall really set the tone," Director of Basketball Operations Martin Newton said. "He and Eric Bledsoe were such hard workers."

They were hard workers who also had a major chip on their shoulders. And for whatever physical gifts that they lacked (mostly size), the one thing they didn't lack was heart. Wall and Bledsoe may have been two of the smallest players on the court. But they refused to back down from anyone.

"I'll never forget the first practices," assistant coach Rod Strickland said. "Everybody's shots got blocked. We were running drills, and John Wall was blocking somebody's shot, Eric Bledsoe was blocking somebody's shot. We had the guards blocking shots."

The intensity that Wall and Bledsoe brought to practice every day was, in a lot of ways, a coach's dream. Sure, every coach has had talented players before, and they've all had hard workers too. But when two of the best players on your team are also two of your hardest workers? Well, it makes everyone else step their game up.

"I remember doing a series of 'Blood drills' is what he would call them," Newton said, describing something similar to "The Perfect Stop" that Hood explained earlier. "It was a series of 1-on-1's, 2-on-1's, 2-on-2's and the competitiveness in those drills; if you didn't play 100 percent, and play as hard as you could, you were going to get embarrassed."

Rod Strickland agreed, and took it one step further.

"They (Wall and Bledsoe) raised the stakes for everyone else," Strickland said. "Because now the older guys you're playing against, you've got to compete or you're going to get embarrassed. And they were freshmen. The older guys are like 'I can't let these young bucks treat me any kind of way.' But then you have these young bucks saying 'Here we are.'"

Yes, the freshmen had arrived, and they had also definitely made their presence felt. But while a ton of credit needs to go to them for coming in and competing right away, Calipari needs credit too, for sticking to his guns, and sticking to the word he gave during the recruiting cycle. If you'll remember, even though Calipari was recruiting some of the best high school players in the country, he refused to promise them anything; no one was guaranteed playing time, a certain number of shots or even a starting spot.

Once the players got to campus, and once practice started, everyone realized that Calipari wasn't kidding.

"We didn't come in thinking we were going to have the No. 1 spot," Wall said. "We had to work for our starting position. I think Coach Cal did a great job of embracing us, but (also) making everyone work."

And work they did. From "Blood Drills" to "The Perfect Stop" the vibe around practice was all about business, all about competition and all about getting better. It was a completely different tone from a season before.

"I was there for some of the 'G' (Billy Gillispie) practices, and they were competitive, they really were," Hood said. "But Coach Cal's practices, that's the way it is. Everything, there is a winner and a loser. He teaches you to be the winner, you *have* to be the winner. You be the winner or there's consequences; you have to run, you have to do push-ups, whatever it is."

Of course while the early season practices were competitive, there's also one thing that Calipari was quick to point out during interviews on the early part of that 2009-2010 season: Those practices weren't always pretty.

Now in defense of the Kentucky Wildcats, that probably should've been expected. After all, early season practices are a bit sloppy at just about every school in the country, and it's definitely become a rite of passage at Kentucky, where the roster has been flipped over in virtually every single season of the John Calipari era.

Yet even by Kentucky's insane standards of roster turnover, the fall of 2009 was different; veterans had to learn to blend with younger players, and all the players were working with the new coaching staff for the first time.

Add in the nuances of the dribble-drive offense, and for lack of a better term, everyone was a freshman.

"Understand this was different," Calipari told Fox Sports. "Now, you have three returning players, maybe four. Well that year, everybody was new. They were new, I was new; they were new to each other. That's why we weren't a great execution team."

No, Kentucky was not a great execution team, and it showed once the games tipped-off.

Those games were coming up fast, and so too was a cram-session with the media.

* * *

DeWayne Peevy is a man who has seen just about everything in college athletics. A former college baseball player, Peevy spent eight years at the SEC offices, right at the time that the conference was emerging as the biggest, baddest, bully in all of college sports. He was there for the beginning of the league's insane run of success in football (which included seven straight National Championships), and also was in charge for media relations for the SEC's basketball teams at a time when Florida won National Championships in both 2006 and 2007.

Add in a year working in the Kentucky basketball pressure-cooker under Billy Gillispie in 2008, and Peevy's resume was about as complete as it could be entering the 2009-2010 season, with more experiences crammed into a decade than many administrators get in a lifetime.

But despite it all, despite those college football titles, Final Four runs and everything in between, even Peevy couldn't believe what he saw when the media descended upon Lexington for Kentucky's media day in October 2009.

The horde which arrived at the Joe Craft Center, was a "horde" in every meaning of the word. The group --- which consisted of local and national media, not to mention print, radio and TV --- was so large Kentucky had to scrap any original plans they had, and do something completely different than anything they'd ever done in the past. Rather than emphasize a player or two, Peevy instead decided to put each player on a stool and space them out evenly around the practice court. John Calipari was in another room altogether.

The setup was unlike anything, anyone had ever seen.

"Our media day that year was crazy," Peevy said. "We had more people at our media day than the SEC media day. I used to run the SEC media day. It was just huge, people were everywhere."

And that media contingent came to see what virtually everyone agreed was the best team in the SEC, by far. While the national polls were uncertain just how good the Wildcats were relative to their competition across the country, 20 out of 25 voters selected Kentucky to win the SEC. Not surprisingly, a pair of Wildcats were preseason favorites for individual awards as well; voters chose Patrick Patterson as the Preseason Player of the Year, Wall, the league's top freshman. That duo was also selected to make the conference's first and second teams respectively.

But despite the hype surrounding Kentucky basketball hitting an all-time high, the Wildcats' spirits were brought back down to reality just weeks before the season was set to begin. That's when news that the team's star, John Wall, would be suspended for the season opener against Morehead State.

Understand that an investigation had been going on for a while, and the truth is, that the results could've been worse. Wall had been found guilty of accepting a small amount of money from an advisor (a little under $800) which he and his family spent to take unofficial visits during his junior year. But because both Wall and Kentucky cooperated with the NCAA, he was given little more than a slap on the wrist as punishment.

Again, it could've been worse.

At the same time, it did strike fear in the Wildcats as they began preparations for their season opener.

"The first game we were worried," Daniel Orton said. "It's like 'we're not going to have everybody, we're not going to have everyone we should have.'"

Even worse was that the Wildcats weren't playing any old mid-major program to open the year, but one that was actually good enough to pull off an upset.

The Morehead State Eagles weren't your father's mid-major darling, but instead one with real talent on the floor, and real coaching chops on the sidelines. The club was led by Kenneth Faried, a star in the paint, who would not only finish second that year nationally in rebounding (he'd finish first the following year), but also later became a first round NBA Draft pick of the Denver Nuggets. Not to mention that Morehead State was also coached by Donnie Tyndall, who eventually climbed the coaching ladder right up to the SEC, where he was in charge of Tennessee during the 2014-2015 season (he was eventually fired for NCAA wrongdoing).

Simply put, Morehead State had enough skill on the court and smarts on the sidelines to pull off the upset, especially with John Wall in street clothes. Or at least that's what everyone thought, right up until tip-off.

Because once the game started, Kentucky fans realized something very important: John Wall wasn't the only star in the Wildcats' backcourt.

That's right, Eric Bledsoe, the guy who many viewed as a "back-up plan" for Wall in recruiting, proved that once the ball was tipped, he took a backseat to no one. In Wall's absence, Bledsoe finished the game with 24 points, the most for a freshman in his Kentucky debut since Sam Bowie in 1979. In the process, he also showed his new teammates exactly what he was capable of.

"One (thing we learned) was how good Eric Bledsoe was," Mark Krebs, a player who himself was awarded a scholarship right before the season, had said. "He stepped up."

Bledsoe did in fact step up. He told Fox Sports last fall that his only memory of the game was being "in the zone," a sentiment that Tyndall --- the man who coached against the Wildcats that night --- agreed with.

"If John Wall is better than him," Donnie Tyndall said. "Wow."

Kentucky won 75-59, but as exciting as the victory was, there was also no time to relax. Just three days after taking down Morehead State, they'd host Miami of Ohio at Rupp. And while Wall would return, the game would prove more difficult than anyone could imagine. Much, much more difficult.

The truth is, that for virtually all 40 minutes of the game, Miami of Ohio was the better team. They jumped out to a shocking 18-point lead in the first half, and even after the Wildcats picked things up, it was still the Redhawks who led 39-36 at the half. Even worse was that for all the work Kentucky did on defense at practice (don't ever forget "The Perfect Stop"), virtually none of it translated on the court that night. The Redhawks hit 15 three's as a team, including a Rupp Arena record eight by Nick Winbush.

It was ugly at times, unwatchable at others, yet maybe the most incredible thing was that the Wildcats were actually in position to put the game away late. Kentucky was up two points with under 20 seconds to play, when the Redhawks fouled Wall, giving him the chance to virtually ice the game if he made both shots.

And that's when things got crazy.

The freshman --- again, playing in his first college game --- went up to the line and calmly sunk the first shot, before the second one rattled off the front rim. With the ball, the Redhawks sprinted up the court, and before Kentucky could get comfortable on defense, Miami's Kenny Haynes pulled up from about 25-feet away and drilled a deep three.

70-70. Tie game.

Now understand, this exact moment is where virtually any coach in college basketball other than John Calipari would call a timeout. Virtually any other coach would've preferred to gather his troops, set something up, and try to win it in regulation, while also conceding that the game might end up in overtime.

The thing was though, John Calipari is no normal coach. And he wasn't going to call a timeout.

"Coach Cal didn't like to call set plays," Wall remembered, when asked about the moment. "So he told me to take the ball up and I attacked."

Wall did attack, catching the ball on the move and sprinting up the left side of the court. He took one quick dribble to the right, only to be met by a slew of Miami defenders, which forced him back to the left.

With the clock about to hit zero, Wall faded away, and let his muscle memory take over. He and Strickland had practiced that shot --- the fade away, with a hand in his face --- time and time again.

John Wall, in his first game was ready for the moment. And it showed.

"I threw it up," Wall said. "And it went in."

The ball hit the bottom of the net with just half a second to go, causing Rupp Arena to explode with excitement, while the Wildcats sprinted back on defense. One final shot by the Redhawks proved to be no good, as Kentucky held on for the second, and most exciting win of the John Calipari era. John Wall had arrived, and proven why he was the most hyped freshman in college basketball.

"It's one of those things that's good to see him step up," student manager Chad Sanders said. "Like yeah, it's a team we should've beaten, but to see him hit a big shot like that, you kind of just felt the presence right there. Like, 'Don't worry, I've got you. I'll take care of it.'

The victory was unforgettable for the fans inside Rupp Arena, and later in the night it also became unforgettable for the media in the press room. That's because for all of Wall's heroics, Miami (OH) head coach Charlie Coles may have stolen the show at the postgame press conference.

Understand that Coles (who passed away in 2013) was at the time, the definition of an "old-school coach," a guy who started coaching ball when he was 27, and never really stopped. Unlike guys who might be breaking into the profession now, there was no money or fame associated with the gig at the time, meaning that if you didn't love basketball, well, coaching probably wasn't for you. At the same time Coles had carved out a nice career for himself at Miami of Ohio, taking the school to the Sweet 16 in

1999, thanks in large part due to Wally Szczerbiak (ironically, the Redhawks actually lost to... you guessed it, Kentucky in that year's Sweet 16!).

But by 2009 however, things were a little bit different. Coles was 67-years-old, and with almost two full decades at Miami, his career was undoubtedly winding down. He wasn't a young up-and-comer with a reputation to protect, or future coaching opportunities to consider. There were no jobs to come after Miami. There were no allies in the media to watch out for.

Therefore, when a media member asked him a question he didn't like in the postgame press conference, well, he let the reporter have it.

The reporter wondered how the Redhawks had let the game "get away" from them, a seemingly innocent question, at least until you remember that they'd entered the game as heavy underdogs, and still almost won.

"I can't believe you asked that," Coles began, stunned.

"I really can't believe it. Let me see here. Kentucky Wildcats, No. 4 in the country. I'm hearing four first round draft choices, and you're asking me how that got away from me? Why don't you ask John (Calipari) why it was so close? I'm not gonna answer that question, man."

Oh, but Charlie Coles wasn't done.

"We come up with a brilliant effort," he continued. "Wow how things change. Before the game, all I heard was 'Boy, this and that.' You know, they start playing. They're the Big Blue. You oughta know that. I'm not mad at you, but where have you been?"

And then finally, after calming down, he decided to actually answer the reporter's question.

"You remember John Wall?" he asked. "I've watched three tapes. From your 'Blue and White (scrimmage),' your two exhibitions and your Morehead game, and John Wall didn't play in a couple of them. And I'm hearing John Wall is the greatest, right? That's how it got away."

Wow.

The funny thing was though, that for anyone who thought the rant was entertaining, well, Calipari had one of his own coming following the

Wildcats next game. That matchup was against Sam Houston State in a preliminary game of the "Cancun Challenge" preseason tournament (the Wildcats would play two tournament games at Rupp Arena as part of the "tournament," before finishing things off with two more games in Cancun).

Kentucky ended up winning 102-92 that night, but if their defensive effort was lousy against Miami (OH), it somehow got worse against Sam Houston. The Wildcats not only gave up 92 points, but also a staggering 18 three-pointers, including 11 from the Bearkats' Corey Allmond.

Yes, you read that correctly. Just one game after Miami (OH)'s Nick Winbush set a Rupp Arena record for three-pointers made by an opposing player, Almond broke it.

Incredible. Well unless you're John Calipari. He was simply furious with the team's effort.

"They have no urgency defensively," Calipari said. "None."

He continued.

"If we don't do better defensively, folks, we are in trouble," Calipari said. "Do you think we can score 100 against everybody? Because we're going to have to. They are going to score 100 against us."

Eventually the emotional plea on the podium ended, and thankfully for Kentucky's players, their coach did eventually calm down (even if it did come after a good old fashioned ass-chewing session in the film room). Prior to the Wildcats' next game against Rider, Calipari was even in a joking mood, telling reporters he had "called the NCAA and asked them to move the (three-point) line back."

Calipari was kidding of course, but his players did take the message to heart in their fourth and final game before heading to Cancun. The Wildcats put forth their best defensive effort to that point in the season by far, holding the Broncs to just 31 percent shooting from the field, and under 25 percent from three. After allowing Corey Allmond to hit 11 three's in the previous game (and Nick Winbush to hit eight the game before that), Kentucky held Rider to just four overall as a team.

With the win, the Wildcats improved to 4-0. It might not have meant much, but it did show the team was moving in the right direction. All the wins weren't pretty, but after the disastrous Billy Gillispie era, where losses to schools like VMI and Garner-Webb became a little bit too common, at least Kentucky was in fact winning games.

Now, it was time to hit the road. After four games at Rupp Arena, the Wildcats would leave the comforts of home, for a different kind of comfort: It was time to hit the beaches of Mexico, for the final two games of the Cancun Challenge.

It seemed all so nice on paper; white sand, aqua blue oceans and a little bit of hoops. What could be better than that?

Not much, but when the team got to Mexico, they came to two quick realizations: The competition was about to get much tougher.

And the playing conditions would be unlike anything, any of them had ever seen.

VIVA MEXICO!

I T WAS A cool, breezy, November day in Cancun, the kind of beautiful afternoon millions of Americans dream of when they book vacations to the Mexican resort town throughout the year. In the distance, the sun beamed off the clear, aqua blue water; a pool the size of some small lakes sat just feet from the hotel room windows of the Moon Palace Resort.

This was the scene of Kentucky's first road trip of the season, and safe to say, there were a lot worse places the Wildcats' basketball team could've been. After two preliminary games at Rupp Arena, the team had flown to Mexico, where they'd open play in the Cancun Challenge the following day. But on this afternoon, both players and coaches were free to do pretty much whatever they pleased. John Calipari himself was in his room relaxing, when he looked out his window and couldn't help but smile at what he saw.

There were his players, walking around the resort, together as a group.

To most coaches, the gesture might have been something small, and to others, insignificant altogether. But for Calipari --- who'd been a head coach for over 20 years at that point --- he knew exactly how important it was.

"The best teams I've coached, they would move in mass," Calipari told reporters the following day. "They would go to a movie and they would all go; they would go to the mall and they'd all go. My best teams, whether they were Massachusetts or Memphis, that's how they were. I was in my hotel room yesterday and I looked out and I see all of them walking around the complex and I thought, `Not bad, maybe it's the start of something.'"

Maybe, indeed. But while the team was quickly bonding off the court, they'd face a different kind of adversity when they stepped on it. For Kentucky, it had nothing to do with the opponent, or even any inner turmoil on their own team. Instead the worries centered on some of the weirdest playing conditions anyone could ever remember.

Before we explain those conditions, it's important to understand that coming to Cancun wasn't John Calipari's idea, or really anyone's who was associated with the team at that point. Kentucky's participation had been booked years in advance, back when Billy Gillispie was the head coach, and back when every detail might not have been as clearly thought out as it was with Calipari in charge. In subsequent years, the Wildcats would take nothing but first-class trips, to places like the Atlantis Resort in the Bahamas and to Hawaii for the Maui Invitational. But in 2009, in Cancun, there was nothing first-class about the conditions that the Wildcats played under.

For starters, games weren't played in an arena, or even a gym, but instead, a ballroom where a court had been laid down smack dab on top of a carpet. On the bench, players sat in standard banquet chairs, and a chandelier hung over the court, making it impossible to even attempt a half-court shot, let alone make one. The scoreboard meanwhile was on the floor, out of view for players and officials on the court.

And yet somehow, as bad as that sounds, the actual playing court was even worse. It had last been used at the same tournament a year earlier, and since then had been kept in storage. By the time it was removed for the start of that year's Cancun Challenge, well, let's just say that it wasn't in the best condition.

"The floor was warped because it was kept in a room that wasn't temperature controlled," DeWayne Peevy said. "There were dead spots in the floor. The three-point line didn't connect fully around when we first got there. It was crazy."

Yikes.

So those were the conditions that Kentucky's team was forced to play under. However, beyond the players, there was good news for the 1,000 Wildcat fans who made the trip down to Mexico to watch the team play. That good news? There was all the free food and alcohol they could consume!

That's right, most fans had purchased an "all-inclusive" travel package, which meant that food and beverages were on the house. And the Moon Palace Resort made sure that the fans were never far from either. Specifically the booze.

"There was a bar behind the bleachers, and a bar in the door on the way in, and you could see the court from both of them," Tucker Max, a best-selling author, and diehard Kentucky fan who traveled to Cancun for the tournament, said. Even all these years later, he still can't believe the set-up. "It was an open bar! You could see the team coming in one door, and the bar in the other corner."

Yes, it was *that* close to the court.

"I could throw a football," he said. "Actually, I could've literally almost hit a long three-pointer from the bar behind the bleachers."

The Wildcats certainly weren't in Lexington anymore, but aside from a tiny distraction like an open bar courtside, they actually looked pretty sharp once they actually hit the floor.

Their opener was against Cleveland State, which in theory probably should have been a tough game; the Vikings were coming off a trip to the NCAA Tournament the previous season, and hadn't just gotten to the Big Dance, but upset Wake Forest once they were there. And while Cleveland State had lost a lot of talent from the previous year's club, they did return a bona-fide star in Norris Cole. Cole would go on to be drafted the following summer, and in both 2012 and 2013 won NBA championships with the Miami Heat.

But while the matchup looked tough on paper, it proved to be anything but when the game tipped. The Wildcats jumped out to a 35-27 lead at halftime, and blew the game open with an 18-4 run to start the second half. DeMarcus Cousins and John Wall combined for 29 points, and Kentucky's defense held Cole to just eight, as the Wildcats cruised to a 73-49 win.

With the victory, the Wildcats advanced to the championship game of the Cancun Challenge. But as easy as the win against Cleveland State was, their matchup with Stanford in the championship game proved to be just as difficult.

Understand that unlike Kentucky's first five opponents of the season, Stanford was no pushover. They were a real team, from a real conference, and regularly faced teams of Kentucky's caliber (although probably not quite as good) during Pac-10 play. They also had a star in Landry Fields; Fields might not have had the raw physical talent of a John Wall or DeMarcus Cousins. But he was plenty skilled, and as he proved by scoring 23 points and adding 13 rebounds that night, he wasn't going to back down from anyone.

"Watching that game I knew, I was like 'that guy is a stud,'" Max said. "'That guy is going to play in the league.'"

Fields' "back down from no one" attitude permeated throughout the team, and helped the Cardinal jump out to a 38-32 halftime lead. Stanford would hold onto that lead for virtually the entire second half, and appeared to be on their way to an upset victory with just a few minutes left on the clock.

But then again this was Kentucky, and like they'd do so many times during the 2009-2010 season, the Wildcats would find a way to claw back into the game. They'd come all the way back to tie things up at 61, courtesy of a John Wall jumper with just over 30 seconds to go.

Now understand that in a lot of games, a tie score with 30 seconds to go would be the end of the action in regulation; but in the case of this game, it was only just the beginning. And it all started a few short seconds later, when senior Ramon Harris was charged with a loose ball foul on Fields. Fields would go to the free throw line and hit both free throws, to give the Cardinal a 63-61 lead.

The Wildcats got the ball back, and just like the Miami (OH) game, Calipari elected not to call a timeout. He wanted to see how his players would react, and to their credit they handled themselves well. Kentucky worked the ball down low to DeMarcus Cousins, where he was fouled with just a few seconds to play. If the freshman forward hit both free throws, the two teams would head to overtime. If he missed the first, well, the coaches would probably instruct him to miss the second one on purpose. And at that point, the Wildcats would need a miracle to win the game.

As it turns out the latter happened; Cousins missed the first, then missed the second on purpose, before Stanford's Jarrett Mann came down with the rebound. Mann headed to the line, and like Cousins, he had a pretty simple task in front of him. If he made one, it would give the Cardinal a comfortable three point lead with just seconds to go. If he made both, the game was essentially over.

So naturally, what did Mann do? He missed them both of course. Kentucky got the ball back with just seconds to go, and as it turned out, "seconds" was all John Wall needed. The freshman guard got the ball on the wing with just a few ticks left on the clock, and proceeded to drive the lane and draw a foul call on Stanford. Wall needed to make both to send the game to overtime. If he missed one or both, Stanford would be the champion of the Cancun Challenge.

Wall stepped to the line. But unlike Cousins and unlike Mann, there was no concern.

Swish, he hit the first.

Swish, he nailed the second one too.

Just like that, the game was headed to overtime. And the "Legend of John Wall" continued to grow.

"This a true freshman, just a couple months out of high school and he drills both free throws," Max said. "It was amazing. I was like 'that dude is going to be an even bigger star than people are predicting.' And people were predicting he was going to be a star, and I was like 'Wow.'"

While the game technically went to overtime, it was basically over as soon as Wall sunk those free throws. Stanford had fired all their bullets in regulation, and by the time they hit overtime were completely out of gas.

Kentucky got ahead early, and when Eric Bledsoe hit a three with just 33 seconds left, it gave the Wildcats a lead they would never relinquish.

Final score: Kentucky 73, Stanford 65.

Kentucky was the Cancun Challenge champs, capping the tournament with a thrilling victory, in one of the wildest games of the season. Even several years later, those in attendance still aren't quite sure how the Wildcats pulled out the win.

"My son is seven, and he doesn't remember John and DeMarcus playing here," DeWayne Peevy began, remembering a game that happened so many years ago. "But we go back and watch old games, and I was showing him the Stanford game, and as I'm watching it 'I'm like, how did we win? I know we didn't lose this game.' But you forget. They had to miss like both free throws, to keep giving us an opportunity."

Yet despite the back-and-forth nature of the game, the Wildcats did get the win, and for those Kentucky fans that made the trek down to Cancun, it turned out to be a spectacular week. A week filled with big victories on the court, and plenty of free, cold beverages off of it.

"We had the best time," Max said. "It was all Kentucky fans. We all got hammered together, and we cheered for Kentucky and they won the tournament."

It was truly unforgettable.

Bizarre, yes. But also unforgettable.

"It was fantastic, don't get me wrong," Max said. "But it was really the weirdest thing I've ever seen in my life."

I Was So Hype

AMONGST ALL THE questionable decisions in the history of modern college basketball, there is one that stands above the rest on the "Man, what was he thinking?" scale. And for those wondering, no, it has nothing to do with Coach K still trying to convince us that he has perfect, jet-black hair after all these years.

Instead it came in the summer, fall and winter of 2008, when John Wall was the No. 1 ranked high school player in the country, living in North Carolina, and yet for some strange reason, the University of North Carolina never seriously recruited him. Sure they showed some interest, but while schools like Memphis (and later Kentucky), Duke, Baylor, and pretty much everyone in the country rolled out the red carpet for Wall, the Tar Heels' coaching staff showed him more of a 'Meh' attitude.

If Wall wanted to come play for them, fine. If not, they felt like they were fine without him.

"I went up there my junior year but they didn't want to offer me," Wall said. "(When they did) they wanted me to commit on the spot. I was like 'I don't want to commit on the spot. If you think I'm good enough, offer me (on my own terms).' But they didn't."

Eventually North Carolina did come around towards the end of Wall's senior year, but by then it was too late. He was the undisputed top player in the country by that point, and virtually every school in the country had put in a year's worth of recruiting work to get him. Wall never seriously considered the Tar Heels, choosing Kentucky over Duke and everyone else in May of 2009. As they say "the rest is history."

And it was that history which was on Wall's mind in early December 2009. The Wildcats were back in the United States, and following their Cancun Challenge win and another against UNC-Asheville, they would then face their toughest challenge to date: On the first Saturday in December, the Wildcats would host North Carolina in front of a national television audience on CBS. The Tar Heels were the No. 10 ranked team in the country, and the defending champs.

And John Wall was ready for them.

"That North Carolina game that was the one John wanted," fellow freshman Jon Hood said. "John wanted that one bad. For whatever reason, he wanted that one more than any other one."

Wall didn't hide his emotions either.

"I was so hype," he told FoxSports.com in February 2015. Even five years later, he hadn't forgotten just how much the game meant to him.

And really, it wasn't just Wall who wanted North Carolina, but the entire Kentucky team, and frankly, the entire state as well. The Wildcats had given the fans everything they could've hoped for in their 7-0 start to the season, but nationally they were still yearning for respect. The narrative still seemed to be "Yeah, Kentucky is good, but wait until they play a real team. We'll find out just how good they are then."

That was the prevailing narrative, and also why the game was so damn important to the program. The questions that had plagued Kentucky since the day John Calipari had been hired would finally be answered. How good were the freshmen? And could they hang with a tough, more experienced team like Carolina?

"North Carolina was also a Top 10 team," team manager Chad Sanders remembered. "That was our first real test. That was the first chance to prove, 'Are these guys all hype? Or can they come out and really play?'"

As America quickly found out, these young Wildcats could in fact play, even if things started off slowly when they fell behind 9-2. But then, just as Kentucky fell behind, just as the doubts grew louder, a funny thing happened.

Well, correction: John Wall happened.

Down by those seven points just three minutes into the game, Wall sensed his team needed a play, and went out and made one. Off a North Carolina miss Wall caught the rebound, and in a blur, beat just about everyone up court on the fast-break. The last defender was Larry Drew II, and after a quick dribble left, he crossed over to the right… and in the blink of an eye took off. He jumped from just inside the foul line, and threw down a spectacular slam dunk with two hands. Kentucky fans burst out into cheers, just as North Carolina's players tried to figure out what had just happened to them.

But before they got the chance, Wall did it again.

On the very next possession the freshman point guard grabbed a loose ball, and again took off on a one-man fast-break. He started to the right, and cut to the left, but this time, North Carolina wasn't going to be fooled. Right as Wall took off, two defenders met him in mid-air. From there, Wall's natural instincts took over; he somehow (still in mid-air) slithered between the two of them, before ducking under the basket, and laying it in. It was one of the most acrobatic reverse layups anyone had ever seen, pretty much anywhere.

And Kentucky fans were beside themselves. Wall tumbled to the ground, just as Rupp Arena again exploded. The cheers got louder a few minutes later when the game broke for a timeout.

"If there has been a louder moment there," Kentucky Sport Radio's Matt Jones said, describing Rupp Arena, "I don't know when it's been."

It was just four points, two simple buckets that don't look like much in a box score. But on that day, they were so much more. The scoreboard showed the Wildcats still trailed 9-6, but that four-point swing might as well have been 100; the Wildcats had their swag, and from there, the floodgates opened. Darius Miller hit a floater in the lane. Patrick Patterson hit a running jump hook. Miller hit a three, then Miller stuffed home a fast-break dunk off a Wall pass. Sometime later, DeMarcus Cousins got in the mix, with an "and one" layup, and Darnell Dodson hit a couple of threes for good measure.

By the time it was all said and done, the Wildcats had gone on a 28-2 run (yes, you read that correctly, 28-2!!). A 9-2 deficit had turned into a 30-11 lead in the blink of an eye, as the Rupp Arena crowd went into a frenzy.

It all seemed too good to be true, but unfortunately for Kentucky, it was. Because just as the Wildcats went on that epic run, just as it seemed they were going to blow North Carolina right out of the gym and stake their claim as one of the best teams in college basketball, well…

"John Wall started cramping up," DeWayne Peevy remembered.

That's right, the early adrenaline had gotten to Wall, and by halftime he had to be given an IV as he battled dehydration. Wall was able to re-enter the game in the beginning stages of the second half, but by then, he simply wasn't the same player. After scoring 13 points in the first half, Wall went scoreless for the first 14 minutes after intermission, and by that point North Carolina had whittled a 20 point lead down to just seven at 58-51. The Tar Heels would cut the lead to three at the under four timeout.

However the Wildcats had been resilient all year, and even on a national stage, in front of the entire college basketball world, they would display that resiliency against Carolina. Eric Bledsoe scored seven points in the final three minutes (including five free throws), as the Wildcats kept the Tar Heels at bay. A pair of foul shots by (who else) John Wall, gave Kentucky their final margin of victory at 68-63.

Eventually the final horn sounded and Rupp Arena exploded. Kentucky had improved to 8-0 but this win was different than any other that the Wildcats had picked up all year. Against a big-time opponent, on a big-time stage, in front of a big-time audience, Kentucky had not only won the game, but at times, dominated.

They had also put the college basketball world on notice: They could play with, and beat anyone in the country. Kentucky was for real.

"(It) was a moment of 'we're here,'" Jones said.

Kentucky could no longer be looked past, no longer be dismissed as a novelty or circus act, or a group of talented individuals that weren't truly a "team." The Wildcats had just beaten a Top 10 club, fresh off a National

Championship, and done it frankly, when they hadn't even necessarily played their best game.

And really, that only added to the importance of that North Carolina win: It not only proved to fans that Kentucky could play with anyone in the country. It helped the players believe it as well.

"It was like everything that Cal came to do, and all his preseason quotes, the messages he has in his interviews, they all seemed to be coming true in that game," Mark Krebs said. "That's where I was getting calls from family members, like 'You guys are for real.'"

Oh, and one more thing.

"(People were) like, 'Who's that John Wall guy?'"

* * *

The hype was officially starting to build in Kentucky, but unfortunately there was no time to let up, and no easy next opponent to beat up on while savoring the North Carolina victory. The Wildcats' next game was against another national powerhouse, and it would come on the biggest stage in basketball.

No literally, it came on the biggest stage in basketball.

The game was against the No. 14 ranked UConn Huskies, a school that had a National Championship pedigree, and like North Carolina, was coming off a Final Four berth the season before. The game itself would be played at Madison Square Garden, "The World's Most Famous Arena" and broadcast on ESPN. ESPN's top college basketball broadcasting team of Dan Shulman and Dick Vitale were on the call, only adding to the hype.

But even despite the hype, the Wildcats kept things pretty cool once they got to New York. It was the Christmas season and the entire city was in a festive move; why wouldn't the Wildcats be festive as well? The players spent their free time shopping and walking around the city, and if you hadn't known any better, you could have never guessed that a huge, potentially season-altering game awaited the Wildcats.

The team was definitely relaxed, but even amongst a group of easy-going guys, there was one player who took it to an extreme: DeMarcus Cousins. As Kentucky fans were quickly learning, while "Boogie" might have been the biggest guy on the team, he also had the most playful nature.

And it was on full display in New York.

"We walked around in the city together as a team," Peevy said. "We were doing stuff for our coaches TV show and DeMarcus Cousins had a microphone, and he's asking fans 'Do you know who John Calipari is? Do you know who John Wall is? Have you ever heard of Kentucky basketball?' This is the middle of the year, this is December, and there are a lot of people who didn't know who John Calipari or John Wall were…. There were plenty of Kentucky fans around, but when you ran into random people, it was one of the funniest skits ever."

It was indeed funny (the video is available on YouTube if you search "Coach Cal TV: New York), but as much fun as the players were having, the tone changed later that night. The Wildcats were still in New York City, still hanging out and still keeping loose, but as Kentucky fans began to trickle into town, the team began to realize the magnitude of the game.

"The night before we were in Times Square just walking around," senior guard Ramon Harris said. "The hotel was right around the corner from Times Square. All these people were like, 'Oh, we just saw UConn. They're talking a lot of trash.' They were coming up to us and saying like 'We just saw Kemba Walker and he said they're gonna beat your ass.'"

Did UConn's players actually say any of that? Who knows?

But it certainly caught the player's attention.

"We have people in the streets trying to hype it up," Harris said. "Whether they (UConn) said it or not, that's when it really hit us like 'Oh, this is a real game.'"

If Kentucky's players didn't know it at that point, they found out the following day, as the team began to leave for the arena. Thousands of fans (yes thousands) greeted the team outside the hotel; the players had to walk through a virtual tunnel of royal blue just to get to their bus. By that point, it was impossible to ignore how important this game was for both Kentucky's fans, and the program.

It had been a long time since the Wildcats had been on a stage like this. For so long they'd been on the fringes of the college basketball discussion; good but never great under Tubby Smith before turning into a punch-line under Billy Gillispie. For a team which had spent most of the 1990's as one of the "it" programs in college basketball, the Wildcats had taken on the worst kind of national profile: For the previous decade they were at times, irrelevant.

Which is exactly why this game meant so much. For the first time in a long time Kentucky fans had the chance to travel with friends and family and build a mini-vacation around 'Cats basketball. And not just 'Cats basketball really, but *this kind* of 'Cats basketball, and a matchup of this magnitude: A huge game, on a huge stage, with a legitimately good opponent. And unlike in previous years, they wouldn't be an underdog, hoping to keep things close, but instead a heavyweight ready and willing to trade blows with another championship-caliber prizefighter.

Add in the fact that it was a primetime game, when no other major sporting events were on TV and the game became even more important. As much as North Carolina was a statement game, this one held even more weight; North Carolina was played on a Saturday afternoon on the same day that college football would later take center stage. But against UConn, it was Kentucky who was on center stage. If they were able to get a win, no one could deny the Wildcats' arrival on the national landscape.

And it was that as a background, which explains why this game meant so damn much to Kentucky fans.

Boy were they ready.

"Kentucky plays in New York every year (before and since) and I've been there every year, and it was never like *that,*" Matt Jones said. "It was like every Kentucky fan *had* to be at that game, because it was the first like, "here we are" basketball game. It was insane. It was insane."

The insanity only grew once the team arrived at the arena. UConn is a fan base which prides itself on owning Madison Square Garden, and bringing more fans than the opponent every time they play in the 'World's Most Famous Arena.' But on this night, there was no denying Kentucky's presence. UK fans were everywhere; in the upper bowl and lower bowl, seemingly spilling out of their seats into the aisles. Heck Wildcats fans drowned out everyone else before the game even began; the fans who got to Madison Square Garden early chanted "Go Big Blue!" while Georgia and St. John's were still on the court for the evening's first game.

Once the game did tip off, well, the Wildcats gave their fans plenty to cheer about. Patrick Patterson hit a quick bucket just seconds in to give Kentucky an early lead, and a John Wall steal led to an Eric Bledsoe layup which gave the Wildcats a quick 4-0 lead. Just 29 seconds into the game, UConn coach Jim Calhoun called a timeout, trying to slow down his opponent's momentum.

It didn't work.

Even after the timeout, there was no slowing down Kentucky. From there, Wall got another bucket. Then another. Patterson hit a two-point jumper, before Wall got another layup on a fast-break.

Before anyone knew what happened, the score was 12-0 as Madison Square Garden went up in a frenzy. UConn called another timeout, but there was no quieting Kentucky's fans. They yelled and screamed and hugged each other, and after that, they did it all over again.

The scene was indescribable. But as someone who was in the building that night, I did my best, describing the scene this way, in an article I wrote the day after the game.

> *It was honestly like watching a bad crowd shot from a sports movie, everyone erupting in unison, almost like a director was yelling, "And action!" Only it was real life.*

But as happy as Wildcats' fans were, the excitement died down just a few minutes later. Out of the timeout UConn began to battle. Gavin Edwards hit a quick, two-point jumper, followed by a Jerome Dyson layup. In the same way that no one was quite sure how Kentucky had jumped out to a

12-0 lead, UConn made an equally surprising run to even things up just a short time later. Even worse for Kentucky, their best player had to watch it all from the sidelines. John Wall picked up his second foul with eight minutes left in the first half and was forced to grab a seat next to Calipari.

"We started out on a 12-0 run," Wall remembered. "Then I got two fouls and Coach Cal was mad at me early in the game."

Wall would have his chance to atone, although it didn't happen right away. UConn had wrestled the lead back and was up 29-23 heading into halftime. From there, the two teams spent most of the second half battling back and forth. As the clock ticked into the final minutes, the game was at a standstill.

The good news was, this was nothing new for Kentucky; at that point, it seemed like just about every game the Wildcats played came down to the final few minutes. And when it did, the Wildcats had a game-plan for these exact moments: Get the ball to John Wall. This game was no different, and Wall was ready for the moment. He started things off with a spinning bank shot with just under four minutes left to play. Next, he took Kemba Walker off the dribble, before coming to a quick stop and hitting an 18-foot jumper.

Kentucky was doing what they always did, but unlike some of their earlier opponents, UConn didn't back down, and seemed to have an answer for every move the Wildcats made. Despite getting nine points from Wall between the eight minute mark and the one minute mark in the game, Kentucky still trailed 61-60 when they got the ball back with a little more than 60 seconds to play. The Wildcats tried to move quickly but had little success; Darius Miller missed a three-pointer, before Ramon Harris' put-back attempt was blocked out of bounds.

Kentucky got the ball back, and this time there was no messing around. They were going to get the ball to John Wall.

Kentucky inbounded the ball to Miller, while Wall stood at the top of the key (by that point UConn had switched the 6'9 Stanley Robinson onto Wall, since none of their guards could defend him); after a few seconds Miller got the ball to Wall, who dribbled down the clock until there was about 35 seconds to play. Wall then passed the ball quickly back to Miller, who grabbed it, and slowly took two dribbles to his right.

Then in a flash, it happened.

As soon as Miller put the ball on the floor, Wall bolted from right to left, and caught a pass from Miller; Miller then used his body to ever so slightly brush the defender, as soon as he gave up the ball to Wall. That brush created just enough space, and just enough separation for Wall, who attacked the hoop. He drove hard with his left hand and threw the ball off the glass, right as he was fouled by UConn's Alex Oriahki.

The ball rolled through the hoop. Wall hit the ground and the crowd erupted. Kentucky had jumped ahead 62-61. Patterson immediately grabbed Wall and pulled him, as his teammates mobbed him from the side. Dick Vitale could be heard screaming "Oh, oh, oh!" on the TV, while Kentucky fans inside Madison Square Garden made the building nearly inaudible.

Wall would proceed to make his free throw to give Kentucky a two point lead, and after a missed basket by UConn, Ramon Harris made one of two free throws to put the Wildcats up 64-61. With just a few seconds left, the Huskies had one last shot; Walker rushed the ball up, and after a quick scramble, passed it to Gavin Edwards who's three clanged off the side of the rim. Kemba got the rebound, but by the time he got a shot off from the perimeter, the clock had sounded. DeMarcus Cousins caught the miss, and threw the ball up in the air.

Kentucky had won again. Final score, 64-61.

The Wildcats had won another thriller, but this one was different. For Kentucky fans, this victory really was everything they'd hoped for when John Calipari had agreed to be their head coach. Their team had just played a big-time opponent, on a big-time stage, and found a way to get a big-time win. It was away from Rupp Arena, so no one could argue that the Wildcats had the benefit of a home-court advantage, and it also came on a night where their highly-ranked opponent had played something close to their best game.

Simply put, this was it. This was the win everybody had been waiting for, hoping for... *praying* for. At this point, there was no true argument against Kentucky; it was impossible to say that they were too young or too immature, talented but a step behind the nation's best. As it turned out they *were* the nation's best; maybe not the absolute best team in college basketball, but they were in the short conversation of true title contenders.

It was a seminal moment for Kentucky basketball, a turning point for the whole program.

"It was the first time in a couple years that I felt like two big teams colliding in a really good match-up, and we came out ahead," Krebs said. "I was like 'This is why I came to Kentucky!'"

Beyond just the win though, the game was important for this reason: Kentucky was again one of the "it" programs in college basketball. It wasn't just that they were good, or even a National Championship contender. It was that they were relevant; no real conversation about college basketball could be had without them. As Scott Padgett said when John Calipari was hired, Kentucky had stopped being *Kentucky*, they had stopped being on the tip of everyone's tongues. But in just a few short months, Calipari had completely flipped that narrative. On a mid-week night in December when not much else was going on, Kentucky was *the story* in all of sports. They led *SportsCenter*. They were what everyone was talking about.

The game also provided another turning point in the season too. The UConn game was the game that John Wall became a *star*; not just a player to be enjoyed by Kentucky fans, but a player that everyone, even casual college basketball fans had an opinion on. Like his team, Wall was the talk of the sport.

And with good reason. Wall had the perfect blend of charisma and talent, not just a star... but a player with *star power*. Kentucky fans had seen it as early as Big Blue Madness. The rest of the world saw it that night.

"John Wall went off in that game," Jones said. "There was a big sense of like, 'Wow, we also have maybe the best player in the country.'"

That's right, John Wall was indeed a star, and his team was now the talk of college basketball.

It was something new, something enjoyable, something refreshing for Kentucky basketball.

But it quickly became more of a challenge than anyone could've anticipated.

John Calipari welcomes Drake and Tayshaun
Prince to his first 'Big Blue Madness'
Photo Courtesy: UK Athletics

John Wall proved he was worth the hype, with a
game-winner in his first game as a Wildcat
Photo Courtesy: UK Athletics

Things weren't always easy in the relationship with Coach Calipari and
DeMarcus Cousins, but each learned to grow and appreciate each other
Photo Courtesy: UK Athletics

UK basketball got a surprise appearance when LeBron
James showed up for a game against Vanderbilt
Photo Courtesy: UK Athletics

Senior Day is always a special day in Lexington, but it
had extra meaning for Mark Krebs in 2010
Photo Courtesy: UK Athletics

Sometimes the only guy who didn't realize how good Eric Bledsoe
was, was Eric Bledsoe himself. Here he's seen hugging John Wall
Photo Courtesy: UK Athletics

Getting on the cover of "Slam Magazine" was a seminal moment for the 2009-2010 Kentucky Wildcats. Not just because it proved the program had "arrived" but because it proved how close the players had truly come.
Photo Courtesy: SLAM Magazine/Issue 137
Cover as Shot by Atiba Jefferson

Patrick Patterson returned for his junior year, hoping to win big. He did just that, as he's seen holding the SEC Championship trophy
Photo Courtesy: UK Athletics

It takes a village to raise a child, and win an SEC title. Here
the team is seen celebrating the championship
Photo Courtesy: UK Athletics

No two people played a bigger role in the "rebirth" of
Kentucky basketball than John Calipari and John Wall
Photo Courtesy: UK Athletics

THE GREAT WALL OF KENTUCKY

I F IT WASN'T clear that John Wall was a bona-fide star following the back-to-back wins over North Carolina and UConn, it was impossible to ignore a few weeks later when the face of the Kentucky superstar magically appeared in thousands of mailboxes across the country. There, on the cover of an early January edition of *Sports Illustrated* was a picture of a leaping, out-stretched Wall, next to a headline that read "The Great Wall of Kentucky."

Inside, writer Grant Wahl gave the most detailed profile of Wall to date. The freshman point guard discussed it all with SI; his desire to go down as the best point guards to ever play the game, the origins of the John Wall dance, and also how basketball helped him mature as a teenager while dealing with personal tragedy. Maybe most important however, were the slew of quotes from NBA scouts and front office personnel. To a man they all agreed that the Kentucky point guard was not just the best player in college basketball, but also the unquestioned No. 1 pick in the next NBA Draft.

It was an interesting profile to say the least, if only because it was (and is) so rare to see a college basketball player on the cover of *Sports Illustrated* at that time of year. Normally in the middle of January, the national media is focused on other stuff; there are college football bowl games to recap and NFL playoffs to preview. Yet on January 11th, 2010 John Wall was front and center on the cover of the most prominent sports magazine in the country. He was the biggest story in sports.

And really Wall's ascension from relatively unknown college basketball player to bona-fide, national star mirrored Kentucky's rise as a team. After years of being good, but never great, the Wildcats were *back*. And everybody wanted a piece of them.

"That was the year I had to learn how to say 'no,'" DeWayne Peevy said.

Peevy was the basketball team's Sports Information Director that year, meaning that he was in charge of handling all the team's media requests. Things had come 360 degrees from a year earlier. Back during the NCAA Tournament-less 2009 season, Peevy was actually pitching media outlets himself, practically begging them to profile the team and its players.

But in the 2010 season, boy, were things different. Requests were coming in so quickly and in such high volume, that Peevy and his assistant John Hayden had to completely overhaul how they handled them altogether.

"We had these long lists of requests, we had this spreadsheet with Cal's requests, player requests," Peevy said. "People would get frustrated 'I haven't heard back, I haven't gotten an interview with Cal all year.' And we were like, 'Yeah you and 100 other people. There's nothing we can do.'"

Eventually the media crush became overwhelming for players, coaches and staff alike (at a certain point Wall got so burned out from talking to the media that Kentucky cut off requests with him altogether). Yet ironically, the attention from the outside paled in comparison to what the players dealt with every day on campus.

Now understand that's not necessarily a bad thing; the simple truth was that after years of being irrelevant nationally, the students on campus were fired up to have a top-flight basketball team again. But it also meant that as the season wore on and the profile of the team grew, the players couldn't go anywhere on campus without being asked to pose for pictures or sign autographs. The players happily obliged, but at times, it also caused problems. After all, they were still student-athletes, and did have class, study hall and practice to attend.

"Here on campus, the kids would constantly complain that they couldn't get to class because they'd be stopped by students," Peevy said. "That doesn't happen as much now, but back then it was just such a novelty."

Like their dealings with the media, it did eventually become overwhelming. At times, it led players to take extreme measures to make sure and not get noticed.

"I remember John Wall would have to put his headphones in and his hood on, so he wouldn't have to feel like he was being rude to people," Peevy said. "That way he couldn't hear people and he couldn't see them. He'd just keep his head down and go to class. Otherwise he'd never be able to get anywhere."

The whole scene was a circus, and seemingly overnight the players had become rock stars both on campus and around the state. But while things did at times get stressful, that's not to say all interactions were bad. Some were just plain funny.

Take the case of Daniel Orton. One day, the 6'11 freshman was making the short walk from the team's practice facility to his dorm, when he was stopped by a Kentucky fan and his small daughter. Orton was used to these interactions by that point, and was happy to stop and make small talk.

But as normal as these types of run-ins were, nothing could've prepared him for what the small girl said.

"This little girl, she was four or five years old, and she was with her dad," Orton remembered. "And her dad was like, 'Go ahead, show him!'"

A little concerned and also surprised, Orton didn't know what to expect. But when the girl's mouth opened, Orton's jaw dropped.

"She'd know all my stats," Orton said. "My height, like 'You're averaging 5.7 rebounds, points, blocks, steals.'"

Again, this was a four-year-old-girl, who knew Daniel Orton better than he knew himself.

"It's like 'are you serious?'" Orton said.

Even five years after the incident, Orton couldn't help but laugh.

* * *

While pressure mounted off the court, on the court things continued to go smoothly for Kentucky. The Wildcats were 9-0 following the win over UConn, off to their best start since the 1993 season.

But while the wins continued to pile up, there was one man that wasn't happy with the state of Kentucky basketball: John Calipari. Coach Cal noticed a familiar pattern with his team, and the way they played. Just about every game began with a slow start, before the team would go on a big run and build a comfortable lead. Then they'd ease up, and have to find a way to hold on for victory. After a while, it became like clockwork. Every game seemed to follow the same script. And as time went on Calipari had an interesting way of letting his team know exactly what he thought about them, and their "undefeated" record.

"Cal was at the press conferences and he was always talking about 'Our record is 10-6' or 'it should be 11-7,'" Peevy remembered. "He was counting all the games he thought we should've lost."

But while Calipari tried to nudge his team through the media, tried to convince them that they weren't as good as their record said they were, even he couldn't deny that it was good to be undefeated. He also couldn't deny the fact that for all their faults, his team did possess one important trait: Mental toughness.

"We were a team that had a great will to win," Calipari explained to Fox Sports in January 2015. "That's why I was saying all along that we should be 9-6, 9-7. I wasn't lying. We could've easily been that."

Still, as the season rolled on Calipari wasn't ready to give his team too much credit. Even if their return to the court following the UConn game gave him little to complain about.

The Wildcats' next game was against Indiana, and it marked their third showcase game in a row. Just like their matchup with North Carolina a week before, it would be broadcast on a Saturday afternoon by CBS. Once again, the entire country would be watching.

But while the wins over North Carolina and UConn were impressive, the matchup with the Hoosiers was different for one big reason: It was a true road game. The Wildcats would have to leave the cozy confines of Rupp Arena, and wouldn't have a "neutral" court advantage like at Madison Square Garden. They'd have to play in a truly hostile environment at Assembly Hall in Bloomington, a place they'd lost five straight games dating back to 1983 (it's worth noting that for a number of years, the series was played on neutral courts in both Indianapolis and Louisville). And to the credit of Indiana fans, Assembly Hall was rocking that day. Thanks to a major home-court advantage, and a big first half from Maurice Creek (who had 19 points before intermission) the Hoosiers were just one point down heading into halftime.

But then, like they'd done so many times already that season, the Wildcats used the beginning of the second half to jump their opponents, and build a big lead. The defining play came with 17:30 left on the clock, and the Wildcats actually trailing by one. Out of a timeout, John Calipari drew up a perfect play, where Darius Miller stood at the top of the key, before tossing an alley-oop pass to John Wall. With a teammate setting a back-screen for Wall, he caught the ball effortlessly and soared over a couple of stunned Hoosiers' defenders. Wall stuffed the ball home to give the Wildcats a 49-48 lead. They would never trail the rest of the game, and would go on to win 90-73.

The victory was a solid one, the first in a truly tough road environment. But what separated it from earlier victories --- and assuredly pleased Calipari --- was that once Kentucky got the lead, they didn't let up, and did step on the throats of their opponent. It was a killer instinct Calipari hadn't seen much to that point in the season, and he was so happy with the performance that he actually credited the Wildcats a "win" on his personal scorecard. That was no small feat at that point in the year.

With another win over a big-time opponent, the schedule finally eased up. Following a week-long break for final exams, Kentucky cruised past Austin Peay for a 90-69 win. Patrick Patterson led all scorers with 21 points.

Next up was a game that at first glance looked like little more than a mid-week, mid-December beat down of an overmatched opponent, when Kentucky hosted Drexel at Rupp Arena. But while the game didn't seem like much on paper, it carried a ton of weight with both Kentucky's coach and its fans.

For starters there was the coach, and in this game, Calipari would be facing one of his closest friends in the business, Drexel's James "Bruiser" Flint. Flint and Cal's relationship dated back nearly two decades; Flint had served as Calipari's top assistant when the two were at UMass, and when Cal left for the NBA, Flint was named his replacement. Even though it'd been a number of years since they'd worked together, the two still spoke every day on the phone according to an article in the *Lexington Herald-Leader* that ran that week.

Again, the game mattered to Cal. But it probably mattered even more to Kentucky's fans. On that night, the Wildcats were looking to become the first team in college basketball history to record 2,000 wins. North Carolina was just a few victories behind the Wildcats so both the fans and Calipari wanted to make sure and hit the mark before the Tar Heels did.

To the player's credit, they sensed the importance of the game and never let things get close. The Wildcats jumped out to a 56-20 halftime lead, and cruised to an 88-44 victory. The team's three biggest stars --- John Wall, DeMarcus Cousins and Patrick Patterson --- all scored in double figures.

As the clock inched toward zero the fans screamed, and were rewarded with a special moment once the game went final. Confetti fell from the rafters, while the players on the court wore specialty shirts that read "UK2K" on the front, all as the song "Celebration" played over the loudspeakers in Rupp Arena. It was a historic moment, one which technically began back in 1903 with a victory over the Lexington YMCA, and came full circle with John Calipari, John Wall and 24,000 of their closest friends in Rupp Arena over a century later. Following the game, Calipari called the scene "a special moment for the state" while UK legend Dan

Issel added "From the beginning to the end, getting to 2,000 wins proves that Kentucky has been the strongest college basketball program."

It was a nice sentiment from Issel, even if Kentucky looked like the furthest thing from "the greatest program in the history of college basketball" when they took the court two days later against Long Beach State. A combination of too much UK2K celebration and the realization that this would be the final game before a brief Christmas break left the Wildcats feeling groggy…. or at least playing that way. The game was tied at the half, and with just 13:51 remaining in the game, "The Beach" (as they like to call themselves) actually took a 47-45 lead. But then, just when the 49ers hit their peak, they crashed. Long Beach had taken a red eye to Lexington after playing on the West Coast just two nights before and eventually it showed. In the end the 49ers simply ran out of gas, as the Wildcats regained the lead, and eventually held on for an 86-73 win.

The victory improved Kentucky to 13-0 (the school's best start since the 1977-78 season) and left them feeling good heading into Christmas break. They emerged a week later refreshed, and in their last real "cupcake" game of the season, beat up their visitors from the University of Hartford. The win was relatively unremarkable, except for two reasons.

One, John Wall set a Kentucky single-game assist record by tallying 16 dimes.

And two, Hartford coach Dan Leibovitz said this following his team's 104-61 loss.

"Kentucky is one of the best teams I've seen in all my years of coaching in terms of talent."

Hello!

It was no small praise for one of college basketball's top teams that season, but also a sign of how far the Wildcats had come and how quickly they'd done it. Just nine months before, Kentucky --- with many of the same players who were on the 2009-2010 roster --- had missed the NCAA Tournament altogether. Now, they were just one of a handful of teams which entered the New Year undefeated.

But for them to stay undefeated they'd have to get through their final non-conference game unscathed.

That wouldn't be easy against their biggest rival, who was coming for blood... literally.

* * *

Amongst the great rivalries in all of sports, Kentucky and Louisville might be the best. The two schools (and their fan bases) have a genuine hatred for each other, and unlike fans in other rivalries, actually live amongst each other in-state. Kentucky-Louisville isn't like some rivalries where graduates of one school either aren't from the state or routinely leave after graduation (think Duke-Carolina) and it isn't like Ohio State-Michigan, where fans are divided by a state border. Nope, Kentucky and Louisville fans live amongst each other, work together, and in some cases are even married to one another. That also puts added pressure on the two school's basketball teams, because, well, nobody wants to lose and have to deal with the other side for the next 365 days.

Yet as insane as Kentucky-Louisville is pretty much every year, the 2009-2010 edition might just have been the craziest of all. Even veterans of the rivalry had never seen anything like it.

"I've never been in more of an intense environment at a sporting event," senior guard Mark Krebs said. "Like 'I don't know if it's going to come to blows, but I don't know what's going to happen.'"

The rivalry had reached a boiling point, due to a couple different reasons.

For starters, Louisville's players simply weren't happy with all the attention that Kentucky had gotten to that point in the year. Remember, the Cardinals had been the No. 1 overall seed in the NCAA Tournament just one season before (meaning they were the de-facto "favorite" entering the Big Dance) and owned two straight wins over Kentucky coming into the 2009-2010 matchup. But despite all of Louisville's recent success in the rivalry, it was Kentucky who was getting all the acclaim entering that year's game. That tends to happen when you start 14-0 and have five future first-round picks on your roster.

But that was just part of why the rivalry had extra bad blood in 2010. The rest was thanks to the two coaches, Rick Pitino and John Calipari, a pair of men who genuinely did not like each other.

It's funny really, Calipari-Pitino is one of those great coaching rivalries where there's a whole lot of bad blood, but nobody is quite sure where it started. The ironic thing is, by all accounts the relationship actually started on a positive note.

It all began back in the late 1980's, when UMass needed a new head basketball coach, and one of their most prominent alums --- Knicks coach Rick Pitino --- recommended Calipari, a protégé of his at the time. The story has taken on mythic lore through the years, and in some accounts Pitino actually helped pay Calipari's first salary at the school (a rumor that has since been refuted by other UMass officials).

But for a relationship that started with humble beginnings it grew rocky pretty quickly. That's not entirely surprising given that the two coaches had been going head-to-head for virtually 20 years by the time Calipari got the Kentucky job. It started when Pitino himself was in Lexington (Calipari was at UMass), then continued when both were in the NBA, and took on new life when Pitino got to Louisville and Calipari was at Memphis. A rumored riff allegedly stemmed from Calipari accusing Conference USA officials of favoring Pitino's club, and later there were other rumors that Calipari believed Pitino was trying to keep Memphis out of the Big East, after the Cardinals had switched conferences.

Again, no one is quite sure how the beef began (or if the rumors are even true), but the disdain was indeed a thing. It only continued when the Kentucky job opened up in the spring of 2009 and Pitino openly petitioned for two men to get the job. As you've probably guessed, neither was Calipari. Pitino instead thought a pair of his former UK players, Oklahoma State's Travis Ford and John Pelphrey (who was at Arkansas at the time) would be better fits.

So when you add up the dislike between the two coaches, and hatred between the fan bases, it's impossible to argue that the hostility between the clubs was at just about an all-time high when Louisville and Kentucky got together in January of 2010. The jawing between the two teams started in the tunnel before tip-off, and that turned into a near brawl when the two clubs took the court a few minutes later.

The signature play of the game --- the one that set the tone for what was ahead --- came just 45 seconds in, when a loose ball resulted in three --- yes, three --- technical fouls. It happened in pursuit of that loose ball, when Reginald Delk --- the nephew of Wildcats' assistant Director of Basketball Operations and former hoops legend Tony --- shoved DeMarcus Cousins in the back in pursuit of that loose ball. Cousins who was reaching for the ball, got a little extra momentum thanks to the push, and gave a solid forearm to the face of Jared Swopshire. The play turned into sheer pandemonium, and three technicals were awarded before anyone knew what was going on.

"DeMarcus Cousins, he almost put somebody's head through the ground," assistant coach Rod Strickland remembered, when asked about the game.

The announcers on CBS didn't dispute Strickland's claim, arguing that Cousins should be ejected for the forearm. He wasn't, but after the play, there was little doubt that tensions had reached an all-time high. On the sideline, the players were trying to process everything they'd just seen.

"The first 45 seconds, I didn't know what was going to happen," Krebs said. "Everyone is excited, everybody is jacked up. It felt like a football game, like that football intensity."

But with the intensity so high, Krebs felt that it was time for him to step up as one of the veterans on the team. In the huddle, he grabbed the young players and insisted they keep their cool. As Krebs told the freshmen, the physical play was all part of Louisville's plan. The Cardinals wanted to get into Kentucky's heads, and throw them off their game.

Krebs urged his teammates, begging them to stay calm. If the players could keep their cool, they would win the game.

"I was in the huddle screaming," Krebs remembered. "(I was) like 'Calm down, we'll win this if we play normal. Don't get thrown out, don't get in trouble, don't get technical fouls, don't give them points.' That's what they wanted, that's what Louisville wanted, was talking, getting in guy's heads. It worked at the beginning."

To Krebs' credit, he was correct. Once the pandemonium died down after the technical fouls, the Wildcats regrouped and played some of their most inspired basketball of the season. It was certainly their best defensive effort to date; Kentucky forced Louisville into 17 misses on their first 18 shots. Meanwhile on offense, the Wildcats learned a very important lesson: An angry DeMarcus Cousins is the best kind of DeMarcus Cousins. Fueled by the technical fouls, Cousins scored the game's first six points. It gave Kentucky an early lead that they wouldn't relinquish in the first half.

Of course, there was also the second half, and by now, you can probably guess what happened. Kentucky blew the lead. Just like against North Carolina, John Wall cramped up, and to Louisville's credit, they were able to slow the game down, and in the process quiet the loud, Rupp Arena crowd. Furthermore, Louisville --- a team which has always prided itself on defense under Pitino --- had one of their best performances of the season on that end of the court.

"We were preparing for them to foul a lot, grab as you're trying to dribble and be sneaky. That's what Louisville is very good at," Krebs said. "Louisville has always been a good team that, they touch you and they knock the ball away from you, and they hit you, but they (the refs) don't really see it. I think that Pitino always has his team playing in a good way, and it shows."

It showed that day, as Louisville cut an eight point lead down to two with just under 11 minutes to go. And when Edgar Sosa scored a bucket to tie things up with 10:23 left, John Calipari had no choice but to call a timeout.

"We had momentum," Rick Pitino would comment after the game.

But whatever momentum the Cardinals had, Kentucky ripped it away. Specifically, John Wall --- as he'd done all season --- seized control of the game. It started with a mid-range jumper out of the timeout. Then another. Then he got to the foul line where he hit both free throws. Thanks to Wall's personal 6-0 run, the Wildcats went on their own 18-7 run to close out the game, and hold onto victory. Cousins finished with his best stat line of the season (18 points and 18 rebounds) as Kentucky beat Louisville for the first time in three years. Final score, 71-62.

The win was satisfying for the Wildcats, yet as good as it felt, it may have been even more important than it looked on paper. Simply put, this was a different *kind* of win. Sure the victories against North Carolina and UConn and Indiana had been important, but they all took on pretty similar narratives. Those games were all played pretty straight up; those three teams gave Kentucky their best shot, and Kentucky took that shot, punched back and were able to hold on for the win. Simply put, Kentucky was just better than those three.

But Louisville? Louisville was different.

Sure, the Wildcats were better than them too, but Louisville didn't try to play the game straight up. Nope, the Cardinals wanted to muck things up and make things ugly for Kentucky; they weren't interested in trying to be better than Kentucky at their game, but instead, to play a completely different game altogether. They wanted to slow things down, they wanted to play physical, and at times, they wanted to play mean. For Louisville, this wasn't just basketball, but instead, mental warfare. And in getting the win, Kentucky proved that they weren't only physically tough, but mentally tough too.

In addition to another signature win, the victory also marked another national coming out party for John Wall (it was following the Louisville game that Wall ended up on the cover of *Sports Illustrated*). His six points down the stretch changed the entire course of the game. In the process, Wall also picked up a new admirer: Rick Pitino.

In his postgame press conference, Pitino alluded to those six straight points from Wall. As mentioned earlier, Louisville had the momentum at the time. And then the freshman star stepped up.

"He wasn't having a great night," Pitino said. "And the great thing about that young man is it never bothered him, he never lost focus, he stayed with it, and made two killer plays for them. That is the sign of a great one and he certainly is. I've got to give him a lot of credit."

Just like that, the Wildcats non-conference schedule was complete. They would enter SEC play undefeated, which was no small feat, even for a team which entered the season ranked in the Top 10 in every major poll. Even Kentucky's biggest critics couldn't argue that by that point they had exceeded even the most optimistic of expectations. They were undefeated, with two wins over Top 15 teams, and a victory over their most hated rival. They'd won games on home, road, and neutral courts. They'd proven that they could play with just about anyone in the country, and do it anywhere.

Now, it was time to get ready for conference play, and just like the Louisville game, things would get tougher. The opponents would be familiar with Kentucky, and unafraid of them.

But what no one could've anticipated however, is that just as conference play was about to begin, tragedy would strike thousands of miles away.

And all of a sudden, basketball wouldn't seem so important anymore.

HOOPS FOR HAITI

PATRICK PATTERSON WOKE up from a mid-day nap, unsure of exactly where he was. He rubbed his eyes and gazed to the side; there, a few teammates lay next to him. A movie played on a TV a few feet away, the smell of fresh baked cookies filled the air.

It was winter break, and with Kentucky's campus quiet, the player's lives had changed a bit. They spent most of their day at the gym, where two-a-day practices were the norm; the practices were designed partly to help fill the void, but also to get the team ready for conference play.

But once practice was over however, the players experienced something different than they had in previous seasons. Rather than retreating to their dorm rooms to fill the idle time, they instead went over to John Calipari's house as a group, to hang out with the rest of their teammates. There, the players got to lounge in the basement and watch movies. Calipari's wife often spent the afternoon baking for them.

Although it's been a long time since Patterson was at Kentucky, afternoons like these remain some of his most vivid memories from the one year he played for Calipari.

"Definitely hanging out at Coach Cal's house, falling asleep and waking up to brownies or cookies," Patterson said. "Just everything about that year was memorable. (I) had a great group of people around me, a true family."

"Family" is a buzzword that just about every college coach, at every program in the country likes to use to describe his or her program. Only at Kentucky it really is applicable. Players spend just about every waking hour together, but unlike at most schools, that time together doesn't end after class, study hall and practice. At Kentucky, being part of the "family" means actually hanging out like a family does.

"That's just what Coach Cal was raised on," senior guard Ramon Harris said. "I don't know his family personally, but I just know that's what he's used to. He spends so much time with the team that he just wants that atmosphere even if he's not with his immediate family."

It was something the players certainly enjoyed, especially players like Harris and Patterson, who'd seen both sides of the coin. While Kentucky players have probably taken the family atmosphere for granted as the years went on, the 2010 team was filled with guys like Harris and Patterson, who knew that not every college program was run the same way. At most other schools, players don't hang out at the coach's house. But at Kentucky, the Calipari's wouldn't have it any other way.

And in 2010 that quiet time lounging around the house was definitely appreciated. With the pressure from outside growing, Calipari's basement provided the players a retreat. It allowed them a place where they could simply be themselves, away from all the cameras, reporters and fans on campus.

"(We were) just enjoying time at his house," Harris said. "(We were) in the basement, watching movies, laughing, talking about each other. Who had gotten dunked on, who had a bad practice, just having fun."

Days like this would become rarer as the season wore on, but following the Louisville win, the Wildcats had a full week off to relax and recover from a busy few early months of the season. When it was finally time to return to the court for SEC play, they faced a familiar foe in their opener.

That would be the Georgia Bulldogs, the same team which had ruined Senior Night in Lexington the season before. Much like the Wildcats, Georgia was a completely different team than the one that had come to Rupp Arena the previous March. They were no longer the plucky underdog playing for an interim coach, but instead had hit their stride under first year head coach Mark Fox. The Bulldogs featured two future NBA draft picks (Travis Leslie and Trey Thompkins), and entered their matchup with Kentucky fresh off a win over No. 17 ranked Georgia Tech. To the Wildcats' credit, they didn't take Georgia lightly at all. By the middle of the first half they had built an 11-point lead.

Like a lot of games that season, the lead wouldn't last for Kentucky. A combination of poor perimeter shooting (they ended the game just 2 of 14 from three) and equally poor bench play (non-starters combined for just nine points) allowed the Bulldogs to get back into the game. The entire second half turned into a back-and-forth affair; by the time the game went final, the lead had changed hands 12 times.

But eventually, the combination of Kentucky's pressure defense and DeMarcus Cousins down low proved to be too much. The Wildcats forced 26 turnovers, and Cousins scored seven straight points in the closing minutes. It gave Kentucky a 76-68 win, and they improved to 16-0 on the season.

Following the game, Calipari seemed happy with the victory. He called Georgia one of the most improved teams in college basketball, and openly admitted that his team might not have fared so well if the game wasn't at Rupp Arena. But a win is a win, and Calipari was satisfied. He even credited them with a "victory" in the imaginary win-loss column in his head. According to Calipari, the team's record now stood at 9-7.

Beyond the victory, Calipari was impressed with one player specifically. DeMarcus Cousins had again played well, and was emerging as a force down low.

"He was a beast," Calipari told reporters. "We were throwing it to him every single time."

The win served many purposes for Kentucky, but the most important one might be that it showed Cousins' huge game against Louisville hadn't been a fluke. If anything Cousins' strong play was starting to become a trend. For the second straight game, he had been *the* difference in a win.

It was all part of the larger development of Boogie Cousins.

If you ask just about anyone who was involved with Kentucky basketball during the 2009-2010 season they would admit that Cousins could be immature at times when he first arrived at the school. He could take plays off at practice, and pout like a little kid if he didn't get the ball down low.

In his book, "Players First, Coaching From the Inside Out," Calipari tells a great story from Cousins' first day of practice:

> My players have to get through fifteen conditioning drills and meet certain benchmarks before we start practice in the middle of October. The very first day, DeMarcus stopped halfway through and said, "My feet are on fire!" The whole rest of the team was watching this—the new guys who had come in with him, like John Wall and Eric Bledsoe, along with Darius Miller and DeAndre Liggins and some of the others who were already in Lexington when I took over. Everything stopped for a moment, like it does when there's a car accident and traffic comes to a standstill. First I told the other guys, "Keep going. Don't worry about him," and they picked it back up.
>
> I turned around and DeMarcus was sitting against a wall. He had his shoes off. I walked over there and he said it again: "My feet are on fire!"
>
> I said to him very calmly, "DeMarcus, you didn't make that run, so you know you're going to have to make it up. And to be honest with you, I'm okay with that. I know you've got a long way to go. But you do know that you will never start for this basketball team if you can't do the conditioning and you're not in shape. You know that, right? You'll come off the bench, and if you're playing well and in shape, might play thirty minutes. But if you're not, you'll come off the bench and you'll play eight minutes. Either way, you can never start here. You do know that, right?"
>
> He made every conditioning drill after that, every single one. It was one of those things where I could have gone crazy on him. And believe me, I do go crazy sometimes. But right then he just needed to know that, number one, respect what we're doing here. We're a team, we're in this together, and it's not going to work if one guy is sitting down with his shoes off. And number two, I wanted him to feel

like I cared about him enough to encourage him to do the right thing. We were all just getting started and getting to know one another. I didn't need to humiliate him. I trusted him to know what he had to do. If I didn't believe that I would never have recruited him.

Over the first few months of the season, Calipari tried several different approaches to handle Cousins. He gave his tongue-lashings in practice. He benched him in games. At times, he removed him from practice altogether, and had him ride the stationary bike while everyone else continued to work.

But by the middle of the season, all of the tough love had made Boogie mentally tougher. He was learning how to handle himself both in practice and in games, and how to control his temper when things didn't go his way.

He also learned one other very valuable lesson: If nobody was going to get him the ball, he'd just go get it himself.

"Ten or or 11 games in --- and we're winning all these games --- it just clicked with DeMarcus," assistant strength coach Scott Padgett said. "And when they (the guards) didn't get him the ball, he'd just go get it off the boards."

With Cousins' development, Kentucky was just starting to become a complete team… and as Padgett pointed out, that was *after* winning their first 16 games of the season. Wall and Bledsoe were already playing lights out on the perimeter. Darius Miller and Patrick Patterson were providing strong play on the wing. And when Cousins started hitting his stride? It made Kentucky damn near unstoppable.

"It became a team that was dribble-drive, to, 'You've got to get (Cousins) the ball,'" Padgett said. "And we're doing more post up plays for him. And now you have this dynamic perimeter with Wall and Bledsoe, and you team it with a beast in DeMarcus and a big-time player in Patrick Patterson as well, and you see it. You see, 'This team can be big-time.'"

The team was becoming big-time and in their next game against Florida, the Gators got to see just how deep the Wildcats' talent ran. Early on Florida decided to focus their defensive efforts on Wall and Cousins, only to realize that the Wildcats had a third deadly freshman as well. His name was Eric Bledsoe.

Things didn't start out particularly smoothly for Bledsoe or Kentucky, as the Wildcats actually fell down 7-0 just a few minutes into the game. Bledsoe finally stopped the bleeding with a lay-in about four minutes into the game, and from there, the Wildcats were able to rally. They led 38-31 at intermission.

But just like the Georgia game, things would tighten up in the second half.

For the young Wildcats, they were learning just how tough the rigors of conference play really were. Teams weren't intimidated by them or afraid when they saw Kentucky come out of the tunnel. It was actually the opposite; everyone in the SEC was familiar with the Wildcats, and thanks to Billy Gillispie's two disastrous seasons in Lexington most teams had actually beaten Kentucky at least once over the previous two years and played them with no fear. That was especially true for Florida, which had won back-to-back National Championships just a few years earlier. If anyone had a particular bone to pick with Kentucky --- and all the attention they were getting --- it was definitely the Gators. A few years before, it was Florida that was the king of the conference. Now all anyone wanted to talk about was Kentucky.

That's also why the second half of the matchup between the two teams turned into a street fight. Kentucky built a massive 15-point lead, but thanks to the combination of solid shooting, solid defense and a ravenous fan base behind them, Florida battled back. With just under five minutes left the Gators came all the way back and actually took a one-point lead, as the "O-Dome" (the nickname for Florida's O'Connell Center) turned into a mad house.

Thankfully though, Kentucky had been here before.

Just a few games earlier, Louisville had made a similar run on the 'Cats, and Calipari responded by calling a timeout to stop the bleeding. Well this time he let his players play, and they responded about as emphatically as he could've hoped for. Patrick Patterson hit a jumper and was fouled, and even though he missed the foul shot, DeMarcus Cousins grabbed the loose ball. He kicked the ball back out to Darnell Dodson who sank an open three, and all of a sudden, a one-point deficit became a four-point lead for the Wildcats. When Bledsoe hit another three on the next possession, it was the dagger Florida was never able to recover from. Kentucky won 89-77.

The story coming out of the game was of course Bledsoe. The freshman guard didn't just have a night to remember, but put up one of the best stat lines anyone had in college basketball to that point in the season. Kentucky's "other" freshman guard finished the game with 25 points (including three, three-pointers), seven rebounds, five assists and three steals.

It was enough to catch the attention of Florida coach Billy Donovan, who heaped praise on Bledsoe after the game.

"He's as good as any point guard in the country," Donovan said. "He's faster than John Wall, and probably shoots a little better too."

Talk about praise, huh?

But with Bledsoe's emergence along with Cousins, it proved that the Wildcats were no longer just relying on John Wall to bail them out every time something went bad. Instead they were a true "team" and somehow, despite being 17-0, were only now starting to play their best basketball.

But then, just as the Wildcats hit their stride, just as they reached one of the most important moments of their season, something unexpected happened. It was something no one could have planned for or anticipated, and all of a sudden, wins on the court paled in comparison to what was going on off of it.

∗   ∗   ∗

At 17-0, Kentucky was off to a historic start, the best for any Kentucky squad since the 1965-66 season.

But just as the high of the Florida game died down and preparations began for a trip to Auburn that Saturday, John Calipari turned on his TV. Once he did, Auburn quickly became the last thing on his mind.

On the television were images that shocked Cal, and shocked the world too. Haiti --- a small island nation in the Caribbean --- had been rocked by one of the largest earthquakes in recorded history, a 7.0 blast that occurred just hours before the Wildcats took the court against Florida. The tragedy had an immeasurable toll on one of the world's poorest countries, leaving hundreds of thousands dead, hundreds of thousands more missing, and over a million people displaced.

Seeing the images shocked Cal, and got his mind racing. What could he do? How could he and Big Blue Nation help? Eventually he got a call from a local businessman, and the two agreed that something *had* to be done. Calipari always had been a big-thinker, and immediately the wheels began turning.

"That was probably the hardest part of the job (of working for Calipari)," former Director of Basketball Operations Martin Newton said. "He's got 5,620 ideas a week, and (you've got to) figure out how to get them all done. That's just how his mind works. He's constantly thinking."

Remember, Newton had given up a highly successful career working at Nike to take the job at Kentucky, and he had done it in part because of moments like this. Newton knew that Calipari was fearless, unafraid to take on any challenge, no matter how big it might seem. Whether it was rebuilding the Kentucky basketball program from the bottom, or helping a desperate country miles away, Calipari's approach to life intrigued Newton. It also reminded him of one of the core tenants that Nike was built on.

"When I worked at Nike, the old adage was 'If ain't broke, break it,'" Newton said. "And I felt the same way about Cal. Let's not just settle on the way it's always been done, let's always think about doing something different. That's one thing I respect a lot about him."

Eventually Calipari hatched a plan. His team would host a telethon on local television, with all proceeds going directly to those in need in Haiti.

Calipari had arranged to get over an hour of air-time on a local TV station, and had lined up a prominent group of Lexington area business men and women to match whatever funds Kentucky raised that day. A handful of celebrities such as Kentucky super-fan Ashley Judd and Steelers head coach Mike Tomlin (who'd attended a Wildcats' game earlier that season) also offered up items to auction. Oh, and one more thing: Kentucky's players would also help field calls as they came in.

The idea was totally out of left field, totally unlike anything that most coaches would ever dream of doing. Calipari isn't most coaches however. And the telethon, which was dubbed "Hoops for Haiti" was quintessential Cal.

"I grew up around coaches, my dad was a coach," Newton said. "And most coaches, once you get into the season, they're not thinking about anything but basketball. Yet what was amazing about that was that he was thinking about helping this country which had just gone through this catastrophe."

The telethon was set for that upcoming Sunday, which meant that the first order of business was actually playing basketball, with the trip to Auburn next. The Wildcats held on for a 72-67 win against the Tigers, thanks to another double-double from DeMarcus Cousins. He finished the game with 16 points and 11 rebounds, in what served as a little bit of a homecoming for both he and Bledsoe (each was an Alabama native). Calipari didn't admit it at the time, but would later confess that his full attention hadn't been on basketball that day. Part of his focus was on the next day, and "Hoops for Haiti."

That night, Kentucky's traveling party returned to Lexington, and it was at that point when Calipari held a team meeting to tell them what was planned for the next day. He began by laying out the big picture nature of it all; just how serious the situation was in Haiti, and how Kentucky basketball was going to do something to help. He also urged his players to understand that this was bigger than basketball. In this case, lives were at stake.

Then he laid out exactly how they would help. The players would come down to the TV station for the telethon and stand-by. Callers would dial in and speak to a volunteer, who would take down the person's name and payment. Then at that point, when the call was over, a player would step in and thank the individual for their support. Then the next call would come, and they'd do it again.

The players nodded their heads in understanding. Although they didn't really have a choice in the matter, they all seemed eager and happy to help.

"The guys (players) didn't hesitate a bit," DeWayne Peevy said. "They wanted to help out."

Finally, the day had arrived.

The players came to the TV station early the next morning, just as the calls began to pour in. Calipari served as the host for the whole event, and occasionally grabbed one of the guys to come speak to the TV audience. Meanwhile, everyone else stood by the phones as planned, jumping in to offer a quick thanks to the callers.

Little by little the players grew more comfortable with the callers. Within a few minutes, it became second nature.

"It was really remarkable to watch," Kentucky Sports Radio's Matt Jones said. "The kids were really into it. It wasn't some place they felt like they *had* to be."

Instead, they embraced the unique opportunity to make a real difference in the world. They also enjoyed the chance to interact with the fans in a loose and fun (albeit serious in nature) setting. As you can imagine, the phone conversations ranged from serene, to outright absurd.

"Some of them would just talk to you, and they're just happy to talk you, tell you that we're doing good, they're just happy that their program is doing well," freshman center Daniel Orton said. "Some would call and literally try to have a conversation with you. They'd want to know about the program, what practice was like, stuff about the coaches, different players. Some would call giving us tips on what we needed to do the next game."

Some messages got even more personal than that.

"They'd say 'I love you Josh, I love you Jorts! Your time will come!'" Josh Harrellson remembered.

All in all it was a fun day for just about everyone involved, but more importantly the fundraiser was a staggering success. The team raised over $500,000 from the telethon, and when that was tallied with the matching gift from the Lexington area businessmen, it meant that over $1 million had been raised in Haiti relief.

The numbers of it all were mind-blowing. So was the idea that a college basketball team, a bunch of 18 to 21-year-old kids, were the ones who were the driving force behind all the donations.

"Think about the notion that a college basketball team in Kentucky would raise a million dollars on earthquake victims in Haiti during the season," Jones said. "That's kind of insane if you think about it."

It also showed the power of Kentucky basketball. As Calipari later explained to Yahoo's Dan Wetzel, the impact of the telethon had overwhelmed even the coach himself. Fans called in from all corners of the state, with all kinds of different stories. Some were just normal folks happy to help out. Others were unemployed, but still felt the need to help any way they could. Parents were calling in for their children, who wanted to donate that week's allowance. Again, the whole scene overwhelmed Calipari. He told Wetzel that any coach would've done the same. But Kentucky was one of the few schools with a fan base that would allow him to pull off such a feat.

Whatever the case was, Calipari taught his players an important lesson in the process of raising that $1 million: They could make a difference. They could use their platform as Kentucky basketball players to truly help others. While that theme has become common at Kentucky throughout the Calipari era, it was completely new at that particular moment.

"It was an eye-opener for me," senior guard Mark Krebs said. "Like, yes it's cool playing Kentucky basketball, to win games. It's cool to go to

Madison Square Garden. But it's also that we're making a big difference, and people are taking notice."

And boy did people take notice.

Although nobody realized it at the time, the Wildcats' impact had reached well beyond just Lexington.

"We felt good doing it, like 'Wow that was really cool raising money,'" Krebs said. "We didn't realize it was a national thing, we thought it was more or less a thing around the state, around the Commonwealth, even around Lexington, really. We didn't realize how far it reached."

Oh, it reached far.

Straight to the White House.

Hello Mr. President, This is DeMarcus Cousins

With 'Hoops for Haiti' over, it was back to business for the Wildcats. Following the Auburn win, Kentucky had a full week off before their next game against Arkansas. But rather than taking it easy on his players, John Calipari decided to ramp things up. The team may have been 18 games into the season, with an 18-0 record, but the coach still wasn't happy with how his club was playing. Specifically he was upset at how every game seemed to follow the same blueprint: Get up early on an opponent, let the opponent get back into the game, then hold on for dear life and pray for a victory at the end.

In Calipari's eyes, his team wasn't 18-0, but instead closer to 10-8. Therefore he decided to switch things up when they returned to practice that Monday following 'Hoops for Haiti.' Rather than coddle his team, and rather than praise them for their hot start, he decided to flip the script.

"Coach Cal did something that I've never seen a coach do," senior guard Mark Krebs said. "He came in so mad and we were like 18-0, 19-0 and said 'I'm going to act like you guys lost. I'd rather do it now, then do it when we actually lose. So I'm going to act like we lost, and turn this thing.'"

So there the Kentucky Wildcats were, 18-0 after the Auburn win, with their coach treating them like they were a .500 club fighting for an NCAA Tournament berth. The bikes and treadmills came out that week, looming as punishment for any player who showed up not ready to work. Practices went longer. Calipari pushed and prodded his squad, and insisted he needed to see more from them.

Again, he did all this even as his team's record sat at 18-0. Even with a No. 2 ranking in both major polls.

"He said 'I don't want you guys getting complacent,'" Krebs said. "He was using it as a teaching point, a mental thing."

And for at least one game, the bizarre decision by Calipari looked genius.

With the full week off Kentucky returned to the court recharged and refreshed against Arkansas, and after their coach had spent the previous week taking his frustrations out on them, the Wildcats' players took *their* frustrations out on the other team. Kentucky put up a staggering 57 points in the first half against the Razorbacks, on their way to a 101-70 win. All five starters scored in double figures for Kentucky, with Darius Miller tallying a career-high 18 points. Daniel Orton also earned praise for his play off the bench with six points, five rebounds and four blocks.

Clearly Calipari's mind games had worked. At the same time, the Wildcats also had a different kind of motivation that day: The No. 1 ranking in college basketball was up for grabs.

Kentucky had entered the game ranked No. 2 nationally, but after No. 1 ranked Texas had lost earlier that week they seemed poised to move into the top spot. When the Longhorns lost a second straight game that weekend (to the same UConn team the Wildcats had already beaten) it was official. When the new polls came out on Monday, Kentucky would be No. 1.

For better or worse, a shot at No. 1 had motivated the whole team in their win over Arkansas.

"I think it drove us a lot," John Wall admitted to reporters after the game. "Coach Cal said this morning that he woke up and it really hit him that we have the chance to be number one. He said he's a little nervous, so you all (the players) can be a little nervous (too)."

As it turned out, the Wildcats had nothing to be nervous about. They beat Arkansas on Saturday. And when the new polls came out on Monday, Kentucky was indeed No. 1 in the country.

It was a joyous time for Kentucky hoops, a moment to reflect on just how much things had changed in such a short amount of time. And normally the team would have taken a minute or two to celebrate. Yet just as they reached the top of the polls, something *even bigger* happened.

That's right, 'Hoops for Haiti' was still making news and the story had gone national. Apparently it had touched one person specifically, who hoped to reach out and personally congratulate the team on their efforts.

That person was President Barack Obama.

And just as the team got set to leave for a road game against South Carolina, the President's office reached out with a simple request: Obama hoped to speak with the team. Would they be available the next day?

"I want to say we found out right before we left town," DeWayne Peevy said.

Peevy was the man tasked with figuring out the logistics, but thankfully the staff at South Carolina was more than willing to help out. Peevy coordinated everything with the school; they would take the call early the next morning right before shootaround. South Carolina was willing to let the Wildcats use the school's media room, so that reporters could listen in on the call.

"South Carolina was great," Peevy said. "We worked with Emily Feeney, who was the South Carolina basketball contact at the time to be able to get the phone set up. They had to talk to a lot of people on their end."

With the team settled in South Carolina, the big day arrived and Peevy and the Kentucky staff had a game plan for everything. Calipari would greet the President and then let Patrick Patterson, John Wall and DeMarcus Cousins each deliver a quick, personal message. Peevy then asked the players if he'd like them to script anything for them to say. After all, this was the President and he understood the players might be nervous.

To his surprise though, the players didn't feel like they needed anything. President, schesident! They had made a million phone calls before and didn't feel like this would be any different.

"We were in the locker room, making sure those guys were comfortable, knowing what they want to say," Peevy remembered. "And they're all like 'We're fine, we know what we're doing. This is not a big deal.' And I said, ok 'You guys are comfortable? Cool.'"

To the player's credit they did remain comfortable ... at least for another 30 seconds or so. Then the reality set in: This wasn't just any phone call. This was the President of the United States on the other line.

Everyone tightened up. One, more than the others.

"We get ready to go, and DeMarcus starts freaking out, like 'What do I say?'" Peevy said. "Like all of a sudden, he realized this was a big deal. Like, he's getting to talk to the President. He was like 'I forgot what I'm supposed to say. What am I going to do?' So we wrote everything on an index card. And I gave one to him, gave one to John Wall just in case."

Nerves were at an all-time high, but with the call coming, the team and Calipari made their way to the stage. Patterson sat to the side of his coach, with Wall and Cousins close by. The rest of the team stood behind them, with a horde of media in ear shot.

And then finally, the phone rang. John Calipari answered. And even though he was ready for the call, he wasn't ready for just how blunt the President's staff member would be.

"Hi, this is Katie Johnson," the voice on the other end of the phone said. "I'm calling on behalf of President Obama."

The comment drew a crooked head turn from Calipari, who said "OK" and smiled at Ms. Johnson, who seemed blissfully unaware of just how unique her introduction was. Johnson then placed the team on a brief hold while she grabbed the President. Everyone waited anxiously, including Calipari who admitted to his players that even he was nervous.

Then, just moments later, a familiar voice spoke up on the other line.

"Hello?" the President asked.

Once it was clear that he had picked up the right line (we can only imagine what foreign diplomat may have been on the other one) he quickly congratulated the team on their move to the top of the polls.

"I am honored to speak to the No. 1 team in the country just a few days after it happened," Obama said.

Calipari responded and thanked him for the call. He mentioned what a success that the 'Hoops for Haiti' initiative had been, then thanked him and turned it over to his players. From there, Patterson thanked the President on behalf of the players.

Following a brief pause, Calipari got set to introduce Wall. But before he could, the President (who is a huge basketball fan) cut him off. Like Kentucky's basketball players, Obama himself was a little star struck.

"What's going on All-Star?" The President said, clearly aware of Wall's exploits to that point in the season.

Wall responded like any nervous 19-year-old would: By reintroducing himself, even though the President had made it clear that he knew who Wall was.

"Hi Mr. President, this is John Wall," he said.

In the background, the Kentucky traveling party chuckled. As it turns out, John Wall could be intimidated. It just didn't come from an opposing player, but instead, the leader of the free world.

"If you listen closely, (the players) they're kind of robotic, like they froze up," Peevy said. "I didn't think John would; DeMarcus clearly showed he was rattled on the front end, but John ended up showing the same thing. President Obama referenced him, called him by name, and the first thing John says is 'This is John Wall.' That was the funniest part about that, the guys were so nervous."

They were robotic, but to Wall's credit, he read the lines right off his note card like a seasoned Hollywood actor. When the President paused, Wall followed his script, and invited him down to Lexington. Maybe he and Obama could even play "HORSE" together?

"Ahhhh, I don't think I want to play HORSE with you," Obama said, as the entire Kentucky contingent burst out in laughter. "I don't want to lose, and then you'll have bragging rights for a long time. But what we might do is have a little scrimmage at some point. And I'm going to make sure you're on my team."

Again, the team burst out laughing, then after a pause, DeMarcus Cousins stepped to the podium. Like Wall, Cousins showed his age. He may have been a bruising 6'11 low post monster on the court, but off of it he was still a shy, nervous 19-year-old. He leaned into the speaker, with his hands folded behind his back.

"Hello Mr. President, this is DeMarcus Cousins," he said.

Without pausing, he delivered his next line.

"What we're really looking forward to is seeing you at the end of the season," Cousins said.

The comment received even more laughs as the two sides finally began to wrap up their call. The President (not surprisingly) had other business to tend to, but after discovering the team played South Carolina that night, he had one final message to deliver.

"Well, you should be alright," he said. "But there is that tendency once you get to No. 1 to start letting down a bit."

The President's message would prove to be prophetic, although at that particular moment no one seemed to give it a second thought. The truth was that South Carolina was the last thing on anyone's mind. The team had just talked to the President of the United States, and as they departed from the media room to shootaround and later the hotel, everyone was all smiles.

Even Patrick Patterson, the team's stoic, calm, veteran presence was giddy like a little kid.

"Getting to speak to the President even if only for a brief moment was unbelievable," he told Fox Sports in February of 2015.

The Wildcats' leader --- who always set an example for his younger teammates --- was so excited, he may have even broken Presidential code later that day. Not that he cared.

"After that was over and we got back to the room, the first thing I did was text all my friends and then call my family," he said. "Can't remember if I was supposed to do that or not."

* * *

The 2010 Kentucky Wildcats might have been the only team in the history of college basketball to get a call from the President in January, but that meant little to their opponent that evening. The South Carolina Gamecocks were a veteran club, led by the SEC's leading scorer (Devan Downey) and were coming off a near upset of the Florida Gators.

Put simply, the Gamecocks would be ready for the Wildcats. But would Kentucky be ready for them?

"We had a young team, ripe for a letdown," assistant strength coach Scott Padgett said. "And we had a letdown."

It didn't appear the Wildcats would overlook the Gamecocks at first, with Kentucky jumping out to an 11-6 lead just a few minutes into the game. From there, the rest of the half turned into an offensive lull for both teams; just a couple days after the Wildcats put up 57 first half points against Arkansas, they were held to just 29, taking a 29-26 lead into halftime.

The good news was that for the Wildcats this was nothing new; virtually every game that season had been close at halftime, and in every one they had used the opening few minutes of the second half to attack the opponent. The problem was that on this night, the Gamecocks were prepared for the run. Every time Kentucky tried to make a move, South Carolina had an answer. Every time they went on a mini-run, the Gamecocks countered.

"We felt like we were sleepwalking, that nothing we did worked," senior guard Mark Krebs said. "Like we'd go on a six-point run, and they'd hit a three falling out of bounds or something. And then somehow we'd go down, get fouled and miss both free throws, and somehow that six point run was nullified. That was a very weird feeling."

Trailing 39-33, the Wildcats eventually made their move. DeMarcus Cousins scored six of the game's next nine points, with John Wall adding another five after that. Just like that, a six-point deficit had become a two-point lead.

It was a move that surprised no one. By that point in the season, the Wildcats didn't just know they were capable of a quick run. They had come to expect it.

"That team just didn't feel like we could lose," Peevy said. "We had been down so many times, and we didn't feel like we could lose."

The thing was, on this night South Carolina didn't feel like they could lose either.

Following Kentucky's run the Gamecocks made a run of their own. After the two teams traded buckets, Downey tied things up at 47, and then proceeded to score seven of his team's next 11 points. South Carolina gained a 58-54 lead and eventually extended it to 62-56 with just under two minutes to go.

With their first loss looming, the Wildcats made one last gasp effort. Wall got to the foul line and hit a pair of free throws, and then followed it up with a quick bucket out of a timeout. He was fouled while making the shot, which allowed him to head to the line for a free throw. He hit it, to cut South Carolina's lead to just 62-61 with a little over 23 seconds to play.

The Wildcats had to foul and hope for a miracle... a miracle, which ultimately never came. The Gamecocks hit two free throws to take a 64-61 lead, and Kentucky turned the ball over and missed a three on the next two possessions. Ramon Galloway hit two free throws for South Carolina, and then before the Wildcats could move the ball up court the clock hit zero.

South Carolina 68, Kentucky 62. It was the first ever loss of the John Calipari era, as fans stormed the court in Columbia.

Eventually the players made their way back to the locker room, and as the first loss of the season sunk in, many couldn't help but think back to President Obama's message earlier that day.

Remember, it was Obama who warned the team about a letdown.

It had gone down exactly the way the President had drawn it up.

"Since then, I've said 'that was the curse,'" Jon Hood said with a laugh. "Obama never calls anybody during the season, and he called us. We got 30 rung up on us by Devan Downey, and walk out with a loss."

Hood was of course joking, but the truth was that Obama was right: Kentucky hadn't come out focused. They had also made the worst kind of assumption, and figured that no matter how many points they fell behind, they could overcome the deficit.

In Kentucky's defense however, they had done it so many times to that point in the season, they felt sort of invincible.

"That's the thing that was so weird," Krebs said of Kentucky's inability to make a comeback. "If you go back and look at it, the Miami (of Ohio) game, the Stanford game, the UConn game, the North Carolina game when they came back on us, Louisville was close. There were so many games that were close and probably shouldn't have been. And it was like 'If we play, we can just turn it on when we need to turn it on, we're going to be fine.' And that was the one game that we just couldn't turn it on."

With the loss Kentucky fell to 19-1.

The good news was of course, that they would stay No. 1 for a few more days, at least until the polls came out the following Monday.

But the bad news, well, it was much worse.

For Kentucky, they hadn't just suffered their first loss of the season, but for some of their best players, they'd lost something even worse: Their mojo. Some of the Wildcats' biggest stars were dealing with the first major disappointment of their college careers, and as John Calipari would find out, they weren't totally sure how to handle it.

Not that Calipari had time to worry.

He had a very special guest coming to town that weekend.

Just days after speaking to the President, "The King" was coming to Lexington.

THE KING AND I

IF THERE HAS been one theme which has been prevalent throughout John Calipari's time at Kentucky, it's that you just never know who you might see walking around campus, in the Wildcats' locker room or at a game. Celebrity UK fans have become the norm in Lexington, as common as Final Four runs and first round selections at the NBA Draft.

Now several years into the Calipari era at Kentucky, the list seems endless. Jay-Z was seen celebrating with the Wildcats after they clinched a Final Four berth back in 2011 (as partial owner of an NBA team, he was later fined by the league for being there). Kevin Durant and his Oklahoma City Thunder teammates spent part of the NBA lockout working out at Kentucky later that same year. And as mentioned earlier, Drake has been a regular around the program, after first attending Big Blue Madness back in 2009.

At times all the celebrity attention can cause what seems like a little bit of a circus atmosphere around Kentucky's basketball program, but ultimately that's how John Calipari wants it. As they say, "there's no such thing as bad PR." And there's no one in college basketball who is better at marketing his program than John Calipari.

"One of the geniuses of Cal is how creative he is," said Martin Newton, the man who served as the team's Director of Basketball Operations during the 2009-2010 and 2010-2011 seasons. "Cal is a business-savvy, marketing guy at heart. He just happens to be a basketball coach. If Cal was at Nike or at a Fortune 500 company he'd be incredible, because of his creativity and his ability to market."

Newton should know. Remember, he spent over 20 years working for Nike before coming to Kentucky, and got an up-close, first-hand view of how one of the largest companies on the globe operates. And in a lot of ways, Calipari runs his program like a Fortune 500 company. He knows who his "consumer" is (in his case it's 18-year-old high school basketball kids) and knows how to market his program to them.

Specifically, Calipari knows that while he might not be able to identify with guys like Drake or Jay-Z, his "consumers" (again, high school basketball players) do. So if kids can come to Kentucky and rub elbows with their favorite stars, it gives the Wildcats just one more advantage in recruiting.

"They're recognized by the 16, 17, 18-year-old kids," Newton said. "Whereas John Calipari might not be (interested in Drake or Jay-Z), but the players are. And John Calipari was smart to know where their mindsets are. They don't think five, 10 years down the road. They think in the now. They've forgotten things that happened five years ago."

Calipari's marketing savvy isn't something that started at Kentucky; he was doing stuff like this all the way back to his UMass days in the early 1990's. But the 2009-2010 season was the first time that UK fans got to see it all up close and in person. And there might not have been a better example of "entertainment" meeting "basketball" than on the final weekend of January in that season.

The Wildcats returned to campus following the loss to South Carolina mentally fatigued, but got a pick me up from the most unlikely place when they got back to Lexington. As they prepared to play Vanderbilt that Saturday at Rupp Arena, word trickled out that the biggest superstar in basketball might make a surprise guest appearance.

That's right, LeBron James was coming to town.

As it turned out, LeBron had a rare mid-season off-day, and used it to swing by Rupp Arena and check out the spectacle that is Kentucky basketball in person. James' relationship with Calipari had dated back years; Calipari had actually recruited LeBron back when he was in high school and Coach Cal was at Memphis. The two had stayed in touch through mutual friends at Nike, and one of LeBron's closest high school friends (a guy by the name of Brandon Weems) served as a graduate assistant on UK's staff that season. LeBron had even popped by Lexington to play a little pick-up the summer before, shortly after Calipari accepted the head coaching job at Kentucky.

But on this Saturday there would be no pick-up, and instead LeBron was in town to simply hang out and watch some hoops. He was honored shortly after halftime by spelling out the "Y" in Kentucky with the Wildcats' cheerleaders during a timeout, but other than that, he was just a regular bystander. Along with 24,000 of his closest friends at Rupp Arena, he got to watch as DeMarcus Cousins dominated in the paint with 21 points and 10 rebounds, as the Wildcats went on to an 85-72 victory.

It was another big game for Big Cuz, who recorded his 12th straight double-double, which set a new Kentucky freshman record.

But if you think he played hard to impress King James, think again.

"He was always around," Cousins said after the game. "I'm used to seeing him."

Cousins was clearly in a joking mood after the win, but as John Calipari quickly learned, some of Cousins' freshmen teammates were not. Specifically, it was another frustrating afternoon for John Wall, who finished with just 13 points in what amounted to one of his worst shooting performances of the season (he went just 4 of 12 from the field). Following the game, Wall caught a few reporters off-guard when he expressed frustration with his play.

"The last two weeks I haven't been playing well," Wall said following the win. "I haven't been having any fun."

The comments quickly took off like wildfire, and many wondered if there were ulterior motives behind them. Was Wall frustrated with his role in Kentucky's offense? Also, was he frustrated with Calipari specifically? Immediately rumors began to surface and everyone began to wonder: What was behind John Wall's comments?

But as it turned out, Wall was simply a frustrated 19-year-old old, struggling to handle the first true adversity of his basketball career. He even went so far as to personally meet with Calipari after the game to ensure there was no confusion.

"He comes in after the game, and we win but it's an ugly game," Calipari remembered. "Well he walks in and says 'Coach, I want you to know I love you.' And I look at him like 'what did you do? Why did you say that?' And I found out that he said he wasn't having fun, that he'd said it to the media.'"

Calipari lent a sympathetic ear. He then addressed the situation the only way he knew how: With tough love.

"I said 'no kidding,'" Calipari said. "'It's really hard.'"

It was safe to say that for lack of a better term, Wall had hit… a wall (please forgive the bad pun). But the truth was that he had become an overnight superstar, and like anyone in his position, had trouble dealing with all the newfound responsibility that came with it. Everywhere he went, someone demanded something from him; a fan looking for an autograph, another media outlet hoping to profile him, or the coaching staff urging him to do more in practice or a game. It was all overwhelming for a player who had led a relatively normal life just a few months before.

To their credit, Kentucky helped ease Wall's burden, and cut off media access to him midway through the season. He also got some strong advice, from an assistant coach who had been there before.

"I remember telling John, 'This will be the toughest year of your basketball life,'" Rod Strickland said.

If anyone would know, it was Strickland. Like Wall, Strickland was a college All-American, and a guy who went on to have a successful career in the NBA as a point guard which spanned nearly two decades. He knew what Wall was going through; the burden of pressure and expectations.

He also told Wall that it would get easier. He promised. College basketball was a lot more challenging than anyone ever realized.

"In college, people can scheme for you," he told Wall. "The court shrinks for you. We had a lot of great players (at Kentucky) but you're not playing with the same (level of) guys (that you will in the NBA). When you get to the league, you're going to have knockdown shooters, guys who hit shots. In college, teams can focus in. They can say 'this guy isn't a shooter' and pack it in. In the NBA, the court opens up."

The pep talks from both Calipari and Strickland helped ease Wall, but as it turned out he wasn't the only freshman struggling with the emotional adjustment of college basketball. So too did Eric Bledsoe, although his problems were different. While Wall was frustrated because he wasn't doing more, Bledsoe's biggest problem was that he just didn't realize how much he was actually capable of doing.

"How about John Wall comes into my office and says 'Eric Bledsoe doesn't think he's good enough. He doesn't think he's an NBA player,'" Calipari told Fox Sports. "And John and I had to get into him, like 'Do you know how good you are?'"

As it turned out, Kentucky had gotten back in the win column against Vanderbilt. But to get their "swag" back was going to take much more. Thankfully, they had a few manageable games coming up on the schedule to help figure things out.

It started with a visit from No. 25 ranked Ole Miss, and for whatever problems the Wildcats appeared to have entering the game, they all disappeared for at least one day. DeMarcus Cousins again dominated (something that was becoming a theme at that point in the season) with 18 points and 13 rebounds, and Wall bounced back with his best performance in weeks. He finished with 17 points and seven assists and had one big smile when he met with reporters following the game.

"It feels good," Wall said, when asked about his bounce back performance. "Hopefully all the other stuff will go away. But I am back to having fun and winning games."

If Wall had fun against Ole Miss, just about everyone else got to enjoy themselves the following game at LSU. The Wildcats fell down early, but then went on a 22-0 run midway through the first half to blow things open. Kentucky led 42-14 at the break, and the visit to Baton Rouge proved to be the rare game where Kentucky jumped out early on an opponent and didn't let up. With his team hitting full throttle, it allowed Calipari to go deep into his bench. Thirteen players took the court that night, including an emerging DeAndre Liggins who poured in seven points and had eight rebounds off the bench. Overall, the Wildcats got 22 points from their reserves and cruised to an 81-55 victory.

Following the win, LSU's Bo Spencer summed up the Wildcats about as well as anyone could.

"The guys on Kentucky's team are absolute animals," Spencer said. Spencer led all scorers with 25 points that night, yet when pressed by reporters, he was more impressed with Kentucky's play than his own. "Cousins, Patterson, all of them are physical. They are big and wide and they're hard to get around."

The mid-season SEC swing continued a few days later with a comfortable win over Alabama. While John Calipari wasn't happy with certain elements of the Wildcats' game (John Wall's turnovers, a tough night shooting the three), the coaching staff had to be happy overall with the evolution of the team. Since losing to South Carolina they had ripped off four straight wins, all by double-figures. In addition, the team was coming together. Freshmen were getting more mature by the day, and the bench was rounding into form.

If anything, the loss didn't hurt the team. If anything, it might have helped it.

"It could've been one of those, you have a letdown, and you're down in the dumps, and you roll off two or three losses in a row," Scott Padgett said. "Instead we go right back on a winning streak."

But while everyone was all smiles, things would get tougher going forward.

It started with the next game on the schedule. Kentucky was set to get a visit from No. 12 ranked Tennessee, in a game the whole college basketball world would be watching.

* * *

Over the past few decades, there might be no surer way to know you've "made it" as a major college football or basketball program than to see

College GameDay come to your campus. For those who have been living under a rock since the mid-1990's (which almost certainly isn't anyone reading this book), *College GameDay* is one of ESPN's signature programs, a preview show which is broadcast live, on-site from the campus of the biggest game in college basketball (or in the fall, football) that day. To have the show arrive on your campus is a badge of honor; not just a sign that you've made it, but also that you're relevant as a college hoops program.

For Kentucky fans, the arrival of *College GameDay* was nothing new; ESPN had actually broadcast the show from Rupp Arena twice prior to the 2009-2010 season. But even though Kentucky fans were seasoned *College GameDay* veterans by that point, the show still felt bigger and better than ever before when it arrived on campus the second weekend in February.

Well, technically that's not true.

It didn't *feel* bigger than ever before. It was *bigger* than ever before. On most college campuses *College GameDay* will draw a crowd of a couple thousand fans. Only on Saturday February 13th, 2010, 22,000 fans showed up that day.

It was by far the biggest crowd that *College GameDay* had ever drawn for a basketball broadcast to that point. And it left ESPN's broadcasters damn near speechless.

Jay Bilas did his best to provide a little bit of context.

"In 2007 when Tubby Smith left and they were courting Billy Donovan, there was a lot of talk of 'what kind of job is Kentucky,'" Bilas said. "I said this is the best job in America. *This* (the crowd) is the reason why. There's no place like Kentucky."

His colleague Hubert Davis followed up.

"I went to North Carolina," Davis exclaimed, as the crowd behind him broke out into boos. "But nobody does it like Kentucky."

The show ran for the hour, with a few show segments providing a preview for the day's biggest games, and Bilas used another segment to explain how Tennessee hoped to slow down John Wall. Then the camera shifted to the far end of the court, where host Rece Davis had a one-on-one interview with Calipari.

There, Davis asked Calipari one simple question: What was his first "Welcome to Kentucky" moment after he accepted the job the previous year.

Not surprisingly, Calipari was ready with an answer.

"We're playing a team that's 2-9," Calipari began. "And I walk into the arena and there's 24,300 (fans in the stands). There's a snowstorm, it's a 9 o'clock game, it's on TV, and I walk into the building and there's 24,300. We lose to South Carolina and there's a stack of mail. I haven't had the 'For Sale' sign on my front yard yet."

Not yet. But again, Calipari knew what the expectations were when he took the job. And he enjoyed every second of it.

"These fans are crazy," Calipari said, concluding his answer to Davis. "And I love them!"

If the frenzy was through the roof for "College GameDay's" taping at 10 a.m., it was at an all-time high when the game actually tipped off several hours later. Rupp Arena was packed, but Tennessee (which was again, a Top 15 opponent) wasn't fazed at all. The Vols jumped out to a 12-7 lead early, and spent most of the first half trying to slow down Kentucky and take the air out of the ball. The Wildcats pulled ahead to take a 30-29 lead right before the break.

Things stayed tight for most of the second half, before Kentucky finally made their run. It started with a John Wall floater which tied the game up at 52; in real time the bucket didn't look like much, but it turned out to be the exact spark that the Wildcats needed. Before Tennessee could blink, Kentucky had ripped off 10 straight points, and just like that, had a 60-52 lead. A Wayne Chism basket appeared to stop the bleeding for the Vols, but just when Tennessee let up, the Wildcats went on another run. Eric Bledsoe hit a three, and then on the next possession he hit another triple after some quick ball movement by Liggins. The Wildcats 66-56 lead was more than enough, as they went on to take a 73-62 victory.

Following the win, Liggins may have summed things up best.

"I like where we're at," he told reporters following the victory. "We need to take it one game at a time and we'll be fine."

To the Wildcats' credit, they were taking it one game at a time, and were winning games with a newfound perspective and maturity. Following the Tennessee win they now sat at 24-1 overall, and had five straight wins since the loss at South Carolina.

Kentucky was riding a newfound high. But just as they reached that high, they would again be tested.

It started with their next game, which featured a tough road trip to Mississippi State. There they would face a hostile environment, a rowdy fan base and one of the most talented teams they'd play all year.

Oh, and one of Kentucky's best players was about to get "called out."

Big time.

CALL ME

I F YOU WANT to know the biggest difference between Kentucky basket-ball in the late 2000's and Kentucky basketball now, a good place to start might be to take a road trip with the team. Back before John Calipari arrived in Lexington, the Wildcats barely drew a second glance when they went on the road in the SEC. Sure, they were still the biggest name in the conference. And yes, they had more historical cache than anyone else. But after two down years --- in which just about everyone in the confer-ence beat them at least once --- they didn't elicit fear from their oppo-nents. And they certainly didn't elicit the kind of attention they do now.

"Like now, when we go to a bigger city, we might have extra security and bring them with us," DeWayne Peevy said. "We weren't doing that stuff back then. We might have campus police, but we didn't know what we were in for (when we started going on the road in 2010)."

No they didn't, although in Kentucky's defense, there was never a need for extra security before Calipari arrived. While the Wildcats are now mobbed everywhere they go on the road, that just wasn't the case back before 2010.

"In future years, we took out of our media guide where we were stay-ing," Peevy said. "That year we had a list of where we were staying on the road."

Yes, you read that correctly: Right up until 2010, if a Kentucky fan (or any fan for that matter) wanted to know where the Wildcats were stay-ing on the road, all they had to do is pick up the team's media guide. Listed there, in big, bold letters (or at least normal sized, non-bold letters) were the team's lodging accommodations. It's something that's laughable now; the Wildcats have evolved into one of the biggest road shows in college basketball (if not the biggest) and making that information so readily available would lead to thousands of extra visitors every time the team left Lexington.

Of course things changed drastically that year for Kentucky basketball, and it's doubtful the policy will ever go back to the way it was. That's because (as you've probably figured out by now) by 2010, Kentucky wasn't just *another* team in the SEC, but instead, *the* team that everyone had to see. And boy, did they in fact see them. UK fans --- who've always traveled well to road games even in the down years --- came out in droves to check out the 2010 team in person. And with a slew of future first round draft picks on the roster, opposing fans came out to see them too. It was a phenomenon which started with that huge crowd of Kentucky fans at Madison Square Garden for the UConn game, and turned into a huge crowd period --- of both Kentucky fans, and those of the opponent --- every time the Wildcats went on the road in the SEC.

"As we went on the road and we would show up for shoot-around, there would be students in line the night before, at road games that didn't normally sell out the crowd," former Director of Basketball Operations Martin Newton said. "But Kentucky was coming to town."

That's right, Kentucky had become *the* ultimate road show in the SEC; back in 2010 John Calipari might not have yet coined the term "Kentucky is everybody's Super Bowl" but the feeling was already prevalent. When Kentucky came to town, normally disinterested basketball fan bases came to life. Schools which might only draw 5,000 to most games, would all of a sudden get 10,000 to see the Wildcats in their home building.

And there might not have been a better example of that phenomenon for Kentucky, than a trip to Starkville, Mississippi during the second week of February in 2010.

Understand that Mississippi State's fan base is a lot like most in the SEC. They have a very hot and cold approach to the sport of basketball, even though the school itself actually has a pretty good tradition (at least relative to other SEC schools). The team actually made a Final Four back in 1996, and entering 2009-2010 were coming off two straight NCAA Tournament appearances. They had good players --- center Jarvis Varnado was an All-American, who would be selected in the NBA Draft in 2010 --- and entering a visit from Kentucky, they had a solid, 18-7 record.

Yet despite all that, the best way to describe the fan's interest in the team during that 2009-2010 season would have been best described as "indifferent." The Bulldogs had routinely drawn around 5,000 people to games earlier that season. For their SEC opener, they had just 7,200.

Of course when Kentucky arrived, it was a different story altogether. A record crowd was expected at Humphrey Coliseum when the Wildcats came to town. As Newton alluded to, fans camped outside the arena before a showdown with the No. 2 ranked team in the country. Oh, and there was one more way that Kentucky knew this game was big.

"We got to the arena, and they had all the shirts out," Peevy said. "Most everywhere to this day, they still have some kind of t-shirt giveaway when we go on the road."

Ah yes, the t-shirts. It's the oldest trick in the college basketball play-book, a ploy to let fans know that they are attending a big game and to hopefully give them one unifying feature against the opponent. The hope is also that an arena full of fans all wearing the same shirt will intimidate the opponent.

However, the move clearly didn't rattle one specific Wildcats' opponent.

"DeMarcus is just randomly going around the arena and signing the t-shirts," Peevy said, laughing while remembering that absurd moment in time.

The moment may have been light and loose, but for DeMarcus Cousins, it had been an interesting couple days in the lead-up to the game. That's because as the Wildcats got set to depart for Starkville, something strange happened: DeMarcus Cousins' phone started ringing… and ringing… and ringing some more. As it turned out, someone on Mississippi State's campus had gotten ahold of Cousins' phone number and had passed it all around campus, to the point that it seemed like every single person at Mississippi State had it.

Cousins was already more loathed than any Kentucky player by opposing fans, and the phone number allowed Mississippi State's fans the chance to potentially unleash on Cousins. So they started calling him. And calling, and calling again. The calls came in all shapes and sizes; some were funny, some were mean, and some were outright racist. They began before Kentucky even left campus, and after Cousins turned on his phone after a flight to Starkville, his inbox was essentially full of voicemails.

At first Cousins became enraged by the calls, but then he learned to actually embrace them. As game-time inched closer, Cousins even learned to have a little fun with the whole ordeal.

"He's on the bus, and he's on the phone and we're like, 'Who are you talking to?'" Peevy said. "And he's just answering the phone, and talking to people, and talking to them all. And finally we got him to hang up. But he was just talking to people."

Tensions were high in the lead-up to the game, and they stayed that way as tip-off approached. Again, Mississippi State had a darn good team in 2010 and they took it at the Wildcats early. The two teams traded the lead six times before a TV timeout with just under eight minutes to go.

And it was out of that timeout where things went beyond "chippy" to just plain unforgettable. The Wildcats had possession up 25-21, when John Wall (as he had done so many times that season) took the ball at the top of the key, beat his defender off the dribble, and pulled up for a floater in the lane. This time though, Wall missed the shot, and it was quickly rebounded by Cousins. With two Mississippi State defenders draped on him, Cousins slammed the ball home for a seemingly innocent two point bucket. But then, just as he got set to run back up court, he turned to the student section, and put his hand right up next to his ear.

The message was unmistakable.

"DeMarcus dunked," senior guard Ramon Harris said. "He put his (hand, shaped like a) phone up to his ear and said 'Call me?' And so everybody on the bench did the same thing."

Yup that's right, Cousins had used all those phone calls from Mississippi State fans as fuel, and that exact moment would go down as one of the most unforgettable in Kentucky's season, if not the entire John Calipari era. The game will forever be remembered in Lexington as the "Call Me Game" although what many people have forgotten, is that after DeMarcus Cousins put his hand up to his ear, the "Call Me Game" turned into one of the most competitive games of the season for Kentucky.

The two teams traded blows the rest of the first half, and most of the second half stayed tight as well. At various points it looked like the Bulldogs might hand Kentucky their second loss of the season; just like the South Carolina game, it seemed like every time the Wildcats made a move, Mississippi State had a counter. At different points in the second half, the Bulldogs took leads of 42-40, 47-44 and 49-47. Every time Kentucky gained any momentum, Mississippi State took it right back.

Finally with about 13 minutes left, Kentucky made their move. Cousins (who played one of the best games of his Kentucky career that night in Starkville) went on a personal 5-0 run, and after a Mississippi State bucket, Patrick Patterson hit one of his own. Kentucky had a 58-54 lead, and seemed like they would once again pull away for another close, late win.

Mississippi State had other plans however. They'd seen Kentucky come back on opponents all year and refused to let the Wildcats do the same to them. Instead, they clamped down on 'D,' slowed down the game, and slowly began to chip away at the lead. There was a bucket by guard Barry Stewart. Then, they jammed the ball down low to Varnado who threw down a dunk. He was fouled and hit a free throw, and before anyone knew it, the Bulldogs had gone on a 13-4 run to give them a 67-60 lead with just three minutes to go. Just as quickly as the Wildcats had seized possession, Mississippi State had seized it back. Kentucky was in trouble.

But as John Calipari said earlier in this book (and throughout most of the actual 2009-2010 year) the one thing his team had during the 2009-2010 season was a great will to win. And that will was never more evident than on that February evening against Mississippi State.

Down seven, Kentucky's final run began with a DeAndre Liggins three. Then off a miss, Wall drove the length of the court and hit Eric Bledsoe in stride for a perfectly executed two-on-one fast break. Mississippi State immediately called a timeout to try and stop the bleeding, but even a break in action couldn't slow down the 'Cats. Kentucky got the ball back with just a minute to play and took their time working down the clock. In a final sequence, they swung the ball around the perimeter, where Liggins made a quick final dish to Patterson in the corner. Patterson was wide open, and hit a jumper to tie things up at 67.

Again, Mississippi State called a timeout.

Unfortunately for the Bulldogs, the timeout once again did little to help. Out of the break there were exactly 40 seconds left on the clock and the Bulldogs ran down almost all of the 35 second shot clock. Finally, they put their offense into action, but it was too late. Stewart forced up a three-pointer with just a few seconds left on the shot clock, but it missed the rim completely and fell out of bounds. Kentucky got one last shot, but an attempt by DeAndre Liggins rimmed out. The game was headed to overtime.

In the extra session the two teams traded scores early, before the key sequence came with 1:30 left. The Bulldogs hit a bucket to tie things up at 72, but before they could even blink, John Wall caught the ball on the in-bounds pass and sprinted up court. In just a few quick steps he exploded towards the basket, and as Wall released a quick shot, he was fouled. The ball went in the basket, and Wall made the subsequent free throw to give the Wildcats a 75-72 lead.

It was quintessential John Wall: He had made another play, to essentially seal another win. And then, just when it seemed like Wall had done it all, he somehow topped himself.

Mississippi State got the ball back with the score still 75-72 and had one, last ditch effort to keep the game in reach. For just a brief window it looked like they'd get that much needed bucket, as guard Dee Bost beat his man off the dribble, turned the corner and attacked the basket. He appeared headed in for an uncontested lay-in to cut the Kentucky lead to one, but just as he released the ball, Wall came out of nowhere and pinned it to the basket. After Wall's brilliant defensive play, UK recovered and the Bulldogs would never again be that close.

Final score, Kentucky 81, Mississippi State 75.

After the game, John Calipari was all smiles, and in a season where he never seemed to be content with his team's play (even after wins), well he couldn't help but smile after this one. He also couldn't help but deliver one of the best lines heard at a press conference all season.

"We made plays. We made shots. We made blocks. We did enough to win the game," Calipari said. "And now we're going to get out of here."

It was classic Cal, but as he returned to the locker room, he realized something: His team wasn't ready to leave just yet. They were in the midst of a raucous celebration, one reserved for a young team, coming off an emotional win, in a hostile environment.

The Kentucky support staff had even gone out of their way to treat the team, to a rare, local delicacy for the post-game meal: Popeye's!

"Popeye's Chicken, was the craziest thing that year," DeWayne Peevy said. "If we were somewhere and we got Popeye's Chicken, we could do no better for them. I look at things now, and what we do, but back then it was a big deal. John Wall was always a picky eater, so if we found out they had Popeye's after the game?"

Again, Peevy couldn't help but laugh at the moment all these years later. He also wondered how different things might have turned out, if they had only gotten the team Popeye's Chicken a bit more often.

"If we had told them, 'We're going to have Popeye's in the post-game we might have won a lot more games," he said.

Finally, with their bellies full, and their hearts content the Wildcats made their way back to the bus. The team charter was set to bring them back to Kentucky, but before the flight took off DeMarcus Cousins had some final business to tend to.

"After the game he was (still) answering phone calls," Jon Hood remembered. "The crazy thing was, I don't think he ever changed his phone number. Until he got to the pros, I don't think he ever changed his phone number."

It was typical DeMarcus, and typical Kentucky basketball in 2010.

But as much fun as the Wildcats were having, the season was quickly coming to an end.

THE HIT MAKER

K ENTUCKY'S SEASON WAS rapidly coming to an end, although the players probably didn't fully realize just how quickly things were winding down. They were too busy having fun, too busy busting each other's chops, and too busy being, well, college kids to even notice.

The 2010 Kentucky Wildcats were a very close team, yet over time an extra-special bond had formed between the school's three uber-talented freshmen: John Wall, DeMarcus Cousins and Eric Bledsoe. The trio had known each other to varying degrees from their younger days; Wall and Cousins from the AAU circuit, and Cousins and Bledsoe as old high school rivals in Alabama. But once they got to Kentucky, the three formed a bond that was airtight. And it would last long after they left Lexington.

"We used to call them 'The Three Amigos,'" assistant strength coach Scott Padgett said. "You could not separate John Wall, DeMarcus Cousins and Eric Bledsoe. To be honest with you, other than them playing against each other, they're probably still on the phone with each other all the time (to this day). They're still very tight."

The three became as close as brothers, although as the rest of the Kentucky squad quickly found out, even brothers tend to fight every now and again. 'The Three Amigos' were no exception, with one player in specific taking the brunt of the teasing: DeMarcus Cousins. Cousins wasn't just the biggest player on the team, but had the shortest temper as well.

It made him an easy target for Wall and Bledsoe.

"John and Eric would make fun of DeMarcus," fellow freshman Jon Hood said. "They made fun of the size of his head. DeMarcus has a very small head, so they always said it would fit in a tea cup. They would call him that. They would say 'cup' and he'd get all frustrated."

It was typical kid stuff, but although Cousins' would take it, even he had his breaking point. You know what happens when you pick on the biggest, strongest kid for long enough, right?

"It was like making fun of the bully at recess," Hood said. "They'd make fun of him, and he'd just take it, and take it, and take it. And then he'd start to get mad, and they'd just lay down on their beds and say 'chill, chill, chill, you're huge, calm down.' You tease the big bear until the big bear decides to do something about it. Then you run."

Yes, there was plenty of good-natured ribbing between the three, but as Kentucky's players and coaching staff found out, there was also genuine love and affection. And there was no better example of that, than an incident which popped up toward the end of the regular season.

At that point in the year, Kentucky was far and away the biggest story in college basketball. That was nothing new; Kentucky had been the biggest story in the sport since November, and the media relations staff was used to dealing with it. But in late February of that year, they got a unique request. Even by the insane standard of media requests that the 2010 Wildcats had dealt with all season.

The request was from *Slam Magazine*, one of the most prominent and well-respected basketball-specific magazines in the industry. *Slam* serves as the voice of an entire generation of basketball fans, with most of the magazine's focus on NBA-related stories. They also cover street ball, international hoops and will even occasionally profile an up-and-coming, can't miss high school superstar. But the one area of basketball that *Slam* rarely ever covers is college basketball. That was, until 2010, when the magazine reached out to Kentucky about a potential cover shoot.

The thing was however, that the magazine wasn't so much interested in featuring the whole team. They were interested in putting John Wall on the cover. Wall was the player that just about everyone agreed was the NBA's next great star. He was also the next in line of great John Calipari coached point guards. Derrick Rose was the reigning NBA Rookie of the

Year, and Tyreke Evans was on his way to winning the same award that year. With Wall almost certainly on his way to the NBA, and very likely to NBA superstardom, it made sense to profile him. *Slam* is an NBA-themed magazine, after all.

But what *Slam* hadn't taken the time to consider was that the Wildcats were about much more than *just* John Wall by that point in the season. Kentucky hadn't gotten to the No. 2 ranking based solely on Wall; it was a team effort to not only get to the top, but stay there. It just didn't seem fair to any of Kentucky's administrators to single out Wall for the team's success.

"They had come in and they wanted to do something with John Wall," former Sports Information Director DeWayne Peevy said. "We said we didn't want to divide them (the players) up. We had been a little protective of that, because John had already done the *Sports Illustrated* cover."

Slam Magazine understood, and offered a counter: How about they feature Wall on the cover with John Calipari. Calipari was the common thread between the NBA's present (Rose and Evans) and its future (Wall). It made perfect sense to include Coach Cal on the cover, with his next great NBA superstar.

Slam assumed that compromise would work for Kentucky. The answer they got back surprised them.

"We said 'Well, we really don't want to do it with one player,'" Peevy remembered. "And they said finally, 'We've never put that many players on the cover' and they were willing to add Patrick Patterson and DeMarcus Cousins."

That had to be good, right?

Well not exactly.

As it turned out, the guys felt like there was a fourth star that deserved equal recognition for the team's success. That was Eric Bledsoe. Sure, he didn't have the numbers that the other guys did, and no, he wasn't yet being projected as a top NBA Draft pick either. But Bledsoe's own teammates knew how good he was, and how important his play had been to the success of the team.

Therefore, the players drew a line in the sand: If Eric Bledsoe wasn't on the cover, they weren't going to be either.

"Those three guys refused to do the cover if Eric Bledsoe wasn't included," Peevy said. "So we called *Slam Magazine* and we were ready to turn down the cover. And at the time, that was a big deal for us because they didn't do a lot of college stuff, and they end up deciding to put Eric on it."

Slam did in fact relent, and a few weeks later the magazine arrived in the mail. The headline said it all, calling John Calipari "The Hit Maker" with subtext that said, "He brought you D-Rose and Tyreke. Meet Coach Cal's next NBA Ballers: Patterson, Cousins, Bledsoe and John Wall." The cover has become a bit iconic in Kentucky basketball circles and is still prominently displayed in Kentucky's basketball offices to this day.

But while the cover was just further proof that Kentucky had "arrived," it also provided much deeper symbolism for Peevy. In a season where many in the national media continued to push a narrative that Kentucky's freshman were selfish and egotistical, that one picture showed the exact opposite.

"That was a big moment for us," Peevy said. "Because I felt like 'this isn't fake.' There really is a bond. They really are willing to sacrifice for each other."

＊　＊　＊

The season may have been coming to an end, but plenty of tough games remained for the 'Cats. Now into the second half of their conference schedule, Kentucky would face many teams for the second time. And after handing losses to virtually all of them the first time around, just about everyone was looking for revenge.

The revenge tour started on a Saturday evening at Vanderbilt. By that point in the season, the Commodores had entrenched themselves as a Top 20 club, and had played Kentucky tough the first time around (remember, that was the game LeBron James visited Lexington). Vanderbilt also owned one of the most unique home-court advantages in the sport: The Commodores played at the famed Memorial Gym, an arena where the two team's benches are behind the baskets, not on the sidelines. That one feature has become a huge advantage for Vanderbilt through the years, and has left a number of opponents flustered and out of sync. It's an especially big disadvantage for young teams who've never played there before, like most of John Calipari's squad in 2010.

Therefore, it's no coincidence that the night Kentucky played at Vanderbilt also doubled as one of their sloppiest (yet also most competitive) games of the season. The Wildcats couldn't get anything going offensively, but thankfully supplemented it by playing spectacular defense. That defense is what allowed them to stay in the game, and what proved to be the difference in the final few minutes.

The two teams entered the final minute of the game with the score knotted up at 54. Out of a timeout, John Wall put in a quick put-back layup to take a two point lead, and after a stop defensively, the Commodores had no choice but to foul. Wall hit two more free throws on the next possession, giving the Wildcats a 58-54 lead which seemingly put the game away with just 22 seconds to go.

But then, just when it seemed like Kentucky would eek out another victory, all hell broke loose.

On the next possession, Vandy sharpshooter John Jenkins hit a corner three to cut the Kentucky lead to one, and the Commodores fouled Eric Bledsoe, who proceeded to go to the line and miss his first foul shot. Following a Vanderbilt timeout, Bledsoe went back to the line, but missed his second foul shot as well. When the Commodores grabbed the rebound, it gave them a chance to take the lead after being down by four just seconds earlier.

Vanderbilt rushed the ball up court, and got it into the hands of Jenkins, the same player who'd just hit the three-pointer to cut the lead to one. He gave a quick pump fake, before rising for what could be the go-ahead bucket.

But Jenkins hadn't considered one thing: His defender was John Wall.

Wall didn't bite on his pump fake, and was one of the few players in the country with the quick-twitch reflexes and leaping ability to react the second that Jenkins went up with the jump shot. Wall wasn't fooled, and rose at the same time Jenkins did, getting a clean block on the shot attempt. He came down with the ball, and was immediately fouled. Wall grabbed the ball and sprinted to the other end line. He placed the ball on the baseline, unable to control his excitement. Again, it looked like the Wildcats had sealed the win.

That excitement was short lived though, as Wall missed the first free throw. He hit the second one, but Kentucky had left the door cracked open just a bit for Vanderbilt to steal a victory. The Wildcats were up by two (instead of three, or potentially more had Bledsoe hit his free throws) and the Commodores had one final chance to send the game to overtime, or even potentially win it. They threw the inbounds pass the length of the court, and somehow it fell right into the hands of center A.J. Ogilvy. He took a few dribbles towards the hoop and with just seconds on the clock released a floater that could've potentially tied the game. But it fell just short, as the Wildcats had somehow won another nail-biter.

It was another thrilling win, and after the game all the talk was about Wall's big defensive play. A few days later, it was still the buzz of Lexington with one special visitor even weighing in.

That visitor was NBA legend Magic Johnson.

Johnson was in Kentucky for a political event just a few days after the Vanderbilt win, and decided to stop by Rupp Arena for the Wildcats' next game, which was against South Carolina.

When he was asked prior to tip-off how much he knew about Wall, well, Magic began gushing.

"Let me just say to all the Wildcat fans," Johnson began. "This is probably the best guard we have seen in five or six years to come into college basketball. The thing that I am most impressed with (in) John is his ability to know how to win the game. Let's take last Saturday at Vanderbilt. The big play was when he stole it, got out front and got the layup. The next big play was of course when he got the blocked shot. Just before that, the same player had just hit a big three, the Vanderbilt player. He had a nice pump fake and got John up (off his feet). This time he stayed down, waited, waited and went up the same time as the shooter went up."

It was spot-on analysis by Magic. But he wasn't done praising Wall.

"I have seen this happen over and over again," Johnson said. "When the game is tight for Kentucky, he always comes up with the key play, whether it is on defense and then on offense. He is poised, he is very confident in his ability and he is a great leader among these young players that they have here."

Johnson stuck around to see Wall that night, but the Wildcats needed no additional motivation when they hosted South Carolina. Kentucky was focused and ready to take on the Gamecocks, the only team which had beaten them to that point in the season.

Boy, were things different the second time the two clubs met.

In their first matchup, Kentucky fell down early and never could make up the ground against the Gamecocks. In their rematch, Kentucky jumped out to a 37-26 halftime lead and never looked back. In the first game Kentucky struggled offensively, shooting just 38 percent from the field. In their second game they shot 50 percent, led by a season-high 23 points from Patrick Patterson. In their first game, they let Devan Downey go wild; he torched the Wildcats for 30 points in the Gamecocks' win. In the second game Downey still got buckets (26 points), but Kentucky's defense also forced him into five turnovers.

Most importantly, in the first game, Kentucky suffered its only loss of the season. In their second game, they pulled away for a comfortable 82-61 win. The win was the Wildcats' eighth straight since their only loss of the season.

But the good times wouldn't last. Not with a tough game against Tennessee looming.

As you may remember, the Vols were really good during the 2010 season. When the Wildcats visited Knoxville for their final game in the month of February, Tennessee was ranked No. 12 in the country, and at that point in the season were also the only team in college basketball who'd defeated top ranked Kansas (the Jayhawks were probably the only team in the country that season that the experts liked more than Kentucky to win it all). In addition to raw talent, the Volunteers were well-coached under Bruce Pearl, and definitely had a home-court advantage when they hosted the Wildcats. Kentucky was visiting Knoxville for a mid-afternoon, nationally televised game on CBS. There was no doubt that Thompson-Boling Arena would be rocking.

Basically, Kentucky was walking into a snake pit. And they got bit early.

For Kentucky, it didn't start poorly; UK actually jumped out to a quick 4-0 lead. But in a season where the Wildcats were used to exerting their will, and used to big offensive bursts to blow games wide open, it was Tennessee who blitzed Kentucky with the same. After falling down by four, the Vols went on a shocking 18-0 run that left the Wildcats reeling, and left Knoxville rocking. Thompson-Boling Arena was nearly inaudible by the time Kentucky stopped the bleeding, but by then, the Wildcats were down double-digits. Tennessee went on another run out of halftime and took a commanding 54-35 lead with just 14 minutes to go in the second half.

The 19-point deficit was by far the biggest Kentucky had faced all year, and no one would've blamed them if they had packed things in and let the Vols pull away. The problem was that "giving up" just wasn't in the Wildcats' nature that season.

The rally began when Eric Bledsoe hit a quick bucket. Then John Wall got one of his own, and another, and another. Wall scored seven straight, and all of a sudden that 19-point deficit was cut to 10. A TV timeout came next, but it didn't slow down the 'Cats. The two teams traded baskets before a pair of DeMarcus Cousins free throws cut the Tennessee lead to eight. Sensing his team was losing control, Pearl called a timeout. It temporarily held the Wildcats at bay, and at the four-minute mark, Tennessee still held a comfortable 65-59 lead.

But again, the Wildcats wouldn't be denied. Out of the under four minute TV timeout, the Wildcats made one final run. DeMarcus Cousins scored six straight points, and all of a sudden, a 19-point lead had somehow been whittled down to zero. The Wildcats incredible will to win was again on display, and it seemed like they would once again figure out a way to pull off a wild victory.

On this day though, the Volunteers' will to win was just as great as Kentucky's. And Tennessee had an answer.

After the Wildcats tied things up, the Vols got the ball back. Tennessee --- which wasn't a high-scoring team that season --- calmly moved the ball around the perimeter, as the shot clock ticked down. Then, with just a few seconds left, guard Scotty Hopson made his move. He drove down the lane, and dished it to forward J.P. Prince. Prince made a quick, up-and-under move around the basket, to give Tennessee a two point edge. After a Wildcats' turnover, Tennessee got the ball back and again got it into Hopson's hands as the clock wound down. But this time, instead of driving the lane Hopson decided to pull up. He hit a three-pointer as the shot clock expired and Thompson-Boling Arena exploded. The two buckets had given Tennessee a 70-65 lead, and they would eventually score the final nine points of the game.

Final score: Tennessee 74, Kentucky 65.

For just the second time that season, Kentucky left the arena with a loss. But this one felt different. When the Wildcats' fell to South Carolina it was a bit fluky, and came on a day where the opponent could do nothing wrong, and where the Wildcats were understandably distracted. They had just spoken to the President, after all.

But against Tennessee, real concerns popped up. The Wildcats shot just 35 percent as a team, and for the fourth straight game were terrible from beyond the three-point arc. They went 2 for 22 from downtown against the Vols, and had shot just 12 of 73 over the previous four games.

Most of Lexington was nervous about the recent trend, especially as the team inched closer to the NCAA Tournament. But while concern was rampant, John Calipari remained calm. He had been a head coach for over two decades, and had seen the peaks and valleys that come with a college basketball season before.

When he was asked about the team's shooting woes prior to the team's next game against Georgia, Cal exuded confidence.

"I'm comfortable with Darius (Miller), Darnell (Dodson), John Wall, Eric Bledsoe, DeAndre Liggins," Calipari said prior to the Georgia game. "You're talking about guys who over the season have shot the ball as well as anybody in the country. They hit a spell where they don't shoot it well. I've done this so long it doesn't faze me. Now, if they're buying into what everybody is saying, it might faze them."

Nothing fazed Kentucky when they did in fact take the court to face the Bulldogs. Sure, the Wildcats were playing on the road, and sure they were coming off a loss. But with the calendar turned toward March, the intensity across the team picked up. Especially when Calipari mentioned that the club could clinch a share of the SEC regular season title with a win.

It was all the players needed to hear. They jumped out to an early lead, and capitalized on 14 Georgia turnovers. John Wall led the way with 24 points, Patrick Patterson added 17, and as a team, the Wildcats hit eight of 24 three-pointers.

It wasn't necessarily Kentucky's best effort, but it was an important win none the less. The team got back on track, got back in the win column and had shot better from beyond the arc than they had in weeks. Most importantly they had clinched a share of the SEC title, their 44th in school history.

In their first game in March, Kentucky had passed with flying colors.

But just as the team celebrated their first win in March, they also had to begin preparations for their final game at Rupp Arena.

Incredibly, after roughly 10 months and 30 games together, it was time for Senior Day.

* * *

As discussed earlier in the book, "Senior Day" is a sacred tradition at all schools across college basketball, but nowhere is it more celebrated than at Kentucky. But even as important as "Senior Day" always is in Lexington, it held even greater importance in 2010. It's hard to imagine any seniors, in any year in UK hoops' history, had been through more than the four players who were honored in the Wildcats' final home game on March 7th, 2010 against the Florida Gators.

For starters, there were the four players themselves, four guys who all had slightly different experiences during their time in Lexington, but who would forever share a common bond. There was Mark Krebs Jr., the three-year walk-on, who had been awarded a scholarship by John Calipari in the fall of his senior year. There was Ramon Harris, who enrolled mid-way through freshman season, but had seen more in three-and-a-half years on campus than most players see in a full four years at any other school. There was Perry Stevenson, the only four-year scholarship player in the group. And there was Patrick Patterson. Sure, he was only technically a "junior." But when Patterson elected to return to Kentucky the previous spring, he had vowed to finish his degree in three years. With just a few credits left, Patterson was on course to graduate that spring. Therefore, there would be no fourth year left for Patterson. This would be his final game at Rupp Arena.

Before the game, the four were honored at center court, in a tradition familiar to college basketball fans all across the country. They each stood with their families and were given framed jerseys, as their names were called one final time at Rupp Arena, before "My Old Kentucky Home" was played over the loudspeakers. Over 24,000 adoring fans serenaded them with applause. But while the scene is familiar to college basketball fans, this specific Senior Day was much different than any other in Kentucky history. The road the four had taken to get here was unlike anyone else's in program history.

Remember, Krebs, Harris and Stevenson all had been through two different coaching changes, and three different coaching regimes during their four years at the school. It was something unheard of, even in the modern, high-stakes world of college basketball, but none forgot their humble beginnings. In a pre-game press conference each player thanked

Tubby Smith for bringing them to Kentucky, and allowing them to play for Big Blue Nation.

Patterson hadn't played under Smith, but his path wasn't much different than the other three. He had been through two tumultuous years under Billy Gillispie, and could have easily chosen to leave when Calipari was named head coach the previous spring. No one would've blamed him, especially when it became clear that he wouldn't be the focal point of the team when Calipari brought in his class of super-recruits.

But Patterson stayed, and like the three other seniors, he had thrived in his final year at the school. After a couple years experiencing the worst that college basketball had to offer, the four got to experience what it was like to be one of the best teams in the country, at one of the sport's most historically powerful programs. No one was talking about missed NCAA Tournament's anymore. Instead, they were talking about a potential run at a Final Four.

This group of four had been part of the revival of Kentucky basketball.

"Senior Day for me was extra special," Krebs said. "I felt like I was part of its (Kentucky basketball's) downfall, I felt like I was part of the worst part in Kentucky (history). At least now, I felt like I had some hand --- even if it was a small hand --- I felt like I had some hand in the rebuilding, or at least the first year of what could be a really epic run. I felt like Kentucky basketball was back. That was neat."

Krebs continued.

"If I had been through Senior Day when Coach Gillispie was there, I certainly still would've been sad that it was my last game at Rupp, and I would've been sad that my career was coming to an end," he said. "But to know that we had so much fun my senior year, that made it extra difficult to say good-bye to Rupp Arena."

The moment was special for all four seniors, but for Krebs it carried extra significance. Senior Day allowed him to spend a little extra time with his mom Terri, who had been battling breast cancer since his freshman year in high school.

Krebs chronicled his mom's battle in his own book, "Beyond a Dream" which was released shortly after his senior season. But during the season itself, he mostly kept his mother's condition a secret.

"I was never open when I was at Kentucky, I was never open about my mom," he said. "I didn't want anything to make it seem like I was getting ahead (because of her illness)... I never talked about my mom. It wasn't until they saw my mom in a wheelchair; I think it was John Wall who asked 'What happened to your mom? Is she ok?' And I explained, 'Well, she's sick, she has this going on.'"

From that point on, the entire Kentucky basketball program embraced Terri Krebs as if she were their mother.

"It wasn't until I was actually asked a question and answered it that the guys really, they'd stop and give her a hug every time they saw her," Krebs said. "She loved the guys like sons. There was a real bond through my senior year."

And when the Wildcats took the court on Senior Day, Krebs was in for one final surprise. For the first time in his career he was in the Wildcats' starting lineup, joined by fellow seniors Harris and Stevenson, as well as Patterson and Wall. After a slow start, Kentucky used a 14-0 run to open things in the first half, highlighted by a nifty up-and-under banked in layup by Eric Bledsoe. The Wildcats sputtered a bit early in the second half, but did enough to pull away late. Darius Miller and DeMarcus Cousins each had 14 points for the Wildcats and five Kentucky players total scored in double figures. The Wildcats won 74-66 and had clinched the SEC title outright. Kentucky's 18-0 home record was tied for the best in program history.

Following the game the emotions continued to pour out. Both Calipari and several players discussed the touching embrace of the Krebs family, and Calipari made sure to re-emphasize the role that all the seniors had played that season.

For Kentucky hoops, it was both a happy and sad moment.

But while all the focus was on the seniors (as it should have been), another player stood quietly in the corner, holding back his emotions. He too had played his final game in Rupp Arena. And he was having a tough time accepting it.

"I remember doing a TV interview with John Wall after our last home game against Florida, and him looking up at the rafters and tearing up," DeWayne Peevy said. "I asked him 'you alright?' And he was like 'I'm gonna miss this place."

It took Peevy a second to figure out what Wall was saying.

"And that was the first time I realized that he wasn't ever going to play in Rupp again."

It Was Like a UK Party, Everywhere You Went

THE REGULAR SEASON was over, and the postseason was about to begin for the 'Cats. But before it did, there was some business to tend to. More specifically, there was some hardware to hand out. Not surprisingly, several Kentucky players were up for awards both within the conference and nationally, making it a busy couple days in Lexington.

It all started just days after the regular season ended, when Yahoo Sports named John Wall its National Player of the Year. The timing was a bit different (most outlets elect to wait closer to the end of the postseason to hand out their Player of the Year awards) but the accolade was not. When asked about Wall being named National Player of the Year, John Calipari was blunt.

"Good," he told reporters. "He deserves it."

Next were the SEC's conference awards, and it was near a clean sweep for the Wildcats. John Wall and DeMarcus Cousins were unanimous first team All-SEC selections, while junior Patrick Patterson joined them on the first team. Patterson was also named to the All-SEC Defensive team, with Wall, Cousins and Eric Bledsoe all being honored on the All-SEC Freshman team. DeMarcus Cousins was named the conference's Freshman of the Year, while John Wall took home the league's Player of the Year.

(For those wondering how Wall could be named the league's top player, but not the top freshman, well, the answer is actually pretty simple: John Calipari had to submit "nominees" for each award to the SEC offices and chose to "only" put Wall up for consideration for Player of the Year, not Freshman of the Year. Therefore, if you're going to blame anyone for the snub, blame John Calipari.)

Speaking of Calipari, if there was one notable exception from the end of season SEC awards, it was recognition for him. In a move that has become a bit of an early-spring tradition in Lexington, John Calipari was overlooked for SEC Coach of the Year. The league instead gave the award to Vanderbilt's Kevin Stallings.

Still, it was a good week overall for the Wildcats, and it only got better as the team descended upon Nashville for the SEC Tournament. As usual, there were a lot of Kentucky fans in town for the tournament; many view the trip as a vacation, an easily-drivable getaway to watch their favorite team. And for others, it's quite possibly the only chance all season they'll get to watch their team in person. Tickets to Rupp Arena aren't easy to come by, after all.

Yet even by Kentucky's own insane standards of fan turnout at the SEC Tournament, the 2010 showing was astronomical. It had been a long time since the Wildcats had such a dynamic team, or had entered the conference tournament as such heavy favorites. Therefore it seemed as though every Kentucky fan on the planet wanted to be in Nashville to experience it all. By the end of the weekend some projections said the Wildcats had brought close to *a couple hundred thousand fans* with them. Even though Bridgestone Arena (where the games would be played) didn't even hold 20,000 people.

It also caused an interesting dynamic between Kentucky's players and its coach. In the lead-up to the Wildcats' SEC Tourney opener, John Calipari had said he didn't like playing in conference tournaments. The risk involved simply outweighed the reward.

Yet by the time the team arrived in Nashville, Calipari had changed his tune. Even he realized just how important this week was to his fan base.

"Calipari had said, 'I don't like the SEC Tournament, I hate conference tournaments, I wish we didn't have to play them,'" Kentucky Sports Radio's

Matt Jones remembered. "Then he goes down there, and Nashville has like (all) Kentucky fans."

Clearly, the tournament meant a lot to the fans, but don't underestimate how much it meant to the players as well. The veterans were well aware of Kentucky's historical success at the SEC Tournament, and the team's disappointing performance in previous years. Despite Kentucky owning an SEC record 25 conference tournament championships, they hadn't won a single one since 2004. It was a streak the veterans wanted to end. And the freshmen wanted to help them do it.

"The players wanted it," team manager Chad Sanders remembered. "I don't think Cal made a big deal about it, but I think the players wanted it for the older guys. The younger guys they wanted to prove --- Kentucky hadn't won an SEC title in a while --- they wanted to prove Kentucky was back on top. This was the chance to come back and say 'This is our conference, we got this.'"

That was the statement Kentucky wanted to make, but in their SEC Tournament opener they made a different statement altogether: That they weren't ready for the rigors of the postseason. To put it simply, Kentucky came out flat for a mid-afternoon matchup with Alabama. They fell down to the Crimson Tide 35-30 at halftime and even after taking a lead six minutes into the second half, never could pull away. The Wildcats held on to win by a final score of 73-67. But it wasn't pretty. And John Calipari wasn't happy.

If this was Kentucky's first big test in March, they had failed.

"I'm trying to convince this young team of 19-year-olds that either you want it more than they do, or they want it more than you do," a livid Calipari told reporters following the narrow win.

Calipari --- who was seen on TV repeatedly arguing and pleading with his team throughout a frustrating 40 minutes --- couldn't believe the lack of urgency his club had played with. The Wildcats may have picked up their 30th win of the season that afternoon, but they had once again played down to their opponent, and allowed an inferior team to hang with them.

All season long the Wildcats had been able to flip a switch whenever they wanted to, but Calipari realized it wouldn't always be that way. And he was mortified to know that his players didn't have the same understanding.

"I mean you think you've cracked it, and they've understood," Calipari said. "Then they come out the next game, and you know, 'well, he pushed me, and I tried.' He tried harder. You've got to try harder. All those kinds of things are what we're dealing with right now."

Calipari clearly wasn't happy with his team's effort on Friday. But by the time the semifinals rolled around on Saturday, motivation wouldn't be an issue at all.

The opponent that day was the Tennessee Volunteers, one of the two teams which had beaten the Wildcats that season. But for Kentucky it was more than just the loss to the Vols which motivated them. Understand that Tennessee hadn't only defeated them. They'd mocked the Wildcats in the process. Following the win in Knoxville, Tennessee guard Scotty Hopson had been caught by TV cameras doing the "John Wall Dance" at center court. It was a clear dig at the Wildcats, and clearly an attempt to tell the media 'Oh, you want to give them all your attention? Well we'll show them, and we'll show you too.'

In a certain way it was understandable, the mark of a team trying to earn attention that hadn't been given to them. Of course for Tennessee, there was one big problem: The media weren't the only ones who had seen the celebration. Kentucky's players had too. And when the Wildcats got matched up with the Vols at the SEC Tournament, they were ready to take out their frustrations.

During pregame warm-ups DeMarcus Cousins went out of his way to track down Tennessee starters Scotty Hopson and Brian Williams. He stopped them in layup lines, and let them know exactly what was coming when the game tipped off.

"You have to understand DeMarcus his jokes, and him talking trash," Jon Hood said, explaining Cousins' unique form of smack talk. "But he looked at Brian Williams and Scotty Hopson in lay-up lines and was like 'You know we're up 25 right now.'"

It was a bit of a strange thing to say, but Cousins' point was clear: He was telling Tennessee's players that the Wildcats were so fired up, that it was almost as if they had been given a 25 point head start to begin the game.

But to Tennessee's players, well, they weren't really sure what to make of the comments.

"They looked at him and said 'What are you talking about?'" Hood remembered. "They didn't know what he was talking about. And I was behind him just cracking up."

Kentucky clearly had a mental edge going into the game, to go along with a sheer talent edge as well. And although they didn't need any other advantages, they got one anyway from their fans. As the calendar had turned from Friday to Saturday, even more Kentucky fans had flooded into Nashville for the remainder of the weekend. And they had not only come to town, but gobbled up tickets from fans whose teams had already lost.

After seeing the Kentucky turnout Friday against Alabama, Tennessee guard Bobby Maze had told reporters that Wildcats "travel like the Million Man March." By Saturday, it really did seem like Kentucky had a million fans in the building, even though the game was being played just a couple hours from the Volunteers' campus.

"I knew it was a different level when we played Tennessee, in Nashville, and 90 percent of the people there were in Kentucky blue," DeWayne Peevy said. "And they weren't there all week. Whoever was losing was selling them the tickets, because they (Kentucky fans) couldn't have had that many tickets."

By tip-off there was a sea of blue in Bridgestone Arena, and the Wildcats fed off that emotion. An early John Wall steal and dunk got the crowd fired up, and it seemed like the Wildcats didn't let up throughout the first half. Every loose ball seemed to end up in Kentucky's hands, every 50-50 play turned up in favor of the Wildcats. Just a day after Calipari had complained about his team's energy, Kentucky was full of life. They led 32-19 at the break, with those 19 points marking Tennessee's lowest first half output of the season.

And after the halftime break, the Wildcats' energy level seemed to rise even higher.

It started just a few minutes into the second half, when DeMarcus Cousins backed up his pregame smack talk with one of the most aggressive blocks you'll ever see. After guard Cameron Tatum beat his man off the dribble on the baseline, the sophomore attacked the basket, and when he saw John Wall closing in on him, decided to dip under the basket to attempt a reverse layup attempt. But as he leapt, Tatum didn't see Cousins coming from the other side. Well, Big Cuz was there, and when the Tennessee guard released the ball, Cousins pinned it so hard against the basket it appeared as though the glass would break. Kentucky grabbed the loose ball, and eventually on the other end got it back to Cousins. He flushed it home for a one-handed slam, completing one of the most aggressive back-and-forth plays anyone had seen all season.

Bridgestone Arena went crazy. At least until a few moments later when Cousins followed it up with an even more spectacular play.

This time it was Tennessee forward J.P. Prince who appeared to have an uncontested dunk at the rim. Cousins again stepped in, but it didn't stop Prince from jumping right at him. He leapt and so did Cousins, and with his big right hand, Cousins smacked all leather, right in mid-air as Prince went to jam it home. The Tennessee forward tumbled to the ground, as the whistle blew. The referee had called a foul, because, well, it had to be a foul right? The play had been so violent and Prince had landed so hard, that everyone in the arena assumed it had to be worthy of a whistle. Only replays confirmed it wasn't a foul, and that Cousins got all ball.

The crowd booed, but the truth was Kentucky was in the best position possible. Even with the foul call, the Wildcats had sent their message for the afternoon. And that message was: Don't mess with us.

Then, just when things couldn't seem to get any better for the Wildcats, it did. With the Wildcats up 45-39 and nine minutes to play, Kentucky got hot on offense, going on a blistering 13-2 run, highlighted by eight straight points from Darnell Dodson. As soon as Tennessee stopped that run, the Wildcats went on another, scoring 14 straight points as Bridgestone Arena just about exploded. Kentucky went on to win the game 74-45, outscoring the Vols by a staggering 29-6 margin over the final 11 minutes. And as it turned out, Cousins was right: Kentucky could have spotted Tennessee a 25-point lead and still won.

It was arguably the Wildcats' most dominant win of the season. And even Tennessee coach Bruce Pearl was impressed.

"We got outplayed at every position," Pearl said to reporters following the game. "Kentucky's the No. 2 team in the country for a reason. They're a really, really good team."

Calipari wasn't ready to heap too much praise on his squad, but after such a lackluster win over Alabama, even he was happy with the output against Tennessee. He also was amazed by the support the team had received in Bridgestone Arena that day. He had been at Kentucky for a while at that point. But he was still in awe over just how rabid his fan base really was.

"They tell me 180,000 fans came to Nashville," Calipari said. "Is that true? Kentucky fans? And only 17,000 could get in the building? It's unbelievable. The blue dust is everywhere. It's incredible."

Finally, it was time to prepare for the SEC Tournament championship game. And when Kentucky got there, they'd face a familiar foe: The Mississippi State Bulldogs.

As Kentucky fans undoubtedly remember, the Bulldogs were a good team during that 2010 season, and had played the Wildcats tough in the famed "Call Me Game" a few weeks earlier in Starkville. To their credit Mississippi State was playing some of their most inspired basketball of the season entering that SEC title game. They had beaten Vanderbilt by double-digits just a day earlier, and had the extra motivation with a potential NCAA Tournament berth on the line when they faced Kentucky.

The Bulldogs were clearly on the bubble, and the only way they could guarantee a spot in the Big Dance was with a win over the Wildcats. A loss would leave them sweating on Selection Sunday.

Calipari knew the Bulldogs would be ready to go, but his bigger concern was his own team. Coming off that emotional win over Tennessee, the Wildcats were due for a letdown, especially since many believed the victory had clinched the team a No. 1 seed in the upcoming NCAA Tournament as well. So if they had a No. 1 seed locked up (like every expert on TV was saying), what exactly did they have to play for against Mississippi State?

Well, Calipari had the answer. And he let his players in on it, in an emotional pregame speech.

"I remember Coach Cal coming in and saying 'There are 50 or 100,000 Kentucky fans that travel down here,'" Mark Krebs said. "'This is their vacation, they want to see a victory, they want to see a championship. We're here, why don't we win it all? Why play a game thinking it doesn't matter if you win or lose? Every game matters.'"

The speech hit home. At least for Krebs.

"I remember hearing his speech," Krebs said. "I'm a person who has a good understanding of sports, and how you should never take a game for granted. You never know what happens that night, or in the selection committee process. You just never know. Every game should matter, but with the season we had, we knew we were going to be a No. 1 seed or close to it. Where we were going to play at was pre-destined, or it felt like it. I don't know if that's the case, but it felt like it. But after that speech we went out there and put our hearts into that game."

Following Calipari's speech, Kentucky came out fired up for the title game. But the thing was, Mississippi State was fired up too. In a lot of ways, the beginning stages of the SEC title game played out a lot like the first matchup between the two teams a month earlier; neither squad could get much of an edge. In total, there were five ties in the first half, and eight lead changes. When Mississippi State went into halftime up four points, it tied the largest margin for either team the entire game.

But as they had all season long, Kentucky made a run shortly after half-time. Eric Bledsoe made a three-pointer to open the half and DeMarcus Cousins scored four straight of his own. Before anyone could blink, the Wildcats had gone on an 11-3 run, and led 42-38 just minutes into the second half.

To Mississippi State's credit however, they continued to battle. Following the Wildcats' spurt, the Bulldogs had one of their own. Dee Bost hit a three, and then the Bulldogs forced the ball into their star Jarvis Varnardo in the post, where he scored six straight. Mississippi State regained the lead just minutes after losing it, and for most of the second half they maintained it. When the Bulldogs' Ravern Johnson hit a three to put Mississippi State up five with just over a minute to go, it looked like they might have done enough to knock off Kentucky.

Still, Kentucky continued to battle. Patrick Patterson hit a two-point bucket, and after Mississippi State bricked a pair of free throws and turned the ball over on the next two possessions, the Wildcats were able to cut the lead to one on a John Wall jumper. Mississippi State once again missed another free throw, but after Kentucky got the ball back with under 30 seconds to go, they were unable to take advantage. When Wall missed a jumper and the Bulldogs got the rebound, Kentucky had no choice but to foul. This time, Mississippi State wouldn't struggle at the line; Barry Stewart hit a pair of foul shots, to give Mississippi State a three point lead with just eight seconds to go.

The win seemed in hand for the Bulldogs. All they had to do was make sure to not do anything stupid (like fouling a three-point shooter), and make sure Kentucky didn't pull off a miracle. If they did that, Mississippi State would be the SEC Tournament champions.

The problem of course, was that Kentucky pulled off a miracle. After Stewart hit those two free throws to take a three point lead, Calipari immediately called a timeout. And whether Mississippi State realized it or not, that's when it all began to unravel.

Up three, Bulldogs' coach Rick Stansbury was left with a choice that has plagued basketball coaches for years: Should he foul Kentucky to make sure they didn't get a three-point shot attempt off which could potentially tie the game? Or should he let them dribble up court, and hope that if the Wildcats did attempt a three, it wouldn't go in?

Stansbury chose the first option, and had Stewart foul Eric Bledsoe with about five seconds left on the clock. On paper, the move made sense. Bledsoe had only made one of four foul shots to that point. It was hardly a guarantee that Bledsoe would even make the first foul shot to extend the game.

Well, to his credit, Bledsoe executed the first part flawlessly. He sunk the first free throw, to cut the Mississippi State lead to just two.

Now came the tough part for Bledsoe: He had to miss the second one on purpose, and hope that somehow the Wildcats would be able to secure the rebound. Even if they did, Kentucky would have to get a shot off, and pray it went in. A two-pointer would tie the game. A miracle three would win it.

Simply put, a lot had to go right for Kentucky.

And as it turns out, it did.

Bledsoe got the ball back and lined up for a free throw, but instead of taking a traditional shot, he instead tossed the ball high in the air. It hit off the back of the rim, and then, as if it were a scene right out of a bad sports movie, ricocheted off Patterson's fingertips and right into the hands of Wall. Wall --- who caught the ball as if it was what he had been expecting the whole time --- gave a quick pump fake before stepping back and attempting a three-pointer to win the game. Wall's attempt missed, but somehow it landed just in the reach of DeMarcus Cousins. From a funky angle, Cousins threw a shot off the backboard.

It hit the backboard, and fell through the net as the clock expired.

Somehow, the Wildcats had gotten their miracle. The most improbable play in all of basketball had worked.

"Since I was a kid, in second or third grade, my dad was a high school basketball coach," Mark Krebs explained. "So he always tried the 'off-the-back of the basket, miss a free throw on purpose to try to get extra points' and it never worked! The one time it worked in my entire life was in the SEC Tournament."

The play led to sheer pandemonium. The second that the ball rolled through the basket, Bridgestone Arena erupted, and ABC broadcaster Brad Nessler screamed "It's good! It's good! It's good!" all while Cousins sprinted to the other end of the floor in sheer excitement. His teammates sprinted after him, and when they caught up, John Wall tackled Kentucky's hero to the ground. The celebration was everywhere, as the game was now headed to overtime.

Although to be honest, not everyone was aware of that.

"I think a lot of us thought it was a winner," senior guard Ramon Harris admitted. "Me included."

The excitement permeated through the arena, as players and fans alike celebrated a moment that was way too good to ever be scripted.

But as the celebration continued… and continued… and continued, the excitement turned to concern on the Kentucky bench. Somebody was going to get hurt at the bottom of the pile!

"My job then was substitutions," team manager Chad Sanders said. "I followed substitution patterns for the other team, and I held the clipboard for Cal going into timeouts. Well, DeMarcus hits his shot and everyone's celebrating, and I'm trying to hand Cal his board and trying to watch the other side for substitutions. And I remember Coach Antigua grabbing the guys like 'We've still got to play!"

Antigua didn't disagree.

"I remember two things out of that game," Antigua said. "One, the resolve and the will to win. And two, the fact that I didn't want anybody to get hurt in that damn celebration. We still had overtime! These guys are celebrating and I'm like 'Man, we've got overtime!'"

Once things did settle down and the game moved into overtime, the Wildcats simply overpowered the Bulldogs. John Wall scored seven points in the extra session, including a three which gave Kentucky a five-point lead with about a minute to go. It was more than enough, as a Mississippi State three-pointer with just a second left made the game appear to be closer than it actually was. It was too little, too late for the Bulldogs, as the Wildcats won 75-74 in overtime.

For the first time since 2004, Kentucky was the SEC Tournament champs.

The celebration began for the Wildcats as soon as the final horn sounded. Kentucky's players jumped around at midcourt, and eventually, the festivities moved into the locker room, where the party kept going.

And going.

And going.

"I remember celebrating in the locker room after that Mississippi State game," Sanders said. "The players took a lot of pride in winning that SEC Championship. The players really, really wanted it."

It was a magical moment in time, one of the rare instances the entire season where the pressure was completely off Kentucky. Nobody was talking about NCAA Tournament seeding, potential draft position or whether a run at the Final Four was attainable. Nobody wanted an autograph, and for a few minutes, no media member was demanding an interview or sound bite from one of the players.

Nope, for just a brief moment, Kentucky's players were allowed to be themselves, amongst themselves. No one from the outside was questioning their motives, calling them selfish, or accusing them of only being at Kentucky because NBA rules forced them to be. For that one moment, they were simply kids. Kids who loved basketball. And loved each other.

It's a moment that several players still cherish to this day.

"They have that picture in the practice facility," Ramon Harris said. "Every time I go back I look at that like 'memories.'"

Speaking of memories, Kentucky's players aren't the only ones who have plenty of memories from that week. The fans do too. They had spent the previous few days celebrating in style. Celebrating an SEC championship. And celebrating their return to the top of the conference.

"Nashville those few days was about as fun a time as it could be to be a Kentucky fan," Kentucky Sports Radio's Matt Jones said.

"It was just like a UK party, everywhere you went."

THE BIG DANCE BEGINS

THE KENTUCKY WILDCATS were SEC champs. But while their fans partied long into the night Sunday in Nashville, the team itself took a quick flight home to Lexington. The NCAA Tournament Selection Show started at 6 p.m. ET. And no one wanted to miss it.

As they had done several times that season, the team gathered at John Calipari's house and got comfortable as the Selection Show began. Just minutes in, Wildcats' players and coaches saw "Kentucky" flash across the screen as a No. 1 seed. No one was surprised by the news; a No. 1 seed had been expected for weeks and was all but clinched with the SEC Tournament semifinal win over Tennessee. After seeing their school on the TV, the players calmly clapped, acting like they had been there before. The truth of course is that they hadn't; virtually no one on the Kentucky roster had ever suited up for an NCAA Tournament game in their career.

In terms of the Wildcats' draw, well, it was about what they expected. Kentucky had earned the No. 1 seed in the East region, and would open tournament play Thursday night in New Orleans against East Tennessee State. Assuming they won their opener (like every other No. 1 seed in NCAA Tournament history had before them), they could face a potentially tough matchup in the second round. The No. 8 seed Texas Longhorns had been one of the nation's best teams before a late-season swoon sent them tumbling out of the polls. No. 9 seed Wake Forest was talented, with potential future lottery pick Al-Faroq Aminu in their front court. If the Wildcats beat either of those teams, they would advance to the East regional semifinals and finals, played in Syracuse, New York.

Syracuse was a long way away both literally and figuratively though, and the following day the team began preparations for East Tennessee State. John Calipari hosted a small breakfast at his house that Monday morning and reiterated a point to his players that he had told reporters the previous night: Kentucky's only focus was on the three teams in their little sub-region. There was no reason for them to worry about anyone else. The tournament was way too unpredictable for them to have any idea who they could potentially play down the road.

"He said 'we're going to take one game at a time,'" Mark Krebs remembered. "'Everything's reset right now. We're going to go out and play, here's the hand we're dealt.'"

Krebs continued, explaining Calipari's early tournament approach.

"He had the bracket," Krebs said. "The only thing on there was the first two games, who we were playing, and he just said 'We've got to keep this mentality. Don't worry about what the rest of the country is doing, what the rest of the bracket is doing. Just worry about us.'"

It all made sense, and was a simple and refreshing approach to the Wildcats' players. Again, most had never played in the NCAA Tournament before, and even the veterans who had made the Big Dance in 2007 and 2008 had never been in a position like this. In those years the Wildcats weren't a heavy favorite, but instead, the proverbial underdog. In those years, everything had to go right for them to advance. Somewhere along the way they had to catch a break, or hope a higher-seeded team fell in front of them.

But in 2010, things were different. All Kentucky had to do was worry about themselves. If they played up to their capabilities, everything else would take care of itself.

"We never had that 'It's ours to lose' (mentality)," Krebs said. "It was always 'let's go out there and see what happens!' Even as seniors, we never had that."

After a few days off and a few days of light practice which followed, the Wildcats eventually made their way down to New Orleans. There they would face the East Tennessee State Buccaneers, which had earned an automatic bid after winning the Atlantic Sun Conference. Clearly the Buccaneers were overmatched from a talent perspective, but to the Wildcats' credit they still approached the game with the right attitude. From the moment the pairings had been announced --- and the players cheered confidently from the couch --- they knew that if they were going to reach their goals as a team, they would have to play like one. It wouldn't be about any one individual player, but instead everyone coming together as one.

That attitude started at the top, with the team's most talented individual.

"It's not going to be everybody's night," John Wall had told reporters on the Sunday night the NCAA Tournament pairings were announced. "It could be somebody different. The last two games (in the SEC Tournament) Eric Bledsoe stepped up big for us. It might not be my night, or it might not be somebody else's night. But you just carry the load and stay with your team."

Wall sounded like a seasoned NCAA Tournament veteran with that comment, and when Kentucky's NCAA Tournament actually tipped off, he looked like he could see into the future as well. A Bledsoe three right before the under-16 minute TV timeout gave the Wildcats a 12-10 lead. Little did anyone know at the time that the three-ball would start an epic run for the Wildcats. And a historic night for Bledsoe.

With momentum coming out of the timeout, Kentucky attacked. They got three straight points from Patrick Patterson, then a two by Daniel Orton, and four more from Patterson. Eventually, the Wildcats had gone on one of their patented runs, and scored 14 straight. They turned a 10-9 deficit into a 23-10 lead.

The Buccaneers then slowed down Kentucky --- at least for a second --- with a quick bucket, before the Wildcats went on the attack again. This one was spearheaded by Bledsoe, who hit his second three with just under nine minutes to go in the first half, which gave the Wildcats a 32-14 lead. On the next possession Bledsoe was at it again, attacking the rim for a quick layup, then after the under-eight minute TV timeout, he hit another three. By half-time Kentucky had built their lead to 54-26, and after playing in the shadow of Wall, Cousins and Patterson all year, Bledsoe had emerged as a star with 15 first half points.

And he didn't slow down after intermission, either. Bledsoe hit another three barely a minute into the half, and by the end of the evening Bledsoe had gone from "good" to "historic." He finished the game with eight three-pointers, which broke a Kentucky school record, and ironically, the man who held the record was sitting on the Wildcats' bench that night. Tony Delk held the previous mark with seven three's in a game, and as the assistant Director of Basketball Operations for the 2010 team, had a front row seat for Bledsoe's historic performance. Bledsoe was one of several Kentucky players to fill up the stat sheet that evening. He finished with 29 points, while Patterson added 22, Wall had 17 points and 11 assists and Orton tallied eight points, seven boards and three blocks off the bench. In total Kentucky shot nearly 52 percent from the field, in a 100-71 victory. They also finished 15 for 33 from three, a pretty impressive mark for anyone. Let alone a team which was considered to be a poor three-point shooting club.

"Our scouting report said they couldn't make 3s and they made 15," East Tennessee coach Murry Bartow said. "So, obviously, if the rest of the tournament they shoot the ball the way they did tonight, they're obviously going to be a very tough out."

John Calipari, for the most part agreed. He was thrilled with his team's effort, even if he wasn't sure that they could keep it up.

"They hit a buzzsaw today," Calipari told reporters following the game. "Hopefully we're this good. I'm not sure if we are, but we'll see if we can keep it going."

With a quick and painless victory in the early game of the night session in New Orleans, Kentucky's players returned to the team hotel, while the coaches stuck around for the second game to see who the Wildcats would play next.

Most assumed it would be the Texas Longhorns, one of college basketball's most talented teams that season and one of the few clubs that could (in theory) hang with the Wildcats for 40 minutes. Texas was so good that they had actually been ranked No. 1 in the country earlier that season, before they suffered their first loss, and ironically, Kentucky took over the spot in the polls. And after that first loss the problems continued for Texas. After starting out 17-0, the Longhorns had finished just 7-9 down the stretch, and would add one final loss to their resume against Wake Forest. After all the fear that some Kentucky fans had about facing the ultra-talented Longhorns, Texas fizzled down the stretch against Wake, and lost 81-80 in overtime.

The Wildcats would face the Demon Deacons in a Saturday night showdown in New Orleans.

Like Texas, Wake Forest had plenty of talent (as mentioned, Al-Faroq Aminu went on to be a lottery pick in that summer's draft, and guard Ish Smith eventually carved out a nice NBA career as well), and for a short time the Demon Deacons were able to hang with the Wildcats. Wake Forest led 10-7 at the first TV timeout, and things were tied at 19 when the game went to break at the under 12-minute mark.

But then... oh, who are we kidding? You know what happened, right? Kentucky went on a run. Because of course Kentucky went on a run.

It started with an innocent DeMarcus Cousins dunk, and then John Wall and DeAndre Liggins scored on Kentucky's next two trips down the floor. Sensing his team was about to lose control, Wake Forest coach Dino Gaudio called a timeout, although the stoppage did little to slow down the 'Cats. Kentucky scored seven points before the Demon Deacons scored again, and then went on another 8-0 run to close the half.

The Wildcats led 44-28 at halftime, and then... well, they kept pouring it on. Out of the break Wall hit a three, and from there, the rout was on. Wake Forest was never able to get the lead closer than 17 points again, and by the 10-minute mark, Kentucky had extended the margin to 30, at 70-40. The score would stay that way until the bitter end, as the Wildcats closed things out by a final score of 90-60. Once again it was a stat-stuffing performance for the 'Cats who got a career-high 20 points from Darius Miller, to go along with 19 points and eight boards from Cousins, and 14 points and seven assists from Wall. In total 11 Wildcats scored that day, in one of the team's most dominating wins of the season.

The victory was so dominant, it left veteran Wake Forest coach Dino Gaudio damn near speechless.

"I've been in the ACC 10 years," Gaudio said. "That's as good a basketball team as we played against in the 10 years I've been here."

Simply put, it was a great time to be a Wildcat, and as the team retreated to their locker room, the good news kept pouring in. Right as Kentucky had begun the process of dismantling Wake Forest that Saturday night, another NCAA Tournament game was just starting to wrap up some 700 miles away in Oklahoma City and its result would send shockwaves through the NCAA Tournament going forward.

That result involved Kansas, the No. 1 seed in the Midwest region, and maybe the only team in college basketball that most believed was more talented than Kentucky. At least they *were* the only team that had more talent, right up until they got upset by No. 9 seed Northern Iowa, in a shocking loss that ended in the midst of the Wildcats' blowout of Wake Forest. There would be no Kansas-Kentucky matchup in the Final Four or anywhere. The Jayhawks had been eliminated in the second round of the Big Dance.

To John Calipari's credit he pleaded with his players after the Wake Forest win, begging them not to celebrate Kansas' loss. Instead, they should use it as a learning lesson: The same thing could happen to them if they weren't careful. They too could be the victims of an upset if they weren't focused each and every game.

But while the players listened to their coach, they also couldn't help but see the writing on the wall: Not only did Kentucky have the most talented team in college basketball, but the road to a potential title just got easier. Not only were the Wildcats playing their best ball of the season, but right as they were peaking, their toughest potential opponents were falling to the wayside.

Kentucky was full of confidence. And so too were their fans.

"You didn't worry about anything," Kentucky Sports Radio's Matt Jones said, remembering the Wildcats' run in 2010. "It was just fun. I don't even remember worrying about the NCAA Tournament. You were just like 'this is fun.'"

But as the Wildcats departed New Orleans, "fun" turned into "serious."

Kentucky was set to face a surprise opponent when they arrived in Syracuse.

And they were also about to walk into a surprise controversy.

* * *

There's an old saying amongst media members that "reporters don't care about teams. They care about stories." If that's the case, then the Wildcats' Sweet 16 game was equivalent to college basketball's Super Bowl that year. Not because it was the best matchup of the second weekend of the NCAA Tournament. But because it was by far the best *story*.

In the Sweet 16, Kentucky was set to face the Cornell Big Red, the No. 12 seed in the East Region, who had made a surprising run through their two regional games in Jacksonville. In their opener, the Big Red shocked No. 5 Temple, before flat out dominating fourth-seeded Wisconsin in an 18-point win. By the time Cornell arrived in Syracuse for the East regional semifinals against Kentucky, they were the feel good story of the NCAA Tournament, the Ivy League school with no basketball history and no athletic scholarships, which was competing with college basketball's big boys anyway.

Under any normal circumstances Cornell was an incredible storyline, but the fact they were playing Kentucky only added to the appeal.

Remember, this was back in 2010 when the concept of a "one-and-done" basketball player was still relatively new, and over the course of the season, Kentucky had become the face for everything that was "wrong" about college basketball. For old-school media members, it wasn't that they disliked the players personally, but instead, that they were simply uncomfortable with the rule and what it entailed. Most assumed that the players who planned to leave college after one year were using the rule to their advantage. Many in the media wondered whether they even cared about school, or frankly if they were even attending classes at all. Forget the fact that at least in Kentucky's case, their star player John Wall had a GPA around 4.0, and that Wall, Cousins and Bledsoe would go on to finish their second semester classes, even *after* they eventually declared for the NBA Draft. Many in the media (but certainly not all) didn't know the facts. Many just never cared to learn them.

At the same time, the *perception* of Cornell and the *perception* of Kentucky made for a juicy storyline heading into the Sweet 16. The matchup between the Wildcats and the Big Red turned into a battle of brain vs. brawn. Jocks vs. nerds. Ivy Leaguers vs., well…

"That week the national media really played up the whole 'smart kids versus one-and-done stupid kids' basically," Jones said.

In actuality, the whole scenario meant little to Kentucky. To them, Cornell was just another good team, who they prepared for as if it were a matchup with Kansas, Tennessee or any other big-time opponent. The Wildcats knew that if they weren't careful, the Big Red were good enough to end their season.

Cornell was perfectly capable of pulling an upset, and when Kentucky arrived in Syracuse they were ready to focus on basketball. But unfortunately all the media wanted to talk about was the whole "brains vs. brawn" thing. Everyone kept asking the players about it, and asking, and asking again, hoping to get an interesting quote to spice up their stories. And for the most part the players answered the same way, insisting that they respected the Big Red and wanted to focus on the game at hand.

But eventually, the media asked one too many times, and eventually they got the quote they were hoping for. It came via Boogie Cousins. Cousins was asked about Cornell and responded by calling them a "smart team," which was a reference to their style of play, and not how they performed in the classroom. However, the media heard the word "smart" and decided to ask Cousins one more time for his take on the "nerds vs. jocks" angle.

Cousins gave them an honest answer.

"I mean, I think it's stupid," Cousins said. "But I mean, I'm not going to let it get to me. We're here to play basketball. I mean, it's not a spelling bee."

Ah, the old 'it's not a spelling bee' line.

Understand that while the quote sounds somewhat aggressive on paper, in actuality, that wasn't how Cousins delivered it at all. The video of Cousins answering the question is currently on YouTube, and if you watch it, you can see Boogie answered in a calm, cool voice. There wasn't an ounce of anger in his response.

Not that any of it mattered to the media. They heard it, ran with it, and within hours it had become a huge story. In 2010 the internet was just turning into a never-ending, 24-hour news cycle, and it's safe to say that Cousins had given everyone their headline for the day. It gave the media their perfect "gotcha" moment, a chance to take an innocent quote out of the mouth of a 19-year-old and use it as a referendum on Kentucky's entire team. In essence, the media was saying: "See, Kentucky's players don't care about school! A player from Cornell would never say that!"

One media member who really drove that point home was the *Boston Globe's* Dan Shaughnessy. Just a day before the two teams met, he wrote an article called "Clinging to an Ivy League Climber," which caused quite a little firestorm in Lexington.

Here is an excerpt from that article:

"You can have Kentucky," Shaughnessy wrote. "You can take Ashley Judd, Adolph Rupp, Sam Bowie, Pat Riley, Coach Cal, Refuse to Lose, the one-and-done freshmen bound for the NBA, and all the bags of cash needed to make the Wildcats run. I'll take Cornell and the Ivy League, which has long been a joke in college basketball."

The article went on, but by that point Shaughnessy had made his point: The Big Red were the good guys, everything that was right about the sport of college basketball. Kentucky was the bad guy, the evil empire which had clearly cheated to get to the top. The article quickly had made its way through Kentucky, and within hours Wildcats' fans began reaching out to Shaughnessy, infuriated about what he'd written.

Jones and Kentucky Sports Radio were especially upset.

"That really rallied the fans a lot, including me," Jones said. "I got really upset, and said at the time that I thought a lot of the writing at the time was really....racist. I went at it with Dan Shaughnessy of the *Boston Globe*, because I thought the things he was writing were racist."

The article created such a stir in Kentucky that Shaughnessy actually wrote a follow-up the next day, and even spoke to Jones on the phone to explain the intent of what had been written. At the same time, it didn't matter. The article spoke to the tone of many media members heading into the game.

The funny thing about the whole controversy was that as tip-off approached, Cornell didn't need anyone else on their bandwagon. With the game located in Syracuse, less than an hour from their campus, the Big Red had the majority of fan support in the Carrier Dome that night. When both teams walked out of the tunnel, all they saw was a sea of red.

And when the game tipped off, that home-court advantage allowed them to quickly jump out to a 10-2 lead. The Carrier Dome was rocking, but just as the Big Red had jumped out to a big lead, the Wildcats roared back. Cousins --- the kid who had created so much controversy throughout the week with his quotes --- scored four straight points, prompting a 12-0 Kentucky run. The Wildcats clamped down on defense the rest of the half, and took a 32-16 lead into halftime. They ended the first half on a staggering 30-6 run.

The hot finish to the half felt familiar for UK's players and their fans; in the team's first two tournament games Kentucky had taken big leads into halftime and had used the second half to blow the game wide open. But on this night however, Cornell battled back. The Big Red slowed the game down, and slowly chipped away at the Wildcats' big lead. Eventually they got Kentucky's lead down to just 10 with 10 minutes to go, and when

Louis Dale hit a three with 5:42 left, the Wildcats were ahead by only six points.

Kentucky was facing their first real test of the NCAA Tournament. It was a test they would pass with flying colors.

The Wildcats clamped down on defense, and just as quickly as the lead got down to six, it went back up to double-digits. Cornell never got closer than eight again, and an Eric Bledsoe floater with 2:45 left pushed the lead back into double-digits once and for all. The Wildcats' defense only intensified from there, and Kentucky finished the game by converting 11 of 12 free throws in the final two minutes and change. The 'Cats won 62-45, in a matchup which was much closer than the final score indicated.

The Wildcats had advanced to their first Elite Eight since 2005, and in the process, had proven something to their doubters: They weren't just a team built around offensive fireworks. After averaging over 95 points per game in their first two NCAA Tournament contests, the Wildcats beat Cornell because of their defense. The Big Red entered the game as college basketball's best three-point shooting team, and were coming off an 87-point performance in their second round win over Wisconsin. Yet against Kentucky, Cornell shot just 5 for 21 from three-point range and just 33 percent from the field in general.

In essence, Kentucky was peaking at the perfect time, and after two games of dynamic offense, they were equally dynamic on the other end of the court against Cornell.

It led to high praise from one of the most respected basketball writers in the business.

"Dick 'Hoops' Weiss said to me after the Cornell game, 'I've never seen a college team play better defense than they just did,'" Jones remembered, discussing comments from the famed basketball writer.

And it was at that moment, after their Sweet 16 win, that Kentucky fans finally allowed themselves to dream just a little bit. The entire season had been like a fairy tale. Could it possibly end with a championship?

"It was at that point that you start thinking, 'Ok, we're going to win it,'" Jones said. "Or you thought, 'we're going to play Duke at the Final Four.'"

The feeling was the same in the locker room. Even if no one said it.

"That (Cornell) was probably the game I was worried about the most," team manager Chad Sanders said. "And after that, I was like 'Man, this is ours.' Clearly we weren't talking about it, but I didn't see another team that could beat us."

Just one game stood between Kentucky and a trip to the Final Four.

A game that both fans and players would never forget.

For all the wrong reasons.

Take Me Home, Country Roads

WITH THE WIN over Cornell, Kentucky improved to 35-2 on the season, which at the time, was tied for the most victories in school history. That number matched the win total of both the 1997 and 1998 Wildcats, a pair of teams that played for the National Championship, with the 1998 club winning it. Ironically, 1998 was also the last time that the Wildcats had made the Final Four period, which is exactly where they would go if they picked up win No. 36 during that 2010 season.

But for them to get that win, they would have to beat the best team they faced in weeks, in arguably their toughest game since taking on Tennessee in Knoxville nearly a month before.

Their opponent was the West Virginia Mountaineers, a club which entered their Elite Eight matchup with Kentucky at 30-6, and who appeared to be peaking at the right time. West Virginia had won 11 of 12 entering that Elite Eight game, including a run to the Big East Tournament championship, at a time when the Big East was still by far the best conference in college basketball. They also had plenty of talent, too. Their starting front court of D'Sean Butler, Kevin Jones and Devin Ebanks all at least got a cup of coffee in the NBA.

Simply put, West Virginia was good. Really good. Best-selling author and Kentucky fan Tucker Max might have described them best entering that game.

"(They were) juniors and seniors, a bunch of guys, maybe not great NBA players, but guys that were going to play in the league," Max said. "They had a bunch of old-man muscle. West Virginia had three dudes that went on to play in the league, at least for a while. They were all grown men, and we were still a team full of mostly freshmen."

West Virginia had plenty of skill, but the biggest concern for Kentucky heading into the game was their defense. The Mountaineers had held their previous six opponents under 60 points, and could, at least in theory, exploit UK's biggest weakness: Three-point shooting.

"As we sat down before we got in the NCAA Tournament, we knew that if we hit a bad shooting spell, we better hope it's a team that we can beat anyway," John Calipari remembered. "It was the one Achilles heel we had."

Ah yes, that three-point shooting. It had been a problem the Wildcats had dealt with all year, and one which had never really gone away. As a team UK shot just 33 percent from beyond the arc that season, and Eric Bledsoe was the only regular to make more than 35 percent of his attempts. Not to mention that the entire team had been prone to bad stretches all season long (remember that 12 for 73 stretch in late SEC play?). Thankfully though, by the time the NCAA Tournament began Kentucky had seemed to shoot their way out of any slump. The Wildcats made 15 three's against East Tennessee State, and shot a respectable 7 of 21 behind the arc against Wake Forest.

It was all trending in the right direction... at least until Kentucky went into another funk against Cornell, and missed their final 10 three-point attempts in that Sweet 16 win. While Calipari would be able to recruit around the team's shooting woes in later years by signing guys like Doron Lamb and Devin Booker, there was no hiding it in 2010. As Calipari told Fox Sports, the Wildcats simply had to hope that if they did go into a slump, it wasn't against a team that could beat them.

The fact that the team couldn't miss in warm-ups helped calm any fears (at least briefly) entering the West Virginia game.

"Going back to it, I remember the shoot around the day of that game," team manager Chad Sanders said. "Guys weren't missing. Eric Bledsoe was on fire. Guys weren't missing."

Finally, a little after 7:00 p.m. local time, the game tipped off. Over 22,000 filled the Carrier Dome, many of them dressed in blue supporting

Kentucky, but plenty of others in West Virginia's gold and dark blue as well. Those cheering for the Mountaineers had plenty to get excited about early, as West Virginia's Wellington Smith and Kevin Jones each hit three's to give West Virginia a 6-2 lead just minutes in. From there Kentucky countered however, with John Wall and DeMarcus Cousins combining for the game's next six points, and the Wildcats took an 8-6 lead into the first TV timeout. Kentucky then scored five more unanswered points out of the break to take a 13-6 lead. It was one of UK's patented runs. And early on, it seemed like business as usual for the 'Cats. Even when guard Joe Mazzulla hit a three to end Kentucky's run and cut the Wildcats' lead to 13-9 it didn't seem like much of a big deal.

But off of the make, West Virginia implemented a suffocating 1-3-1 zone that left Kentucky flustered on the offensive end. A missed DeAndre Liggins three proved to be the start of something bad for the Wildcats. Something very, very bad.

"They put that zone on us," junior center Josh Harrellson said.

And?

"Basically we fell into their trap," Patterson said.

Simply put, Kentucky hadn't seen a zone quite like it all year, and certainly hadn't seen one with the caliber of players West Virginia had. The pressure defense extended well beyond the three-point line, and forced Kentucky to get into their offense way earlier than they were accustomed to. In particular, the zone caused two major problems for the Wildcats.

For starters, it took away what UK did best.

"West Virginia just did a great job of not letting them get to the basket," Kentucky Sports Radio's Matt Jones said. "That's one thing that team did great, get to the basket. They had Wall and Bledsoe, and they'd dish it off to Cousins, and they could post guys up, and none of that was working."

More than just taking away what Kentucky did best however, the zone also forced the Wildcats' into the one thing they didn't do well. Which was problem No. 2.

"West Virginia was basically like, 'we're going to give you open threes,'" Jones said. "And they just could not make them."

No they couldn't, and out of the second TV timeout things didn't get any better. John Wall missed a two-pointer then missed a follow-up three-pointer on the same possession, before Darnell Dodson grabbed the rebound. Dodson, who had been Kentucky's most consistent deep threat all year proceeded to miss a three of his own before West Virginia finally regained possession. The Mountaineers' defense was stifling, and even though it was early, the only thing keeping Kentucky from getting blown out was its own strong defensive play. The question of course, was how long would it last.

Unfortunately for Kentucky, they got their answer just minutes later. The Wildcats were up 16-9 out of the under eight minute TV timeout, when West Virginia came out firing. D'Sean Butler hit a three. Then Kevin Jones hit one on the following possession. And off a sloppy DeMarcus Cousins' turnover, Butler hit yet another three-pointer. At that point Calipari had seen enough, and decided to call a timeout; it was one thing for the Wildcats to miss open jumpers, but quite another for them to simply give the ball away with sloppy passing. CBS' cameras showed Butler popping his jersey as the game went to commercial break. West Virginia had taken a 21-18 lead.

Finally, out of the final TV timeout of the half, Kentucky calmed down... sort of. Butler hit another three (his fourth of the half) and was fouled, but the Wildcats were able to cut into the lead on the next possession with a two-point bucket from Liggins. Liggins actually picked up a technical foul later in the half, but even then, it didn't damage the Wildcats as much as it could have. Kentucky was able to close out the half on a 4-1 run, and somehow went into halftime trailing by just two points at 28-26.

Again, Kentucky trailed by just two points. But because West Virginia had been so hot from three-point land, and because Kentucky had been so cold, the margin seemed much wider. In actuality, the Mountaineers weren't just "hot" from three, but "scorching." The three-point shot was basically how they scored all their points that first half.

"The biggest thing I remember from that game was in the first half, they only made three-pointers and free throws," senior guard Mark Krebs remembered. "There were no two-point baskets. It was bizarre."

It truly was bizarre. It also led to panic in the locker room. Even though it wasn't necessary at all.

"We went into halftime only down two, but it felt like it was 10," Krebs said. "It was like we were in quicksand and couldn't get out of it."

And unfortunately for Kentucky, things didn't get better out of the break. On just the second possession of the second half Kevin Jones hit another three, and Mazzulla followed a pair of Kentucky misses with a two-point bucket of his own (incredibly, it was the first two-point field goal West Virginia had hit all day). A John Wall turnover on the next possession led to another three-pointer from the Mountaineers, this one from John Flowers. That three capped an 8-0 run for West Virginia. Incredibly, in less than two and a half minutes, West Virginia had extended their lead to 10 points.

John Calipari again called a timeout. And panic again gripped the Wildcats' bench.

"I felt like in timeouts, you had guys that were usually positive, not necessarily getting on people, but more like 'We've got to do this!'" Krebs said. "It was extra pandemonium, rather than calmness, like 'We've got this, we're going to be fine.'"

Finally, out of that timeout Kentucky put together a mini-run. A quick dish from Eric Bledsoe to Cousins led to an easy bucket, and after John Wall made one of two free throws, Bledsoe again found Cousins for an easy bucket. It was a 5-0 run for Kentucky, and all seemed good again… at least until West Virginia squashed that run with back-to-back buckets by Devin Ebanks and Joe Mazzulla.

In a lot of ways, that little segment was symbolic of the whole game. Every time Kentucky made a run, West Virginia had an answer. Every time the Wildcats hit a bucket, the Mountaineers seemed to make two. No matter what Kentucky did, it just never seemed to be enough.

"It seemed like time was going at triple-speed," Krebs remembered. "Every timeout in the second half, every time we'd try to run something or do something. We'd run it to perfection, but the ball wouldn't go in the basket... Then they'd go down, run 30 seconds off the clock and hit a fade-away three and they'd make it. And it's like 'God, why are we doing that?'"

If there was one possession which symbolized the entire game, and showed just how bad things were going, it may have come with 11:10 left in the second half.

Off a West Virginia miss, John Wall pushed the ball up the court, and like he'd done so many times that season, he attacked the hoop, and threw up a circus shot that somehow went in. It was all so quintessential Wall. Every time the Wildcats had needed a big play all year it seemed like he delivered, and in the most important moment of their season he seemed to do it again. His bucket also cut the lead to single digits at 47-38. If he made the foul shot, the deficit would be down to just eight points.

But in a sign that maybe it just wasn't Kentucky's day, Wall (a 75 percent free throw shooter that season) didn't make the free throw. Thankfully though, even with the miss there was hope. The ball ricocheted to Patrick Patterson, who grabbed it and passed it to Bledsoe for a wide open three.

Bledsoe's three clanged off back rim. Of course it did.

But no worries, Cousins grabbed a second offensive rebound on the possession, and moved the ball to Wall. Wall drove the lane and fired a pass to a wide-open Liggins for an uncontested three.

Clang. Liggins' three-point attempt missed off the front rim.

Bledsoe again got the rebound (the Wildcats' third of the possession), but as he passed the ball over to Cousins, it got tipped and went out of bounds and back to West Virginia. On a night where Kentucky couldn't buy a bucket, this one hurt extra bad. If either of those three-pointers had gone in, it would have cut the Mountaineers' lead to six. Instead, West Virginia scored on the next possession, to push the lead back up to 11.

The worst case scenario was happening for Kentucky.

"The best way to put it was it seemed like a nightmare, you know?" freshman Daniel Orton said. "It's like when you're in a nightmare fighting, fighting, and there's nothing we could do."

Assistant coach Rod Strickland described the scene another way.

"It was almost like, how can I say it?" Strickland asked aloud. "Everything that could go wrong, went wrong that one game."

"And everything that could go right for them did," Patterson said.

For Patterson, the whole scene was especially frustrating. The junior who had stuck around one last year hoping for a deep NCAA Tournament run like this, was watching the final minutes of his Kentucky career slip through the team's fingertips. And it was at that moment, as the threes continued to clang off the rim that he couldn't help but think back to that decision to return to Kentucky, and think about his former teammate who had decided to do the opposite, and declare for the draft the previous spring.

Nobody had talked about Jodie Meeks all that much during the season. But as it turned out, the one player that the 2010 Kentucky Wildcats needed most, was the player they never had to begin with.

"That game particularly I wish Jodie had stayed," Patterson said.

Meeks certainly could have helped the Wildcats that day. Incredibly, Kentucky missed 20 straight threes to open the game. DeAndre Liggins finally hit one with a little over three minutes to go, ending a run of futility that was almost incomprehensible to think about.

"Now you have to understand that after the Cornell game, we missed 10 straight threes to end that game," Calipari told Fox Sports. "Then 20 straight threes to start the next game. That's 0 for 30. Now how do you go 0 for 30? But we did it. And we knew it could happen."

The Liggins three allowed one last ditch effort for the Wildcats. After his deep ball, Dodson followed it up with one of his own, before Wall hit another three to cut the lead to 68-61. Suddenly, the Wildcats had life, and West Virginia helped the rally by missing five of eight free throws during that stretch. Another Dodson three got the lead down to just four with less than 30 seconds to play.

But then, just when the Wildcats got hot from behind the arc, their offense abandoned them. A Dodson three-point attempt was blocked and with two West Virginia made free throws later, the Mountaineers' lead was insurmountable. Down seven with just 13 seconds left, Kentucky's final possession summed up the afternoon perfectly. Patterson missed a three-point attempt, then even after an offensive rebound, Dodson missed another. The Mountaineers grabbed one final rebound and sprinted up the court, arms raised in the air as the clock expired.

In a game that remains one of the most shocking results in recent NCAA Tournament history, the Mountaineers had pulled off the upset. The final score was 73-66, West Virginia. Kentucky finished the game just 4 of 32 from beyond the three-point arc, a number which still haunts many in Lexington to this day. In a season where the Wildcats seemed to be able to flick the switch whenever they wanted, and score points at will whenever they needed, they never did make that run to push them over the top.

"That's where it felt like the finality of a postseason game got to us," Krebs said. "Because every game that season if we got down six points with a minute left, it felt like we were going to win it."

But on this day there would be no rally, no wild last-ditch spurt to put the Wildcats over the top.

The season was over.

And Kentucky had no one to blame but themselves.

"We could make up all the excuses in the world," Eric Bledsoe told Fox Sports. "But they executed their job well. They were the better team that night."

＊　＊　＊

While CBS' cameras remained fixated on West Virginia and their Final Four celebration, a different kind of emotion poured out in the bowels of the Carrier Dome, inside the four walls of Kentucky's locker room.

That emotion was sadness. Raw, real, crushing sadness. The season was over and no one was exactly sure what to do, or how they got there. Players sat by themselves in silence. No one said a word. Everyone replayed the game in their heads, thinking about a season which had slipped through their fingertips. The only sound that could be heard were scattered sniffles, belonging to teenagers who looked like grown men, but who cried like babies that day.

"I was in the locker room after that game," Kentucky Sports Radio's Matt Jones said. "That was the most devastated locker room I've ever seen. DeMarcus Cousins and John Wall were inconsolable. People talk about 'one and done' whatever, those guys were just inconsolable."

Just about everyone who was in the Kentucky locker room that evening has similar memories. Team manager Chad Sanders can't forget the towels draped over player's heads. Assistant coach Rod Strickland still thinks about the flood of tears streaming down star player's faces. No one could move. All they could do was cry and hug, and try to help each other through those final few moments together as teammates.

"I vividly remember Patrick Patterson trying to get DeMarcus to stop crying so he could talk to the media," Jones said. "Ramon Harris had a towel over his head, with his jersey on, and would not look up at any point."

For Kentucky, it simply wasn't supposed to end this way. The entire season had been such a joyride for the fans and the players, a group who had formed a bond since the moment the freshmen arrived on campus the previous spring. Sure, it was all going to end at some point, maybe with a National Championship, and maybe not. But to see it end like this? In the Elite Eight? In Syracuse? When they seemed destined to play on the final weekend of the college basketball season?

It was all so much to handle. And it all came way too soon.

"It was abrupt," Jones said. "It was very abrupt. It was like, 'Oh it's over.'… The assumption was, 'Oh, we're just going to roll.' So we'll go to the Final Four and play Duke, and that'll be fun. Kentucky fans hoped Duke would beat Baylor, because I think they were more worried about Baylor than they were Duke. I don't think there was ever a notion that we would lose that game."

And really, it wasn't just that they lost, but how it happened. All year long Kentucky hadn't just been one of the best teams in college basketball, but one of the most clutch as well. Simply put, the Wildcats played their best basketball in the biggest games of the season. North Carolina, UConn, Tennessee in the SEC Tournament, it didn't matter. The bigger the stage, the brighter Kentucky shined. Just not on this day.

In a lot of ways, that's also what made the West Virginia loss so frustrating. Ask any athlete who's competed at a high level and they'll tell you this: It's one thing when you play your best, and simply lose to a team which is better than you. It's quite another when you lose to any team, and know you haven't played anywhere close to your best basketball.

"It's also extra hard to know that the season was ours to lose," Krebs said. "It's not like it was going to take an amazing effort, amazing feats of strength or athleticism to win certain games. We felt like 'we've just got to play our game and it's ours.'"

It was Kentucky's, and especially after Kansas lost earlier in the tournament, the path to a championship (or at the very least the Final Four) had been laid out in front of them. Through the years, it has also has left many Wildcats' players and coaches wondering one thing: If they could have somehow beaten West Virginia, how different would history have been?

"I think if we had gotten past that West Virginia game we would've won the whole thing," Strickland said. "But it was that one moment where the pressure may have gotten to us a little bit."

Forget that one moment, on that one day. Many still wonder what would have happened if they had played West Virginia any *other* day.

"I think if we played them again, I think we beat West Virginia nine times out of 10," Scott Padgett said. "But they did it when they had to do it. But that's as good of an Elite Eight team as you'll ever see, that 09-10 team."

Kentucky wasn't just as good of an Elite Eight team as you'll ever see, but based on how many of the player's NBA careers have played out, as good of a college team as you'll see period. Some might even make the case that 2010 was the best team Calipari ever coached. The Wildcats won a National Championship in 2012. But even with a title, was the 2012 club really a better *team* than 2010?

Some still wonder.

"I feel bad for that team because, I believe this," Padgett began. "If you lined up 2009-10, and 2011-12, and they're both there in college, and you get to play it like they're in college…. (Sigh)…. I don't know that 2009-10 doesn't beat them."

Of course none of that mattered then and the truth is, none of it matters now. What it simply boils down to is that the 2010 Kentucky Wildcats simply played the wrong team, on the wrong day. Even all these years later, just about everyone involved with the 2010 Kentucky Wildcats --- from coaches, to players and even John Calipari himself --- still looks back on that season and wonders "what if." But ironically, it's someone who wasn't affiliated with that team who might have the best perspective of all.

"That season, it was just, it felt like that was a team of destiny that somehow ended up in the wrong universe," best-selling author and Kentucky fan Tucker Max said. "In every other alternate universe that team wins the national title."

"Just not the universe we live in."

Saying Goodbye

I T WAS A calm, cool spring morning in Lexington, just a day or two after the Kentucky Wildcats returned from Syracuse, and that crushing,
season-ending loss to West Virginia. As the sun rose, Josh Harrellson
awoke and moved about his day slowly. For the first time in months he
didn't have practice to attend or a game to prepare for. Outside of class
and study hall, he wasn't sure what he was supposed to do, or how he was
supposed to spend all his newfound free time.

"It really doesn't hit you for the next day or two," Harrellson said.
"You wake up and you don't have practice, you don't have games. It's
hard to accept reality when it first hits you. It takes a couple days to set in
like 'Wow, it really is over.'"

Harrellson wasn't the only player who felt that way, as the whole team
dealt with free time that they hadn't planned for, and also dealt with the
reality that the joyride really was over. Just about every player handled
themselves differently. Eric Bledsoe didn't watch much TV that week; he
simply couldn't bear to see anything related to basketball or the NCAA
Tournament. Seniors like Ramon Harris and Mark Krebs had to prepare
for graduation, and start figuring out what life after Kentucky would look
like. As Harris told Fox Sports, it was time to "go make money."

Meanwhile John Calipari and his coaching staff were beginning to
try and figure out what their roster would look like the following season.
While Calipari was fully prepared for the roster turnover that awaited him,
many Kentucky fans weren't. As the years went on, it would become commonplace for the program to lose a bunch of underclassmen off their

roster, but in 2010, it was still a novelty. Although the school had lost underclassmen off their roster before, this was the first time they could lose a whole boatload of them.

"You have to remember that this was pre-everyone leaving," Kentucky Sports Radio's Matt Jones said. "Nowadays when Kentucky loses, they know that Kentucky is going to lose a bunch of players. Back then, I think everybody knew we were going to lose Wall and Cousins, but you didn't expect to lose Bledsoe, and you just didn't think about the notion of 'next year's team is going to be a completely different team.' That mindset hadn't crept in yet."

Not only had it not crept in for the fans, frankly it hadn't fully crept in for Kentucky's players either.

Sure, as Jones pointed out, just about everyone knew that John Wall would be leaving. As the projected first overall pick in the upcoming NBA Draft there wasn't a single, logical reason for him to return to college. And yes, it was also a mostly foregone conclusion that Patrick Patterson would turn professional as well. Patterson had nearly left the year before, but decided to return to campus to expand his game, play in the NCAA Tournament and get his degree. With the first two accomplished, and his degree nearly in hand, Patterson was on his way out of Lexington as well.

But while the local and national media spent the weeks following Kentucky's NCAA Tournament loss to West Virginia trying to figure out who would join those two, the NBA was actually the last thing on any of the player's minds. Most were trying to delay the inevitable as long as possible, and soak in as much of the college life as they could.

"I'll tell you what," team manager Chad Sanders said. "All those guys contemplated coming back. Everybody (on the outside) said they were gone. Eric, John and DeMarcus, we used to go to get crab legs at Hooters all the time. We used to go once or twice a week. They didn't have a car, so we'd just go grab lunch or grab dinner and they would talk about how much they loved Kentucky."

Oh, they talked about more than just how much they loved Kentucky. They talked about bringing the 2011 National Championship back to Lexington as well.

"I know it probably wasn't realistic," Sanders said. "But it was like, 'Let's do this again. We can do this again.' They did have conversations about it."

Eventually though, those conversations died down and reality began to set in. Each freshman had a tough decision to make. And it wasn't nearly as easy as anyone imagined.

For Wall, the choice was a virtual no-brainer. Wall was no dummy (literally, or figuratively: his GPA hovered right around a 4.0 in his final semester in Lexington), and again, seemed like a lock to not only go high in the NBA Draft, but be the No. 1 pick overall. When Wall committed to Kentucky he had vowed to be the next Derrick Rose or Tyreke Evans, the point guard who led a John Calipari coached club deep into the NCAA Tournament, before leaving for the NBA after one season.

But even with that season over and millions waiting for him in the NBA, his decision still wasn't as easy as everyone assumed. Remember, he was the same kid that held back tears against Florida on Senior Day, knowing it was his final game at Rupp Arena. Even though Wall knew it was time to say goodbye, he just wasn't totally ready to do it yet.

"John was having difficulty just saying that 'it's over,'" DeWayne Peevy remembered. "He just didn't want it to end."

If Wall was having trouble admitting it was over, DeMarcus Cousins was outright defiant: He was coming back for his sophomore year. He loved Kentucky, he loved his teammates, and after some early battles, yes he loved Calipari as well. So why give it all up? There was no reason to in Cousins' mind, which is why he let the Kentucky coaching staff know throughout the season that his mind was in fact made up. There were no questions about it. He was ready to play another year in Lexington.

"DeMarcus had been telling us through the end of the SEC Tournament and into the NCAA Tournament 'don't recruit another big guy. I'm coming back.'" Peevy said. "He was convinced he was coming back."

But while he convinced himself he was coming back, Kentucky's coaching staff had to convince him otherwise. No, they didn't force him to leave, but they were also blunt with him: If Cousins wanted to come back, they would welcome him with open arms, but there would also be raised expectations. It wasn't going to be a joyride. It wasn't going to be all fun and games. He was already being projected as possibly the second or third pick in the NBA Draft. Therefore, if he wasn't coming back to be the best player in college basketball, well, he probably should reconsider.

"Cal wanted to make sure he knew what it could be," Peevy said. "(Cal said) 'If you want to come back, you better come back to work. If you're not coming back to be the No. 1 pick in the draft next year, then you need to strike while the iron's hot.'"

Whether Cousins was ready or not, eventually he realized the coaching staff was right. Like Wall, declaring for the draft was the smart thing to do. He too would go pro.

For Eric Bledsoe there was genuine internal debate on whether he should declare or not, and unlike Wall and Cousins, there was actually a good reason for him to return to college. Yes, Bledsoe had as much raw talent as anyone on the team (including John Wall), but he also wasn't blessed with the 6'4 frame that Wall was, which made him tougher to project as a professional. Bledsoe was right around 6'0, and after he had spent most of the season playing off the ball because of Wall, many in the NBA wondered if he could make the transition to play point guard in the NBA, and even if he could, if he had the size to last.

When it came time to declare for the draft, many mock NBA Draft websites didn't have him projected as a first round pick at all. It also left Bledsoe in a bind. Could he really declare for the pros?

"For me," Bledsoe said, "I wasn't in the position like John and them where I knew I was gone, that I'd be drafted in the first round or whatever."

Bledsoe was genuinely torn, and was genuinely listening to the critics, which as it turned out, was much to his own detriment. Both players and coaches at Kentucky had seen up close just how good Bledsoe was, and they knew how good he could be going forward. This was the guy who went at John Wall every day in practice for six months, who had taken over a handful of games against really good teams, and who could have been a star at any other school in the country. Simply put, Eric Bledsoe was an NBA player.

The only person who needed the convincing was actually Eric Bledsoe.

"Eric Bledsoe, the thing with him was just that *he* didn't believe," Peevy said. "Cal, John Wall, they were always telling him that he was just as good as any of them. And he should be going in the draft too. Eric was a quiet confidence guy. He had confidence on the court, in his game, but off the court he was quiet."

After several meetings with Calipari, Bledsoe also decided to go pro. He was going to take the plunge.

"I was talking to Coach Cal (a lot)," Bledsoe said. "He was telling me, 'We'd love to have you back, but at the end of the day it's your decision to make. You've got to do what's best for you.'"

Finally, there was the interesting case of Daniel Orton. The fourth member of Kentucky's vaunted freshman class, Orton also had a decision to make, and his might have been most unique of all. Unlike Wall and Cousins, Orton wasn't a surefire guarantee to go in the first round, and unlike Bledsoe he didn't have big stat lines, or a slew of impressive game film to wow scouts with either. Orton had averaged a modest three points and three rebounds that season.

But at 6'11, the one thing Orton did have was an NBA body. There's an old saying in basketball that "the one thing you can't teach is size" and Orton certainly had that. He also had a skill-set that led many NBA front office personnel to believe that with a little work, he could eventually be a good player in the post. Even if he didn't make it as a full-fledged starter, he could stick as a rotation player, someone who provided valuable minutes off the bench.

Simply put, Orton was so big, and so skilled that somebody would take a chance on him at the next level. Orton too was going pro.

"For me, it was one of the hardest decisions of my life," Orton told Fox Sports. "It was harder than choosing schools."

They made it official together, first in a press release, and then a press conference on April 7th, 2010: All five Kentucky players were turning pro. Technically, they could pull out of the draft right up until the middle of May, but for all intents and purposes, their Kentucky careers were over. All five were leaving under slightly different circumstances, but they were in fact leaving a place they loved, before they were ready to do it.

Yet while the decision felt sudden for the players, it was a day that John Calipari had prepared for, for almost a year. The truth was, he had envisioned this moment since the day John Wall committed to Kentucky back in May of 2009, and told Wall exactly that when he arrived in Lexington.

"I made a statement to John Wall," Calipari remembered. "I said 'don't come here leaving by yourself. You take a bunch of these guys with you.'"

Calipari's point was simple: For Kentucky to achieve the success they were capable of, Wall couldn't do it by himself. He needed help from his teammates, and as the most talented player on the squad, it was Wall's job to put them in a position to succeed. If Wall's teammates succeeded, he would succeed as well. So too, would the team.

Well, with the announcement that five guys were going pro, it's safe to say that Wall fulfilled Calipari's request.

As a matter of fact, Wall was good, he left Kentucky a little more short-handed heading into the 2011 season than Calipari had expected.

"Now I didn't know he'd take four other guys," Calipari said with a laugh. "But I told him 'don't leave by yourself.' My point was, bring guys with you. Learn to be that guy. And he did it."

There's no doubt that he did, and there's also no doubt that with a little bit of hindsight on our side, just about everyone who decided to go pro that day made the right decision. Of the five players who declared for the draft on April 7th, 2010, four are still in the NBA, with Wall and Cousins both named All-Stars in 2015. Eric Bledsoe (the guy who wrestled with his decision to go pro) isn't doing too bad for himself either; he joined Wall and Cousins by signing a max contract extension in the summer of 2014. When you combine the salaries of those three with Patrick Patterson (a valuable role player for the Toronto Raptors), they made just a shade under $50 million during the 2015 season.

Not bad.

But more than just the money though, those five players, plus teammates like Ramon Harris, DeAndre Liggins, Darius Miller, Mark Krebs and everyone else on the 2010 Kentucky Wildcats' roster, did something much bigger: They set the tone for everything that has come at Kentucky since.

It's safe to say that the 2010 Kentucky Wildcats changed the face of UK basketball as we know it.

Some believe they changed the entire sport of basketball, too.

Epilogue

O N THE SURFACE, most assume that the story of the 2010 Kentucky Wildcats ends where this book began: On the night of the 2010 NBA Draft. On the night where Kentucky became the first school to ever have five players selected in the first round of the draft. On the night that John Wall became the first ever Wildcat to be selected first overall, and the night that John Calipari called "The biggest day in the history of Kentucky's program."

But to say the story of the 2010 Kentucky Wildcats ends there isn't entirely true. If anything, the better ending point might be on the night of April 2nd, 2012, in a game played at the Louisiana Superdome in New Orleans.

It was a matchup between Kentucky and Kansas for the 2012 NCAA Championship, and a game that the Wildcats had largely dominated. Kentucky led from the opening tip, and built a lead as big as 18 points in the first half, but as the clock ticked down, Kansas was rallying. The Jayhawks had cut their deficit to just 63-57 with a little over a minute to go, and appeared ready to cut into Kentucky's lead by even more when Elijah Johnson hit Tyshawn Taylor with a beautiful backdoor pass. Taylor caught the ball a few feet from the basket, for what appeared to be an uncontested layup.

But while the shot seemed uncontested, Michael Kidd-Gilchrist had other plans. Kidd-Gilchrist had been beaten by Taylor's initial cut to the basket, but realized it instantly, put his head down, and made a beeline toward the basket. Just as Taylor went in for an up-and-under layup,

Kidd-Gilchrist emerged, and pinned the ball against the backboard for a clean block. Kentucky got the ball back, and Kansas never was able to get closer than those six points.

Final score, 67-59. The Kentucky Wildcats were the 2012 National Champions.

It was a fairytale ending, one that UK fans still cherish to this day. Yet many reading this book are still probably wondering one thing: What does that 2012 championship have to do with the 2010 team? Outside of a few holdover players like Darius Miller and Jon Hood, what does one club have to do with the other?

It's a fair question, but also probably the wrong question to ask altogether.

Instead of saying "What do the 2012 Kentucky Wildcats have to do with the 2010 squad," the better question might be this: Would the 2012 team have existed, if the 2010 team had not come before them? Heck, would anything that Kentucky is doing right now --- the 2012 title, an undefeated regular season in 2015, the slew of NBA lottery picks and SEC Championships --- would any of it be possible without the 2010 team?

It's a fair question. And it's one I posed to John Calipari during my initial interview with him for Fox Sports.

His answer says it all.

"If 2010 doesn't allow this to happen, none of this happens," John Calipari said.

It was a bold statement from Calipari, but to fully understand it, you've got to step back and look at the bigger picture of the "John Calipari era" in Lexington as a whole. Do that and you'll see just how big of an impact that 2010 team had, and you'll also see the impact that team continues to have to this day.

Let's start with the obvious, and say that on a very surface-level, the 2010 Kentucky Wildcats were the class which made Kentucky "cool" again. As Kentucky Sports Radio's Matt Jones mentioned earlier in the book, Kentucky was always "good" under Tubby Smith (and to a much, much smaller degree Billy Gillispie), but never elite, and certainly not where the best players, with the biggest star power wanted to come play college basketball. Prior to Calipari's arrival, Kentucky had signed just one McDonald's All-American in the previous four recruiting classes (Patrick Patterson), and had signed just five in the decade before his arrival. Rarely did the biggest stars in high school basketball seriously consider coming to Lexington, let alone actually enroll there.

But that all changed when John Calipari arrived, when he brought John Wall, DeMarcus Cousins and Eric Bledsoe with him. All of a sudden, UK was the "cool" school and the one that virtually every big-time high school recruit at least considered, even if they didn't actually commit to them.

It was a trend that began as soon as John Wall did his dance at Big Blue Madness. Yet the ramifications weren't fully felt until right around that 2010 NBA Draft.

"Right around that time (of the draft) he got commitments from Brandon Knight, Michael Kidd-Gilchrist, Anthony Davis," Jones said. "Those three guys all of whom are NBA players, a couple of whom are star NBA players, committed within a few months of that NBA Draft, and set the tone for the next couple years, and the title that came after."

Simply put, those guys (and the guys who later followed them) saw what Wall, Cousins, Patterson and the 2010 team did. And they wanted to be "next."

"Kids saw us and were like 'We want to go to Kentucky,'" Patrick Patterson said. "'We want to be John Wall or Demarcus Cousins. We want to play for Coach Cal.'"

That's true. But beyond just creating a buzz about the program, the 2010 team did much more than that. They also created the "culture" that came at Kentucky as well. It wasn't just about playing basketball, or getting ready for the pros, but the work ethic that came with it. Sure, you might come to Kentucky with NBA dreams. But you also had to work once you got there.

It's something that future generations didn't totally find out until they arrived on campus.

"I remember talking to Willie (Cauley-Stein) that freshman year," DeWayne Peevy said. "And him saying 'This is harder than I thought it'd be,'" DeWayne Peevy said.

He continued, remembering what Cauley-Stein said back in the fall of 2012.

"'I know Cal told me it'd be hard,'" Cauley-Stein told Peevy. "'But I thought it'd be easy. From the outside it looked like it'd be fun, you just go out here and win games.'"

No, no, no. At Kentucky you work. And you also sacrifice, which is another trait that the 2010 team passed down. John Calipari famously tells recruits that if they want a guaranteed starting spot, a guaranteed number of minutes played or the opportunity to shoot 30 times a game, then Kentucky might not be the school for them. But while it's one thing for Calipari to say it, the 2010 team actually lived it. Eric Bledsoe decided that he'd rather play off the ball and in John Wall's shadow then go somewhere else and be a star. DeMarcus Cousins and Daniel Orton decided to share the paint, when either could have dominated it for virtually any other team. Patrick Patterson could have gone to the NBA after his sophomore year, but decided to come back and play a supporting role as a junior. Ramon Harris and Perry Stevenson gladly gave up starting spots in 2009, because they knew it's what was best for the team in 2010.

Each player on the 2010 team sacrificed in some way, and as it turned out, Calipari was right: Nobody was worse off for it.

"They put individual needs below team needs," former Director of Basketball Operations Martin Newton said. "They realized 'You know, if I do what this guy tells me to do, my dreams will come true.' And you know what? It played out."

Even better, it's an attitude that has trickled down to future generations at Kentucky. As Calipari famously says, Anthony Davis and Michael Kidd-Gilchrist took the fourth and fifth most shots on that 2012 title team, and they ended up being the No. 1 and No. 2 overall selections in the following draft. Heck, when a number of big-name underclassmen unexpectedly decided to come back to school, Kentucky went so far as to use a platoon system in 2015. Although guys like Devin Booker and Trey Lyles started the season on the bench, it didn't impact them in the long-term. Both ended up as lottery picks in 2015.

Certainly that's a credit to all the players who have come to Kentucky since 2010, who for the most part have bought in. But it's also a credit to the 2010 team for laying the foundation for what was expected in Lexington.

"People said it would never work," Calipari said. "Well, we went to the Final Four the next year (in 2011)! Then we lose four more guys, and we win the national title."

He continued.

"It proved you can do this, and it's still good for the program," he said. "On top of that, they set the tone, Brandon Knight and others, academically. We've had a 3.0 since then."

Ah yes, the academics. Let's not forget about that either.

Remember, back in 2010, many in the national media believed that Kentucky's one-and-done players (and guys like them around the country) simply didn't take their academics seriously. Most assumed that a one-and-done player like John Wall would simply be pushed through his classes for a semester to remain eligible, then would skip class altogether once the second semester started.

That might have been the case at some schools. Just not Kentucky.

"One thing that came up a lot during that year was… trying to debunk the myth of why they choose Kentucky," Peevy said. "(The media was) trying to turn us into this one-and-done factory that they (the players) don't care."

If anything, it's been the opposite in Lexington.

"We immediately debunked that myth, that they're only going to be here a short time and they don't care about this university," Peevy said. "John Wall in that second semester, I think he either had a 4.0 or 3.8, in a year where he was probably the one guy on that team that knew that he was probably, pretty much going to leave. The guy got his work done. That's part of it."

Unprompted, Wall echoed the same sentiments.

"Even after the season was over, we were still doing schoolwork and stuff," Wall said. "Guys stayed in school. In the back of our minds, a lot of us knew we could be gone in one year. But our mindset was to go in there and do whatever we can to try and win a championship, and do everything in the classroom and outside the classroom."

And although many of the players on the 2010 team were only at Kentucky for one year, that trend continued long after they left. As Calipari mentioned, Knight was an extraordinary student (carrying a 4.0 GPA at Kentucky) the following year, and according to Coach Cal, 10 players graduated in the first five years he and his staff were there. Even better, guys who had left Kentucky years ago, long before Calipari arrived, were motivated by what they saw their younger peers doing. A number of former UK players, guys who were completely unaffiliated with the Calipari era, have decided to come back to school and finish their degrees. And Kentucky has welcomed them with open arms.

"I think it (the 2010 team) motivated the guys even before them to come back too," Peevy said. "There were guys who were here for four years, or even three, who are coming back to get their degrees. Jodie (Meeks) came back to get his degree, Kelenna Azubuike just came back to school this semester to finish. Gerald Fitch (too)."

In so many ways, the 2010 team really did change Kentucky basketball forever, also brings us to a larger question: Did they change all of college basketball as well? It might sound crazy, but Calipari thinks so. It all points back to those famous words he uttered at the 2010 NBA Draft, that it was "the biggest day in the history of Kentucky basketball."

With a little hindsight, it may have been a turning point in college basketball as well.

"These five just changed the whole, they changed the landscape," Calipari said. "Now we're a 'non-traditional' program. What makes us non-traditional? We broke the 40 year model."

Calipari talks about breaking that 40-year model often, by building what he calls "A Player's First" program. The tenants of that motto are simple: Basically, everything that Kentucky does, is with the mindset of putting the player's first. It's about their wants and their needs, not what's best for the university or basketball program as a whole. It's about using the player's short time at Kentucky to prepare them for the next 40 years of their lives, not just one game or season.

If Kentucky truly does that, and truly lives up to its own tenants, then in Calipari's eyes everything else will work itself out. Including wins.

"I know what he meant now," Kentucky Sports Radio's Matt Jones said. "He had a vision of this place. That he was going to essentially make Kentucky, the minor leagues of the NBA in a way that no one else has done. What he's done here has never been done before, this notion of 'I'm going to worry about producing NBA talent, and if I do that, we're going to be really damn good.'"

Jones continued.

"That offends some people that the first priority in his mind is producing NBA talent, but he used to say 'We'll drag the team to success,' and he's right about that. I think he's been proven right about that."

If there's anything that has proven Calipari's methods do work, and shown that the 2010 Kentucky Wildcats really did change college basketball, it might actually come from other schools. Taking a look around the landscape of college basketball in 2015, it's amazing how many other programs are taking a similar approach to what Calipari and Kentucky do. What they've been doing since he arrived in 2009.

Arizona and Kansas routinely recruit the same players Kentucky does, and Arizona has actually gone so far as to use the "Player's First" motto themselves. Heck, how about the fact that Duke --- yes, Duke! --- won a National Championship in 2015 with three freshmen in their starting lineup, who all went to the NBA after one season. Once upon a time Duke liked to give off the aura that they "held themselves to a higher standard" than other schools, that they put academics above anything, and scoffed at the idea of recruiting players who only planned to stay in college basketball for one year. Well that all changed right around 2009 when they aggressively recruited John Wall, and came to full fruition in 2015, when they won a title with Jahlil Okafor, Tyus Jones and Justise Winslow in their starting lineup.

And ultimately that's not a knock on Duke. If anything (and I hate to do this) it's a credit to Coach K for seeing a trend, and realizing that he could either start following that trend or risk becoming irrelevant.

But it is in fact a trend that really did start with the 2010 Kentucky team. And while it hasn't always been easy, Calipari wouldn't have it any other way. Even if it might be slowly driving Coach Cal insane.

"You age quicker," Calipari said with a laugh. "My daughters are like 'Dad, you've aged more than Obama.' It's hard. It's not a 20-year run doing it this way."

Calipari is of course being Calipari, but he knows the role the 2010 team played in it all. Everyone in the Kentucky basketball program does.

"There's no doubt in my mind that the 2010 team is the reason we're enjoying all the success that we are today," Peevy said. "Players have worked their tails off (after them), and the coaching staff has coached them up."

And it's because of that, because of all these factors, that the 2010 team remains beloved in Kentucky to this day. It's also worth noting that Kentucky --- the state, the people, the school and its fans --- remains beloved by the players as well.

"They truly, truly, truly loved Kentucky," former team manager Chad Sanders said. "That's why I think you see them coming back all the time now. John's back every year, DeMarcus is back every year, Eric comes back. They all come back."

Matt Jones, who has covered the Wildcats since before Calipari arrived, and has had a front row seat for the entire Calipari era, agreed. He also added a little further context.

"That's the other thing," Jones began. "Kentucky was never a place where guys came back and hung out. Mediocre players did that, but the stars didn't. Tayshaun Prince and Keith Bogans have both been back within the last year to get inducted into the Hall of Fame. I think that's the first time they'd been back period. Both of them said 'Now we feel like we can finally come back.' It wasn't like Carolina, where guys came back every summer and played. But they do now."

Oh, they do indeed. And it's impossible to walk across campus on a summer day without bumping into a few of them.

"Those guys (the 2010 team) started that trend," Jones said. "So if you came to Lexington now, on any given day there will be six or eight former Kentucky guys working out in the facility. That never happened before. But it kind of started with those guys."

In the end, it's easy to talk about the "big picture" issues which come with the 2010 Kentucky Wildcats. The idea that they changed everything we thought we knew about the sport of college basketball, and started a golden age of Kentucky hoops too. Yet, the most important elements of the 2010 team might be what we just discussed over the previous few paragraphs: How much that team loved Kentucky, and how the state loved them back.

That's also why whenever you bring up the 2010 team to those who were around them every day, they talk about one thing more than all others, and it's not necessarily what you think. They don't discuss the history that was made, the culture that was changed, or the number of NBA Draft picks that the team produced. Instead, they talk about how fun that season was.

More than anything else, if there was one word to encapsulate the entire 2009-2010 Kentucky Wildcats' season, it would be "fun."

"That was a fun year," Peevy said. "I tell Cal all the time, that 2012 championship year was not as fun as that first, 2010 year."

Peevy paused, thinking back to a different era in Kentucky hoops. Those were the days long before National Championships were expected, and before years like 2015, when ESPN would spend hours trying to figure out when the Wildcats' first loss would come.

Everybody was just happy to be good, happy to be along for the ride.

"I just remember, it was so much more fun," Peevy said. "John, DeMarcus and Eric were always keeping it light. The other guys who had been there, the Perry Stevenson's, the Ramon Harris's, the Patrick

Patterson's, those guys, they enjoyed it. It was refreshing. We saw different sides of them too."

Ultimately, that might be the legacy of the 2010 Kentucky Wildcats.

Yes, they won a lot of games, and sure they set the tone for everything else that has come in Lexington.

But more than anything, they had fun along the way.

Acknowledgments

THE STORY OF the 2010 Kentucky Wildcats wasn't just fun for the players and coaches who lived it, but for the guy who spent close to a year writing about it. That's me, and when it comes to all the people who made this book possible, I guess it's best to start at the beginning.

This whole book began as a story idea for FoxSports.com back in September 2014, with the idea being to chronicle "the team that changed college basketball." But while that concept sounded great in my head, I had no idea if it would translate in print. I also had no idea --- because of the way things ended --- what the reaction would be to it. Would fans want to re-live the season? Would players and coaches be willing to talk about it?

Therefore, I did what I basically always do whenever I have a question about something related to Kentucky hoops: I consulted with my buddy Matt Jones. Before I could even finish my spiel, Matt cut me off, and told me that this was a story I should absolutely do. And then, to top it off, he started re-wracking the season in his brain, and giving me a bunch of little stories that I should pursue while working on the article. For example, did I know that the "John Wall dance" was originally intended to be the "DeMarcus Cousins dance?" No, I did not. Did I know that Cousins had made national headlines before the Cornell game? I vaguely remembered, but probably would have missed it otherwise.

Again, Matt peppered me with stuff that only a diehard Kentucky fan would know… and stuff that undoubtedly made the original article (and now this book), so much better. To Matt, I cannot thank you enough for all your support throughout this process.

I also cannot thank the folks in UK athletics for not only being receptive to this story, but literally doing whatever they could to help me along the way. I have worked with dozens of Division I athletic departments across the country, and can honestly say that not a single one has been anything as close to helpful as Kentucky's was during this process.

For starters, a huge, huge, HUGE thanks goes out to DeWayne Peevy, a man who in my eyes, is the star of this book. First, there was his initial interview (which might have been my favorite), and all the little nuggets of information that came with it (the "Popeye's Chicken" story at Mississippi State was probably my favorite excerpt of the entire book). Then, as if that wasn't enough (believe me, it was), DeWayne then spent the next few weeks doing absolutely everything he could to help me connect with players from the team. Texts, phone calls, e-mails, follow-ups, whatever it took, DeWayne did it. To the fans who enjoyed this book, please know that the book wouldn't exist, and the original article wouldn't have been half as good as it turned out without DeWayne's help.

Staying at UK, another quick shout out goes to my guy Eric Lindsey. I can only imagine how many hundreds of requests Eric gets to interview Coach Calipari every year, yet I can honestly say that he treated me as if my request was the most important on his list (an emotion that I can say for certain a lot of other writers feel as well). We eventually did track Coach Cal down (during an undefeated regular season, none the less), and then as if that weren't enough, he (and DeWayne) helped me gather some final things over the summer months, as the book got set to go to print. Again, I cannot thank you both enough for your help.

I'd also be remiss if I didn't thank the players and coaches who took the time to speak with me for the story. John Calipari gave me more time than I probably deserved, especially since again…. He was coaching the No. 1 ranked team in the country, in the midst of an undefeated regular season when he talked me. Special thanks also to assistant coaches Orlando Antigua, Scott Padgett, Rod Strickland and Martin Newton for taking time to chat as well, and provide me with more context than I would have ever been able to get without them (Fun fact: Orlando Antigua was the first person I officially interviewed for the Fox Sports story. Never in a million years would I have imagined that his words would one day end up in a book).

Thanks to the others who helped too; Tywanna Patterson, who was interviewed for the original story (and later helped connect me with her son Patrick), Tucker Max, and Chad Sanders, who might have been the single most important interview I did for the book. The information I learned from that one interview, gave me a foundation for all the interviews that came after it.

And of course, thank you to the 2010 Kentucky Wildcats, for not only being one of the most dynamic teams in modern college hoops history, but for allowing me to be the one to tell your story. I can honestly say that I would have never taken on the initial project (let alone the book) if your squad wasn't so damn fun to write and talk about, but you guys definitely, definitely were. People ask me why I would ever want to write a 70,000 word book, but to me the question was "Why wouldn't I?" I loved every second of it. I honestly did. There wasn't a single moment during this entire process that writing this book ever felt like "work" to me.

So with that said, thank you to the members of the team who agreed to interviews: Ramon Harris, Mark Krebs, Patrick Patterson, Josh Harrellson, John Wall, Eric Bledsoe and Daniel Orton. To the players on the team I was unable to connect with, I apologize that we were never able to work it out, but want to thank you none the less. Although I never formally interviewed DeMarcus Cousins, Darius Miller, DeAndre Liggins and a few others, you are as important to this book as anyone I officially spoke with. Same to the assistant coaches, managers, walk-ons and anyone else I may have missed as well. My apologies that we were never able to connect.

Finally, I want to thank a few people in my personal life as well.

Thanks to Barry, my editor at Fox. When I came to you with a convoluted, half-baked idea about writing about the 2010 Kentucky Wildcats, you could have easily said no. But you didn't. You saw the forest through the trees, and saw the importance of this team. Again, there would have been no original article (let alone a book) without your help. Thank you also to my book editor Maria, who dealt with a lot of frantic e-mails and frustrated texts in the short window we had to put the finishing touches on this bad boy. I appreciate your professionalism and patience in dealing with a lunatic like me.

Speaking of "dealing with me" I want to thank everyone in my family who I love and adore, and who yes, do spend their lives "dealing with me." Yeni, thank you for everything you do on a daily basis. Same to you Gloria, Matt and Uncle Matt, who continue to be my biggest supporters.

And finally, I want to finish this book the way I began it, by thanking my parents.

I love you both in ways that you can't imagine, and while I say it a lot, it cannot be reiterated enough: Without your support I wouldn't be here today.

I can honestly say that everything I do in life is with one goal in mind: Making you guys proud.

I hope I've done that here.

Prologue:

"UK basketball notebook: 'Old guard' begs to differ with Cal," Lexington Herald Leader, Jerry Tipton. June 25th, 2010.

Chapter 1:

"A Look at a Blue Blood on the Bubble," ESPN.com, Dana O'Neil. March 11, 2009.

"Coach's 'Unhealthy' Obsession Has Led to Success at Texas A&M," New York Times, Pete Thamel. March 22, 2007.

"Gillispie Says He Is Ready for Kentucky's Expectations," New York Times, Ray Glier and Thayer Evans. April 7, 2007.

Chapter 2:

Memphis Tigers Boosters Work to Block Kentucky's Shot at Calipari," Memphis Commercial Appeal, Dan Wolken. March 30, 2009.

"Memphis Tigers coach John Calipari Will Take Kentucky Basketball Job," Memphis Commercial Appeal, Dan Wolken. March 31, 2009.

"Tigers' Calipari to Decide This Afternoon on Kentucky," Memphis Commercial Appeal, Geoff Calkins. March 31st, 2009.

"We learned a little more about John Calipari," Memphis Commercial Appeal, Geoff Calkins. April 1, 2009.

Chapter 3:
"Calipari Taking Kentucky Job," AP. April 9th, 2009.

Chapter 5:
"Cousins Makes the Call," Rivals.com, Jerry Meyer. April 8th, 2009.

"John Wall's Announcement to Come to University of Kentucky Wildcats," YouTube. May 27th, 2009.

"Nation's Top PG Finds Answers In Meeting," Scout.com, John Watson. March 30th, 2009.

"Tigers Get Commitment From 6'11 Cousins," Memphis Commercial Appeal, Dan Wolken. March 8th, 2009.

"Top Basketball Prospect DeMarcus Cousins Commits to UAB," AL.com, February 29th, 2008.

"Wall Names Leader," Rivals.com, Jerry Meyer. March 8th, 2009.

"Wall Gives UM High Marks," Miami Herald, Manny Navarro. April 28th, 2009.

"Xavier Henry commits to KU at press conference," Lawrence Journal-World YouTube Channel. April 24th, 2009.

Chapter 6:
"John Robic Is an Assistant Happy to Sweat the Small Stuff for Kentucky," New York Times, Marc Tracy. March 25th, 2015.

Chapter 7:
"Kentucky Turnover: Six Players Moved on After Calipari's Arrival," USA Today, Marlen Garcia. March 17th, 2010.

"Three Walk-Ons Leave Calipari's Wildcats," YMMT TV Mountain News, Steve Moss. August 1st, 2009.

Chapter 8:

"Nation's #1 High School Prospect Michael Gilchrist to Attend Big Blue Madness," KentuckySportsRadio.com, Dustin Rumbaugh. October 1, 2009.

Chapter 9:

"Sports Illustrated's Top 20 Scouting Reports," Sports Illustrated, Grant Wahl. November 23rd, 2009.

"Kentucky Picked to Win SEC, Patterson Player of the Year," WKYT. October 19th, 2009.

"Kentucky Freshman John Wall to be Suspended Two Games by NCAA," The Sporting News, Mike DeCourcy. October 31st, 2009.

"UK-Miami postgame with Miami coach Charlie Coles," Cleveland.com. November 18th, 2009.

Chapter 10:

"UConn-Kentucky: A Final Four in December," AaronTorres-Sports.com, Aaron Torres. December 10th, 2009.

Chapter 12:

"Cal in the ACC?" Yahoo.com, Dan Wetzel. April 11th, 2006.

"He's the Shizz," Sports Illustrated, Grant Wahl. January 11th, 2010.

"Drexel's 'Bruiser' on Coach Cal: 'He's a fighter,'" Lexington Herald Leader, Jerry Tipton. December 21, 2009.

"Kentucky beats Drexel to become first college team to reach 2,000 wins," Associated Press. December 21, 2009.

"The Very Best of Enemies," Sports Illustrated, Grant Wahl. November 23rd, 2009.

CHAPTER 13:

"Players First: Coaching from the Inside Out," Penguin Press, John Calipari and Michael Sokolove. April 15th, 2014.

"Calipari, UK score with 'Hoops for Haiti,'" Yahoo.com, Dan Wetzel. January 21st, 2010.

"Haiti Earthquake Fast Facts," CNN.com. January 6th, 2015.

CHAPTER 17:

"Beyond a Dream: A Mother's Courage, A Family's Fight, A Son's Determination," Beyond a Dream Publishing, Mark Krebs Jr. and Dr. James Conrad.

CHAPTER 18:

"'Big Game Bruce' Strikes Again," ESPN.com, Pat Forde. March 1st, 2010.

"UK's Wall named SEC Player of the Year," Lexington Herald Leader. March 9th, 2010.

"Yahoo! Sports All-American Team," Yahoo.com, Jason King. March 8th, 2010.

CHAPTER 19:

"Clinging to an Ivy Climber," Boston Globe, Dan Shaughnessy. March 24th, 2010.

"Dan Shaughnessy Puts on His Elitist/Racist Hat," KentuckySportsRadio.com, Matt Jones. March 24th, 2010.

"Wildcat Strike Incited: Kentucky Loyalists Pounce on Column," Boston Globe, Dan Shaughnessy. March 25th, 2010.

Made in the USA
Columbia, SC
13 October 2022

69428244R00143